Egan's Skilled Helper M

D0153478

The skilled helper model of counselling is hugely influential in the helping professions. *Egan's Skilled Helper Model* brings a number of new and challenging perspectives to bear on Egan's work and makes a major contribution to the development of this problem-management and opportunity-development approach to helping.

Val Wosket draws on over twenty years' experience of counselling, training and supervising to provide a clear exposition of the model and situate it in contemporary counselling practice. Numerous case studies are provided throughout, along with contributions from experienced practitioners, illustrating how the model can be applied in a variety of clinical settings and with a range of counselling issues. *Egan's Skilled Helper Model* builds on and extends the aims of Egan's original work, covering key topics, including:

- Developing a client-responsive approach that places the therapeutic relationship at the heart of the model
- Applying the skilled helper model in research, training and supervision
- Translating the model into more accessible and adaptable language

This book provides an invaluable resource for trainees, trainers, supervisors and experienced practitioners wishing to update their knowledge of the model. It will also be of great interest to anyone in the helping professions looking for a pragmatic integrative framework that is adaptable to a diverse range of client issues and contexts.

Dr Val Wosket is Senior Lecturer in Counselling at York St John University College. She is a BACP accredited Counsellor, Supervisor and Trainer and also works in private practice. Her previous publications include *The Therapeutic Use of Self: Counselling Practice, Research and Supervision* and, with Steve Page, *Supervising the Counsellor: A Cyclical Model*.

Egan's Skilled Helper Model

Developments and Applications in Counselling

Val Wosket

Routledge
Taylor & Francis Group

LONDON AND NEW YORK

First published 2006 by Routledge
27 Church Lane, Hove, East Sussex, BN3 2FA

Simultaneously published in the USA and Canada
by Routledge
270 Madison Avenue, New York, NY 10016

Routledge is an imprint of the Taylor & Francis Group, an informa business

© 2006 Val Wosket

Typeset in Sabon by Garfield Morgan, Mumbles, Swansea
Printed and bound in Great Britain by TJ International Ltd, Padstow,
Cornwall
Paperback cover design by Sandra Heath

This publication has been produced with paper manufactured to strict
environmental standards and with pulp derived from sustainable forests.

British Library Cataloguing in Publication Data
A catalogue record for this book is available from the British Library

Library of Congress Cataloging in Publication Data
Wosket, Val, 1954–
   Egan's skilled helper model : developments and applications in
counselling / Val Wosket.
        p. cm.
   Includes bibliographical references and index.
   ISBN-13: 978-1-58391-203-4 (hbk)
   ISBN-10: 1-58391-203-7 (hbk)
   ISBN-13: 978-1-58391-204-1 (pbk)
   ISBN-10: 1-58391-204-5 (pbk)
   1. Counseling. 2. Helping behavior. I. Title.

BF637.C6W675 2006
158'.3–dc22
                                                              2006002514

ISBN13: 978-1-58391-203-4 (hbk)
ISBN13: 978-1-58391-204-1 (pbk)

ISBN10: 1-58391-203-7 (hbk)
ISBN10: 1-58391-204-5 (pbk)

Contents

Tables and figures

Exercises and guidelines

Contributors to Chapter 7

Dr Alan Dunnett
Dr Lynne Gabriel
Trish Hobman
Lynne Lacock
Andy Pendle
Dr Emma Roberts
Lindsay Smith
Peter Storr
Carol Warren

Foreword

I feel a bit strange writing a foreword to a book that is about one of my own books. However, Val Wosket's book is really a book about an *approach to helping* that I have been developing over the years. In her book she champions this approach, looks at it from a number of different angles, corroborates it, challenges it, complements it, illustrates it, clears up misconceptions about it, dismisses nonsense about it, enlarges on it and provides suggestions on how to use it, how to train others to use it and how to supervise those who are using it. It is a wonderfully rich book, a very professional book, and a very useful book. I found her first chapters so interesting that I delayed work on the eighth edition of *The Skilled Helper* until I could read all of them. Its wisdom will certainly influence me as I write my next edition.

I have read Val's book, learned from it, admired her research, challenged some of her premises, noted what seemed to me to be a couple of contradictions and agreed to disagree about a few issues. In reading her book, I have come to realise more fully the cultural differences between the helping professions in the UK and the United States.

I smiled when she described my language as 'muscular' and fretted when I thought she was aiding and abetting both client and counsellor self-indulgence. Yet, though we might differ somewhat conceptually, we seem to be on the same page practically. As I read examples of her interactions with clients, I kept saying to myself things like, 'Now that's spot on' or 'I think she's responded better than I would have'.

The skilled helper model deals with the basics, the fundamentals of helping. The model is, therefore, a starting point. In highlighting the flexibility of the problem-management and opportunity-development model I espouse, Val makes the point that individuals will and must find ways of making it their own – putting their own stamp on it, as she has in her own practice. Indeed, in the last chapter she listens to the voices of a number of helpers who have been trained in, or exposed to, or even dragged kicking and screaming through the skilled helper model. The diversity of these voices speaks for itself. My job is to listen to these many voices and learn from them.

Helping is not about helping models but about the needs of clients. Helping is not about helpers but about healthy catalytic relationships that enable clients to improve their lives. Helping is not about communication skills but the balance between support and challenge that helps clients redirect their energies. Helping is not about stages and steps but about helping clients find direction in their lives. Helping is not about good sessions but about outcomes that improve clients' lives. Helping is not about exploring but about challenging clients to act on what they are learning. Val's book is a timely reminder that there is no one right way of doing all of this.

Gerard Egan

Acknowledgements

I would like to thank Professor Gerard Egan for his support, constructive criticism and generosity in sharing his own work-in-progress during the writing of this book – and, above all, for agreeing to write a Foreword to the text.

I would also like to thank Dr Emma Roberts for offering to step in, at very short notice, as my writing review partner and for commenting on drafts of the manuscript. Her skill and sensitivity in giving supportive and challenging feedback and her exquisite attention to detail have rescued me from a number of muddles, contradictions and omissions.

A particular thank you is due to York and District Mind for assisting me in my pilot research. Finally, I would like to thank all my clients, students, supervisees and colleagues who have, intentionally or otherwise, made valuable contributions to the material contained in these chapters. This book is as much their story as mine.

The author and publisher wish to thank the copyright holder for permission to include an illustration from *The Skilled Helper: A Problem Management Approach to Helping*, 7th edition, by Egan © 2002. This is reprinted with permission of Wadsworth, a division of Thomson Learning: www.thomsonrights.com; fax: 800 730-2215.

Introduction

I would like say something about what this book is and what it is not. This publication is not intended as a substitute for reading Egan's original work on *The Skilled Helper*, now in its seventh edition. Neither is it intended as a comprehensive skills manual covering how to do counselling or use counselling skills. It does not cover all the basic and essential building blocks of interpersonal communication and counselling skills, although it does attempt to explore and illustrate a number of these.

Beginning counsellors and helpers are strongly advised to study Egan's *Skilled Helper* book (2002a) and companion training manual (2002b), and are encouraged to undertake thorough training in these skills on a course pitched to their level of engagement with the counselling or helping process (e.g. introductory, certificate or diploma). As Egan emphasises again and again in all that he writes about the skilled helper model, the helper's level of competence in the use of a wide range of communication skills determines his or her ability to use the model with humanity, sensitivity and flexibility.

The skilled helper model cannot be divorced from the communication skills that underpin it or the key values (client empowerment and the Rogerian core qualities of respect, genuineness and empathy) that suffuse it. This emphasis on dialogue and relationship is often missed by those who quibble with what they consider to be the mechanistic and reductionist elements of the model (see Chapters 4 and 5). The point is again strongly emphasised in Egan's most recent publication on the skilled helper model, *Essentials of Skilled Helping* (Egan 2006), and illustrated by the fact that, of the eleven chapters that comprise that publication, the first seven concentrate on the skills and values of helping and the therapeutic dialogue, while the model itself is condensed into the final four chapters.

What I *have* attempted to do in the present volume is to give some ideas and suggestions for counselling strategies, guidelines and exercises for developing competency, awareness and facility in using the skilled helper model. The text also provides numerous real examples from counselling practice to illustrate how the model can be applied in a variety of clinical settings and with a range of counselling issues. Several chapters show how the model can be used as an integrative framework for developing a person- ally authentic style of counselling. I have also attempted to outline ways in which perspectives from other counselling approaches can be usefully integrated into the model.

In the chapters that follow I have tried to recapture something of the clarity and simplicity of the model that some commentators have remarked are more apparent in early editions of *The Skilled Helper* than in Egan's later work. There is always a danger that precision of articulation, when over-refined, can slip into jargon. Jargon, by its very nature, is culture-bound in that it emerges from the idiom of the day that is current in its locale of origin.

It might be argued that as Egan has further honed the model through its various revisions, some of its peculiarly American (and masculine) language has begun to alienate an audience of coun- sellors in the UK who find it difficult to think and work in the language of empathic highlights, screening and leverage, change agendas, balance-sheets, strategy sampling and the technology of constructive change. Somewhat ironically, a model that was origin- ally developed to de-mystify the helping process has begun to be seen, by some critics, as overly complex and impenetrable in the way it is currently articulated. In the following chapters I have tried to give priority to explaining the model in the language that I – a female, British counsellor – use to teach and apply it. Conscious of my privileged, white, background I have also tried to give some attention to its uses and limitations as a transcultural counselling approach.

In attempting all of this I see myself as a translator and developer of the skilled helper model and hopefully not as a hijacker of it. Two key aims I have held in mind as I have been writing are, first, to reinstate the skilled helper model as a dynamic, integrative approach for individual counsellors and, second, to re-evaluate its contribution to the development of counselling in the UK. I have also endeavoured to address some of the perceived omissions in the conceptualisation and development of the model through a consideration of how it can evolve and adapt to fit a range of client issues and counselling contexts.

My acquaintance with the model and with Professor Egan began through the 'Becoming a Skilled Helper' counselling summer schools held annually for a decade from 1986 to 1996 at York St John University College (or the College of Ripon and York St John as it was then) under the leadership of Dr Mary Connor. As noted by Jenkins (2000) these summer schools have had a major impact on the development of the skilled helper model in the UK. To each of these annual training events, Gerry Egan came as key speaker and consultant to the training team. It was through listening to Egan talk about the skilled helper model that the approach really came alive for me and I have taken the liberty of reproducing in these pages a number of his observations recorded from the lecture notes I made at the time.

In its finished state I think I have produced a book that is something of a hybrid. It is both a theoretical and a practical text. While not specifically a training manual, it incorporates guidelines and exercises that can be used in training. It is a book about counselling that also includes chapters on training and supervision (Chapters 5 and 6). At the heart of the book (Chapters 2 and 3) sits a presentation and explanation of the skilled helper model. These chapters are meant to be practical and include many examples from actual counselling sessions to illustrate how the model can be applied in clinical settings. This material is sandwiched between two chapters (Chapters 1 and 4) that are of a more discursive and theoretical nature. Chapter 1 situates the model in contemporary counselling practice and explores Egan's concept of the person within a people-in-systems framework. Chapter 4 addresses contemporary debates and critiques of the model and looks at how the therapeutic relationship and working with issues located in the past can figure more prominently in the skilled helper framework. The book concludes (Chapter 7) with a round-table chapter of contributions from a number of trainers, experienced in using the skilled helper model, who each write about the way that they have adapted and developed the model in their work as tutors, counsellors and supervisors. This is a 'warts and all' chapter that, in a very real way, illustrates some of the challenges and satisfactions that practitioners may encounter in finding a comfortable fit with the model.

A note on permissions: all client examples included in the text are based on real work from my own counselling practice. I hope and intend that all the case material included is done in a way that honours and respects the dignity and anonymity of my clients. Clinical material that has been minimally changed, or is written as a near-accurate account of what actually occurred, is included with clients' express permissions. Other illustrations of case material have been slightly altered or combined with different examples to ensure that individual clients and their particular personal details are not identifiable.

A note on terminology: where references to *The Skilled Helper* are capitalised and italicised this refers to Egan's book with the same title. Where the skilled helper model is referred to in lower case this means that I am writing about the generic model, rather than the book. At times I have used the words 'counselling', 'psychotherapy' and 'helping' interchangeably in the text – not because I believe they are necessarily the same thing but because I want to highlight that the skilled helper model can provide an effective framework for different levels and degrees of therapeutic and helping intervention. Often, I use the words 'therapy' or 'therapist' as inclusive terms to denote this range. I have attempted to spread my use of female and male pronouns equally throughout the book rather than resort to the clumsy device of 's/he'.

Finally, I hope that some of the exercises and guidelines included at the end of most of the chapters will appeal sufficiently that you may wish to use them in your own work. If so, I would be grateful if you would acknowledge their source.

Val Wosket

Chapter 1

Background and context to the skilled helper model

This first chapter attempts to place the skilled helper model in context, both historically and in terms of contemporary counselling practice. It includes an overview of the evolution of the model and its relationship to recent key developments in the field of counselling theory and practice. In particular there is an exploration of where the skilled helper model is situated in relation to the 'common factors' paradigm and developments in integrative and eclectic counselling. There then follows a discussion of the nature of process models of counselling and psychotherapy and their relationship to the skilled helper model. Consideration is also given to the key values, principles and assumptions underpinning the model. The chapter concludes with a presentation of Egan's view of the person within a people-in-systems framework. Included at the end of the chapter and in subsequent chapters throughout the book are suggested exercises that can be used in training to raise awareness and develop skills relating to the model.

In the closing decades of the twentieth century it became possible to observe a welcome shift taking place in the field of counselling and psychotherapy as some of the more rigid territorial boundaries that have traditionally separated the various 'pure' schools of therapy began to dissolve and break down. This process of dissolution started to come about largely as a result of researchers and practitioners moving away from the seemingly redundant search to find *the* most effective counselling approach and, instead, moving towards the more productive aim of attempting to identify those common therapeutic factors that appear to be universally effective in *all* mainstream counselling approaches (Aebi 1993; Connor-Greene 1993; Duncan *et al.* 1992; Frank 1961; Goldfried 1982a; Miller *et al.* 1997; Shepherd and Sartorious 1989; Strupp and

Hadley 1979; Wills 1982). This endeavour has become widely known as the search for the *common* or *non-specific* factors that appear to contribute to the effectiveness of therapy.

The observable shift in focus from favouring purist theories to valuing common factors underpins the development and increasing popularity of integrative and eclectic approaches, of which Egan's skilled helper model is one. Before moving on to consider the skilled helper model in more detail, I will attempt to outline some of the key influences on the development of the common factors paradigm, as this will help us to consider the context in which the model is currently situated.

Common factors in therapy

The non-specific or common factors approach to integration seeks to uncover and make best use of what have been revealed as the universal, core ingredients of effective therapy across all major counselling approaches. Importantly, this paradigm attempts to take greater account of what clients themselves consider to be the effective ingredients of therapy, rather than relying merely on what therapists and researchers think (Duncan *et al.* 1992).

Common factors have been selected and presented in different ways in the professional literature. Grencavage and Norcross (1990) reviewed fifty publications to identify common factors across therapies and categorised them into five groups which appeared to feature most prominently. These are:

1 *Client characteristics*, e.g. positive expectations; distressed client actively seeking help.
2 *Therapist qualities*, e.g. warmth, empathy, acceptance; a socially sanctioned healer and cultivator of hope.
3 *Change processes*, e.g. opportunity for catharsis; acquisition and practice of new behaviours; fostering of insight/awareness; success and mastery experiences; emotional and interpersonal learning.
4 *Treatment structures*, e.g. the use of techniques/rituals; a healing setting; the provision of a sound rationale for change; a focus on inner world and exploration of emotional issues.
5 *Relationship elements*, e.g. the development of a therapeutic alliance; engagement and transference.

From this list we can begin to see that a complex interplay of factors is at work in any effective therapeutic approach and that techniques and strategies may form only a small part of the whole change-inducing package.

The growth of eclectic and integrative approaches

The growing recognition that common factors appear in all major counselling approaches as universal change agents has contributed significantly to the observable movement towards eclecticism and integration in the counselling world. In a survey of eclecticism among counsellors in Britain undertaken in 1999, Hollanders and McLeod (1999) found that from a sample of 309 therapists, 87 per cent revealed, either explicitly or implicitly, their engagement in eclectic or integrative practice. The exponential increase in the popularity of eclectic and integrative approaches in recent years has been bolstered by a range of factors, including:

- The ever-increasing proliferation of therapies
- The inadequacy of single theories to account for therapeutic change
- The impossibility of identifying one counselling approach as more effective than the rest
- Socio-economic contingencies (in particular the requirement of service providers to be accountable and cost effective).

The integrative/eclectic movement, while taking much of its initial shape from the common factors paradigm, continues to be moulded by an increasing accumulation of research evidence, some key findings from which are summarised below. This body of research (see Wosket 1999 for a detailed discussion and full references to individual studies) includes, but also extends well beyond, those findings that support the notion of universal change agents occurring in all therapeutic approaches. Findings from this research indicate:

- that whereas counselling and psychotherapy are generally effective, they are not differentially so. This means that it has proved impossible to ascertain which approach (or approaches) are more effective than others

- the existence of what is known as the 'equal outcomes phenomenon' – this is the notion that different therapeutic approaches can achieve similar outcomes
- that it is those common factors across approaches, as outlined above, that largely account for this equivalence of outcomes
- that therapist and client matching across a range of variables (see Chapter 4) is an important predictor of outcomes
- the 'paradox of equivalence', which suggests that experienced therapists (regardless of orientation) are more similar than different in the way that they practise and that the more experienced the practitioner, the more likely he or she is to work in an integrative fashion
- that experience, rather than theory, drives the practice of more seasoned therapists
- that para-professional (minimally trained) helpers using a variety of skills may be equally as effective as professionally trained therapists in some contexts
- that the major change agent of effective counselling or psychotherapy is the personality of the therapist, rather than the theory or model employed – particularly the ability to form a warm, supportive relationship
- that a number of studies may have mis-attributed therapeutic change to a therapeutic approach where the change was actually effected by the individual therapist.

A personal approach to integration

Alongside the growing popularity of integrative and eclectic models has emerged a perceptible movement towards transtheoretical and deconstructionist approaches. These are essentially ways of working that are personally shaped by the individual therapist (Duncan *et al.* 1992; House 1999; Karasu 1996; LeShan 1996; Miller *et al.* 1997; Parker 1999). From within this movement can be heard a strengthening argument that personal integration undertaken by individual counsellors and psychotherapists may be a more meaningful and effective response to the dilemmas of pluralism than the further proliferation of 'grand' theories and models of therapy (Horton 2000b; Lapworth *et al.* 2001; Lomas 1981; O'Brien and Houston 2000; Wosket 1999).

More about developing a personally integrated style of counselling within the framework of the skilled helper model is said in

Chapters 5 and 6 where we will turn to considering aspects of the training and supervision of helpers. In the following section I will begin to look at the place that the skilled helper model occupies in the current world of integrative and eclectic practice.

Eclecticism, integration and the skilled helper model

Since it first appeared on the counselling scene in the mid-1970s, Egan's skilled helper model has been continuously revised and expanded. The model evolved from Egan's early writings on interpersonal skills within group and individual contexts (Egan 1970, 1973, 1976, 1977; Egan and Cowan 1980) and has moved through the presentation of a sequential process model for individual counselling to the development of change agent models and skills within the broader field of organisational change.

Early and enduring influences on the skilled helper model are drawn from the work of Rogers (1951, 1957, 1965) and Carkhuff (1969, 1971, 1987), which provide both its person-centred values and principles and its emphasis on the client-centred use of counselling skills. The model's cognitive-behavioural elements are closely informed by figures such as Bandura, Beck, Ellis, Seligman and Strong.

A three-stage map of the helping process, as outlined later in Chapters 2 and 3, has remained a constant during the various editions of *The Skilled Helper* although Egan has made a number of significant adjustments to the model over the years to take account of emerging research and developments in integrative practice. So, for instance, the third edition, which was published in 1986, evidenced a shift from problem management to opportunity development, while in 1990 the fourth edition carried an increased emphasis on challenge and action as running through all stages of the counselling process. In 1994 the fifth edition engaged more forcefully with debates about eclecticism and integrationism. This edition also highlighted the fundamentally flexible, non-linear characteristics of the model together with the importance of addressing shadow-side elements of the helping process. In the seventh edition (2002a) Egan has noticeably adopted a positive psychology approach to helping. This is discussed at more length later in the chapter.

At the time of writing, an eighth edition of *The Skilled Helper*, in which the importance of therapeutic dialogue and of paying attention to the counselling relationship is emphasised, is in preparation (Egan: personal communication). This forthcoming edition also has some notable changes in terminology, as currently outlined in Egan's newest text *Essentials of Skilled Helping* (2006), and these changes are incorporated in the following two chapters that describe the model.

Is the skilled helper model eclectic or integrative?

This is a question that is often asked but one that I believe is becoming less relevant as developments in integrative and eclectic practice increasingly show that making an absolute distinction between the two may be simplistic, inaccurate, outdated and based more on semantics than real differences (Lapworth *et al.* 2001). While agreeing with this argument to the point of acknowledging that firm distinctions between integration and eclecticism are unrealistic and unhelpful, Hollanders (2003) nonetheless considers the skilled helper model to be an essentially eclectic framework. This is based on the argument that the model enables the helper to systematically use a variety of skills and strategies matched to different stages of the counselling process. He refers to this as systematic or technical eclecticism. Jenkins (2000) prefers to see the model as integrative in so far as it provides an overarching framework for the helping process yet does not have an over-reliance on theory.

The divisions between eclecticism and integration are not always clear-cut, therefore my own preference is to think of the terms as shading into one another on a continuum rather than as being distinctly different. Adopting this perspective, I would suggest that the skilled helper model sits somewhere towards the middle of the continuum between integrative and eclectic approaches. In saying this I agree in principle with Lapworth and colleagues (2001), who state that integration is now a useful umbrella term to accommodate a range of approaches that extend beyond purist forms of therapy to include pluralism, transtheoreticism, common factors, eclecticism, relational and deconstructionist approaches. A number of what might be considered to be the integrative elements of the skilled helper model are considered below.

The skilled helper model as an integrating framework

The skilled helper model is derivative in that it draws predominantly on person-centred values and principles and on cognitive-behavioural approaches. Egan himself has described the model as 'atheoretical' (York St John University College counselling summer school 1990) – meaning it moves beyond theory in searching for a framework or map that is built on pragmatism (what has been shown to work) rather than on theoretical constructions. In a sense, the model might be thought of as something of a nomad of the counselling world. It tends to turn up all over the place and seems not to have a fixed abode or place of origin. It has been variously described as 'humanistic-existential' (Franklin 2003: 64) due to its focus on the present whilst being inclusive of the past and future; as 'cognitive-behavioural' and 'person-centred' (Jenkins 2000: 163) and as drawing on 'psychodynamic, humanistic and behavioural theory' (Connor 1994: 69). Coles (2003: 21) has written about the capacity of the model to integrate 'psychodynamic notions of the unconscious' with 'cognitive-behavioural' and 'humanistic' perspectives.

My own preferred term is the one that Egan himself uses to describe the model, which is an 'integrating framework' (Egan 2002a: 37). As such, I consider that the model can provide a consistent and coherent container for a personally integrated approach to helping (more about this is said in Chapter 5). I particularly like what Egan (1998) says on the back cover of the sixth edition of *The Skilled Helper* – that here is a model that will help students and practitioners 'develop a solid foundation for forming your own counselling orientation'.

As well as providing a useful framework for personal integration, Egan's skills-based approach has influenced the development of a number of generic integrative and eclectic models of counselling (e.g. Culley 1991; Culley and Bond 2004; Nelson-Jones 1982, 1990, 2000, 2002; O'Connell 1998; Russell 1993), of training (e.g. Connor 1994; Dainow and Bailey 1988; Frankland and Sanders 1995; Inskipp 1996) and of supervision (e.g. Dexter and Russell 1989; Jones 1998; Page and Wosket 2001; Wosket and Page 2001).

In addition to influencing models of counselling, training and supervision, the skilled helper model has been applied to specialist client populations and contexts including sexual abuse (Hall and

Lloyd 1993), dream work (Hill 1996, 2004), student counselling (Stein 1999), counselling in primary health care (Hudson-Allez 1997), counselling in the voluntary sector (Tyndall 1993), counselling children and young people (Mabey and Sorensen 1995; Plummer 1999), mentoring (Dancer 2003), careers counselling (Kidd 2003) and workplace counselling (Coles 2003; Franklin 2003; Hayes 2002; Martin 1997; Reddy 1987). It has been particularly influential in the field of training nurses and other health professionals (e.g. Arnold and Boggs 1995; Burnard 1996; Freshwater 2003; Rollnick *et al.* 1999).

Egan himself has stated that he sees the model not as competing with other approaches but as providing a solid foundation and direction for the development of the integrative practitioner as he or she draws on a number of different approaches (Coles 1996). In offering this form of accommodation the skilled helper model has had some surprising bedfellows. Inskipp (1993), for instance, has happily married the model to the transpersonal approach and integrated it into a Diploma in Psychosynthesis, while Hill (1996, 2004) uses it as the basis for dream interpretation. Perhaps a particular facility of the skilled helper model, as Frankland and Sanders have remarked, lies in its generic process that many have found 'would hold for *any* assisted change' (1995: 61, original emphasis).

Process models and the skilled helper model

Egan has defined a model both as (1) 'a visual portrait of how things actually work or how they should work under ideal conditions' (Egan 1984a: 25); and as (2) 'a framework or cognitive map with delivery potential' (*ibid.*). Thus the skilled helper model provides both a picture of the helping process and a methodology for implementing that process. Egan has also referred to the model as giving us a 'geography of learning' (York St John University College, counselling summer school 1991). By this he means that the model can enable helpers to map at any point where they are in the process of assisting their clients to be better problem managers and skill learners. Egan has explicitly stated that he actually prefers the term 'framework' to 'model' (Egan 1984b: 135) because this more accurately reflects the two core functions of the approach that are:

1 providing a 'geographical' map for the terrain of helping, and
2 outlining the tasks of helping and how these tasks interrelate.

The model is, then, best thought of as a framework within which a counsellor or helper utilises his or her own unique blend of skills and awareness to assist the client. It provides a map to guide the helper and the client through the problem management stages of the helping process and some strategies that can assist that process to unfold.

The skilled helper is one of a number of models that view the process of counselling as unfolding over definable stages. There is an occasional misperception that process and stage models are limited to the field of cognitive therapy. This is inaccurate. Process and stage models and frameworks exist in abundance across the whole range of cognitive, humanistic, biodynamic, psychodynamic and integrative schools of therapy (Feltham and Horton 2000; Palmer and Woolfe 2000; Totton 2003). As Nelson-Jones (2002) has pointed out, process models tend to work on the cumulative principle that the therapist needs to acquire certain skills for each stage and that 'insufficient application of skills in the earlier stage or stages results in insufficient ability to help in later stages' (Nelson-Jones 2002: 24). At their best, process models are closely tied to, and mediated by, the quality of the counselling relationship and this is something that Egan emphasises in all that he writes about the skilled helper model. Lindon and Lindon (2000: 121) have put this rather well when, in discussing the skilled helper model, they state that 'a staged model creates a framework for helping that grows with the relationship between client and helper'.

Process models and communication skills

The emphasis on skills learning that is apparent in the skilled helper and other process models can suggest a disjointed and mechanistic approach. In his own writing, Egan is at pains to highlight the need for helpers to mediate their use of skills through spontaneous engagement with the client.

> The trouble with dealing with skills one at a time is that each skill is taken out of context. In the give-and-take of any helping session, however, a helper must intermingle the skills

in a natural way. In actual sessions, skilled helpers continually tune in, listen actively, and use a matrix of probes and empathy to help clients clarify and come to grips with their concerns, deal with blind spots, set goals, make plans, and get things done. There is no formula for the right mix; it depends on the client, client needs, the problem situation, possible opportunities, the stage, and the step.

(Egan 2002a: 129–130)

Egan further asserts that it is a mistake to over-identify the helping process with the communication skills that are merely 'the tools that serve it' (Egan 2002a: 135). As Carr (2004: 119) has suggested, communication skills are 'essential for empathising with others, for understanding their concerns and for setting the stage for interpersonal problem solving'. However, they do not, of themselves, constitute the problem management process and, as Egan himself states, 'being good at communication skills is not the same as being good at helping' (Egan 2002a: 135). Communication skills, then, are principally helpful in establishing a good working relationship with the client and the working alliance provides the solid foundation for the helping process – a process that Egan views, first and foremost, as one of systematic 'social-emotional reeducation' (*ibid.*). More about the educative emphasis of the skilled helper model is said later in this chapter where further consideration is given to the values, principles and assumptions underpinning the model.

In the chapters that follow I will show how the model can enable counsellors to develop a sensitive and diverse range of therapeutic competencies. I prefer to use the term 'competencies' rather than 'skills' in relation to the skilled helper model. This is because the notion of competencies extends beyond a toolkit of skills and allows for the inclusion of a broad range of clinical strategies that can be used to translate theory into practice.

In this respect I am in agreement with Goldfried, who understands the search for common factors to be situated on 'determining common therapeutic principles' (1982b: 132) rather than skills. He considers that the best way to uncover these common therapeutic principles is 'by focusing on a level of abstraction somewhere between theory and technique' (*ibid.*), for instance by identifying the clinical strategies most frequently employed by experienced and effective therapists. This idea suggests that effective helpers do not confine their interventions to familiar skills-based techniques but are able to develop a whole repertoire of ways of being and doing with which they are then able to improvise in response to the needs of different clients and helping contexts.

So, far from seeing the skilled helper model, as some critics have asserted, as a constraining and mechanical approach, I believe that the model can provide a versatile and adaptable framework for developing a personal style of working that takes proper account of different client populations, issues and contexts. Egan puts it like this:

> The structure of the helping model is the very foundation for flexibility; it is the underlying 'system' that keeps helping from being a set of random events. A helping model is like a map that informs you, at any given moment, 'where you are' with a client and what kinds of interventions would be most useful. In the map metaphor, the stages and steps of the model are orientation devices. At its best, it is a *shared* map that helps clients participate more fully in the helping process.
>
> (Egan 2002a: 35, original emphasis)

This quotation from the seventh edition of *The Skilled Helper* brings in the element of collaboration with the client that is so fundamental to a proper understanding of Egan's work. His view expressed here about the importance of sharing the process of counselling with the client is supported by research evidence that suggests that when clients are encouraged to take more responsibility for the content and direction of the counselling – that is, when they are encouraged to become collaborators in the process – then the working alliance is enhanced (Kivlighan 1990). Conversely, this same research indicates that when counsellors use interventions that encourage client passivity and deference to the therapist, the therapeutic alliance may be disrupted and undermined. I hope that subsequent chapters will show how the model can be used in a client-responsive and collaborative manner that builds and maintains the working relationship between therapist and client while also promoting optimum change for the client. I will now move to a consideration of the underlying philosophy of the skilled helper model and to Egan's view of the person that is fundamental to his conceptualisation of the helping process.

Key values, principles and assumptions underpinning the skilled helper model

Positive psychology

Over recent years Egan has increasingly adopted a positive psychology approach to helping (Carr 2004; Seligman and Csikszentmihalyi 2000) and this is particularly evident in the seventh edition of *The Skilled Helper*. Positive psychology according to Carr (2004: unnumbered) is 'concerned with the enhancement of happiness and well-being, involving the scientific study of the role of personal strengths and positive social systems in the promotion of optimal well-being'. Positive psychology stands in opposition to the traditional remedial focus of clinical and counselling psychology. Instead of focusing on psychological deficits and dysfunction, positive psychology emphasises instead clients' 'resilience, resourcefulness and capacity for renewal' (Carr 2004: xvii).

It has been shown that psychological adjustment is enhanced by the acquisition of problem-solving skills (D'Zurilla and Nezu 1999). In the light of this research, Egan suggests that taking a positive psychology approach to helping should involve 'seeing problem management as life-enhancing learning and treating all encounters with clients as opportunity development sessions' (Egan 2002a: 6). This is the kind of slightly convoluted phraseology that counsellors sometimes have difficulty with. In 'translation' I think Egan is saying that managing problems is more a proactive than a re-active process in that it provides opportunities for clients to learn effective skills that will stand them in good stead for the future.

The positive psychology approach fits well with both the emphasis on problem management and opportunity development evident in Egan's work and with the person-centred roots of the skilled helper model. Both positive psychology and person-centred therapy share an aversion to the dominant ideology of the medical model of human distress and both approaches are fashioned on an ideology of human potential rather than one of illness and psychopathology (Joseph and Worsley 2005a). Indeed, Joseph and Worsley (2005b) have argued that there is great potential for fruitful collaboration between the positive psychology movement and the person-centred movement based on many shared ideas and goals.

Egan's positive psychology approach has grown out of the values and principles that closely inform his understanding of the culture of helping. A number of these are discussed below.

Values and the culture of helping

Egan defines values, at their simplest, as 'what people prize' (Egan 2002a: 45). These may be principles, standards or ideals such as political freedom, personal security or fair treatment of others. He sees values as interacting with shared beliefs and assumptions to produce cultural norms that influence patterns of behaviour and attitudes. As counsellors work predominantly on an individual rather than societal level with clients, he suggests that a further definition that is relevant in helping relationships is that values are 'also a set of practical criteria for making decisions. As such they are drivers of behavior' (Egan 2002a: 45).

Values in this sense constitute the personal cultures of both helpers and clients and will also influence the culture of counselling. For example, the British Association for Counselling and Psychotherapy (BACP) has developed an 'Ethical Framework for Good Practice in Counselling and Psychotherapy' (BACP 2002) and the values and principles outlined in this document represent the culture of counselling as defined by one professional association in the UK. This framework provides ethical guidelines that govern the professional conduct (that is, drive the behaviour) of its members. Practitioners who adhere to this framework will draw on its values and principles to guide their interactions with clients on a professional basis. At the same time, individual counsellors will have their own 'personal culture' of helping that significantly influences their interventions with clients and the ways in which they understand and apply the ethical framework.

A counsellor's personal culture of helping will be fluid and malleable to the degree that it is mediated by the evolving professional self and the therapist's use of self (Skovholt and Rønnestad 1992; Wosket 1999). Personal culture forms the basis of the therapist's ability to respond with sensitivity to difference and diversity in their clinical practice. A further important point that Egan makes about values is that they are significantly mediated by the quality of the therapeutic relationship since 'the relationship is the vehicle through which values come alive' (Egan

2002a: 44). More about Egan's view of the counselling relationship is said in subsequent chapters, with a particular focus in Chapter 4.

Core values and empathy

Within the framework of the skilled helper model the key values that underpin the culture of helping as understood by Egan are client empowerment and the Rogerian core qualities of respect, genuineness and empathy. These core values suffuse the communication skills that drive the model. Whereas Rogers considered empathy to be a facilitative condition and one of the core qualities of the helping relationship, Egan views empathy both as 'a basic *value* that informs and drives *all* helping behavior' and as 'an *interpersonal communication skill*' (Egan 2002a: 48, original emphasis). To differentiate the latter from the former, Egan has adopted the somewhat unwieldy phrase 'sharing empathic highlights' in the seventh edition of his book to describe the communication skill through which helpers share their understanding of clients' experiences, behaviours and feelings. As a value, empathy places a requirement on the counsellor to understand clients as fully as possible in three particular ways:

1 Understanding the client from her or his point of view
2 Understanding the client in and through the context (the social setting) of her or his life
3 Understanding the dissonance wherever it appears to exist between the client's point of view and reality.

Understood in these terms, empathy incorporates acceptance of difference and diversity and also challenge. While empathy puts a requirement on the counsellor to understand the client from that client's personal and cultural frame of reference, it also allows for the helper to respectfully 'reality test' that frame of reference where it may appear to be limited, inaccurate or self-defeating. Egan asserts that in order 'to be client-centred, helpers must first be reality-centred' (Egan 2002a: 87).

I think it is important to inject a note of caution here about who determines 'reality' in relation to Egan's third requirement above. The considerable danger that is present in any therapist-determined reality is of the client being socialised into the coun-sellor's model of what is real. As Safran and Segal (1990) have pointed out, therapists have to work with the tension between challenging apparently distorted cognitions and accepting that clients are the final arbiters of their own reality. This is a post-modern view that challenges the traditional notion that the therapist has some privileged understanding of the client's internal and/or external reality. For instance, a therapist who is too intent on challenging cognitive distortions, on the assumption that it is these that cause the client's problems, may miss other relevant contextual factors (such as a dysfunctional family system or subtle forms of political oppression) and thereby unwittingly condone an unhealthy status quo. The optimal stance for the counsellor to adopt is a questioning position of 'not knowing' and of preparing to 'be informed' by the client about his or her world view, mean-ings and understandings (Anderson and Goolishian 1992; Kaye 1999; Morss and Nichterlein 1999).

Here, my take on Egan's third point above would align closely with those constructivist therapists (e.g. DeYoung 2003; Safran and Muran 2000; Safran and Segal 1990) who view therapy as a dialectical process involving the meeting of two, sometimes similar, sometimes different, constructions of reality. This view emphasises the creation and experiencing of meanings (rather than fixed realities) between therapist and client in dialogue with one another (Anderson and Goolishian 1992; Friedman 1992; Hycner 1991). I am reminded that it is important for therapists to bear in mind that their own and their clients' accounts of the world and reality are culturally determined and, at best, consist of local knowledge and conventions rather than universal truths (Gergen 1985, 1994c, 1999; Gergen and Gergen 2000; Gergen and Kaye 1992). This becomes very apparent wherever counsellors work with clients whose experience of the world significantly diverges from their own.

Client empowerment

Egan describes client empowerment as 'an outcome value' (Egan 2002a: 55), which is linked to the goal of helping clients to become better problem solvers in their everyday lives. Counsellors, by virtue of their very role and status, occupy a more powerful position than those who seek their help. Helpers misuse their power wherever they encourage deference or dependency and when they oppress others. On the other hand, counsellors can use the power inherent in their position within a social-influence process (Strong 1968) to empower clients to become more effective at managing their own problems.

A 'positive psychology' approach encourages helpers not to see their clients as victims 'even if victimising circumstances have diminished a client's degree of freedom' (Egan 2002a: 56) but instead to 'work with the freedom that is left' (*ibid.*). Egan therefore suggests that helpers who use the model should think of themselves as consultants and facilitators who provide as much or as little assistance as the client needs in order to manage the problem situations in their lives a little, or even a great deal, better (Egan 1984b). Exercise 1.1, at the end of the chapter, is designed to assist counsellors and helpers to explore their own responses to issues around the use and misuse of power in helping relationships.

Giving psychology away

A key principle informing the skilled helper model is that of 'giving psychology away' (Egan 1984a; Egan and Cowan 1979; Larson, 1984). Pinsof (1995: 100) describes a proactive, skills-learning element as characteristic of counselling approaches that have a problem-management emphasis and suggests that 'as teachers, problem-centered therapists give away their skills and expertise in human problem solving . . . Problem-centered therapists should leave patients stronger than they were before therapy'.

Egan's work figures large within the tradition of psychological approaches that view change not as the mysterious preserve of expert therapists, but as a generic process that clients can own and in which they themselves can become skilled (Dawes 1994; Karasu 1996; LeShan 1996; Nelson-Jones 2002; Spinelli 1994). Egan speaks of a need to de-mystify the profession of counselling and suggests that mystification is often mistaken for professionalism, which may be something very different (Sugarman 1995). In an interview he suggests that the acid test of professionalism is 'the degree that our clients live more effectively, or at least are in a situation where they can choose to live more effectively if they want' (Sugarman 1995: 279).

In a number of ways Egan shows himself to be in favour of the parsimonious principle of counselling – this being that the counsellor should be active only to the point of empowering clients to act on their own behalf. Geller *et al.* (1981–1982: 127) sum up this principle nicely when they state: 'the work of psychotherapy is successfully accomplished if . . . patients can assume roles and carry out functions for themselves which their therapists had previously performed for them'. Whenever that point is reached the therapist must be willing to step out of the limelight and allow the client to take both the initiative and the credit for change. The rationale behind this view is that the more clients are able to own the process of change, the more responsibility they can take for their own growth and development.

Egan has referred to the model as being 'radically client-centred' (Egan 2002a: 39), meaning that when used effectively it is more a client-owned rather than a counsellor-owned approach. The model, then, is designed to be given to the client in the form of skills and a process that can be used post-counselling. Egan recommends that 'clients should leave helping sessions more capable of managing problems and both spotting and developing opportunities' (Egan 2002a: xii) and he asserts that 'helping at its best provides clients with tools to become more effective self-helpers' (*ibid.*: 9). This places a requirement on the therapist to extend his or her therapeutic role to encompass the further roles of skills trainer and consultant. The theme of therapist as skills trainer and consultant is further developed in the chapters that follow.

Concepts of the person

Egan acknowledges an enormous debt to Carl Rogers in his own understanding and development of the counselling relationship and the 'humanizing communication skills' needed to activate the helping process (Egan 2002a: 66). Indeed, he has described himself as standing on the shoulders of Rogers. It is worth taking a moment to consider some of the similarities and differences in the work of Egan and Rogers in relation to the understanding each displays of the person and the helping process. While some direct comparisons of key features are possible, there are also areas where Egan and Rogers part company to the degree that differences are more apparent than similarities. Tables 1.1 and 1.2 give some of the main similarities and differences between the two and summarise the implications of these for the counselling process and relationship.

Table 1.1 A comparison between Rogers' and Egan's view of the person

Basic Assumptions: Rogers	Basic Assumptions: Egan
Human beings have an inherent tendency to progress instinctively towards accomplishment of potential	People become estranged from their capacity to realise their full potential through factors such as passivity, learned helplessness and their experience of undermining social systems and environmental conditions
Human beings' basic needs, capacities and tendencies are good or neutral, not evil, and healthy development means actualising these tendencies	There is a developmental framework within each particular culture so that any individual life cycle tends to fit into a common, culture-specific pattern
People are resourceful and capable of self-direction	Skills and knowledge have to be acquired at each stage of development in order to accomplish increasingly complex tasks and fulfil new roles
A distinction can be made between the real, underlying, organismic self and the self concept	Each individual creates a unique world in which psychological meaning is constructed from their own life events and social systems
Individuals become estranged from their organismic (true) self through internalising conditions of worth	Psychological disturbance is mainly attributed to: • Being out of community – i.e. isolated or alienated from key social systems • The inability to successfully negotiate developmental tasks • Being out of touch with developmental resources (intrapersonal, interpersonal and environmental)
Psychological disturbance is perpetuated where an individual continues to be dependent on the judgement of others for a sense of self-worth	Psychiatry and psychoanalysis have been too much focused on the individual at the expense of the social and cultural setting in which the individual exists. The horizons of the helper should be expanded to include these systems and settings
Behaviour is a function of how the individual feels about him- or herself on the inside	Abnormal behaviour and emotional disturbance are seen as ineffective behaviour and its consequences, arising from lack of knowledge or skills
The best vantage point for understanding behaviour is from the internal frame of reference of the individual	Since each individual creates their own unique world, the person can only be understood if the helper is willing and able to enter their particular frame of reference

From reviewing the differences and similarities in these basic assumptions, as outlined in Table 1.1, we can see that Egan's understanding of the person is located in more of a socio-political context than Rogers' view of the person, which is more situated within notions of intra- and interpersonal relating. This has a number of implications for how Rogers and Egan differently conceptualise the counselling process and relationship; these implications are summarised in Table 1.2.

We can gain a clearer understanding of Egan's working theory of the person if we take a closer look at his views about the causes of psychological disturbance. Inskipp and Johns (1984) reviewed Egan's early work and produced a useful overview of the factors deemed by Egan to cause or perpetuate psychological dis-ease, both internal and external to the person. The following summary draws on their analysis.

Factors within the person that cause and perpetuate psychological disturbance

- Passivity or learned helplessness that discourages self-responsibility.
- Low self-concept and self-defeating attitudes based on past experiences.
- Reinforcement for dysfunctional behaviour that encourages the repeating of old patterns.
- 'The psychopathology of the average' – losing touch with strengths, resources and aspirations needed to fulfil the potential to live more fully.
- Conflict or confusion over core values and beliefs, which may trigger depression and exacerbate indecisiveness and passivity.
- Insufficient learning about how to manage emotions (e.g. fear of moving beyond fixed habits, feelings of dependency on others).
- Lack of problem-management and opportunity-development skills.
- Lack of resources, e.g. support and challenge, to enable movement beyond insight to action.
- Being overwhelmed and immobilised by too many crises.
- Being stuck in a transition period between developmental stages and lacking the ability to make new commitments or risk new roles.

Table 1.2 A comparison between Rogers' and Egan's view of the counselling process

Implications for the Counselling Process and Relationship: Person-Centred Counselling	Implications for the Counselling Process and Relationship: The Skilled Helper Model
Both client and counsellor are trustworthy	The client is the expert on him or herself and the counsellor acts as consultant to and facilitator of the client's process. Reluctance and resistance are natural aspects of the change process
Therapy is essentially non-directive and is more about establishing and maintaining a facilitative person-to-person relationship than about identifying problems and solutions	Counselling is a social influence process. Helpers are skill learners and skill trainers and aim to be directive of the process but not the content of therapy. Opportunity development is as important in counselling as problem management
Individuals develop in a positive and constructive manner when a climate of respect and trust is established by the therapist	The quality of the therapeutic relationship importantly mediates the effectiveness of the change process but is not an end in itself
Since each individual is uniquely complex and different, diagnostic labelling can never be justified	The helper is dealing with unique human beings at particular points in their lives. Pathologising clients is unhelpful and perpetuates a remedial rather than a positive psychology approach to helping
Distortions between self and organism can be healed if therapy provides the unconditional positive regard to the person who lacked this acceptance in childhood	Therapy can help to overcome early developmental deficits by enabling the client to acquire skills in living, in particular interpersonal and problem management skills
Reintegration comes about as an increase in congruence through (i) a decrease in conditions of worth and (ii) an increase in unconditional self-regard	Changes in self-concept come about through empowerment as clients learn to be more effective at problem management and opportunity development
The communicated unconditional positive regard of a significant other (e.g. therapist) is one way of meeting these conditions	People are capable of realising their potential and rising above 'the psychopathology of the average' when given optimum amounts of supportive challenge within a therapeutic relationship
In order to be communicated, unconditional positive regard must exist in a context of empathic understanding	Empathy is a basic value that needs to inform and drive all helping behaviour and is also an interpersonal communication skill used to convey optimum amounts of support and challenge

Environmental factors that cause and perpetuate psychological disturbance

- Being at the mercy of social systems that limit options for action (e.g. inadequate state benefits for childcare or disability).
- Being helped by a therapist to cope with problems and then being returned to a destructive 'system' that raises more problems without the knowledge, skills or power to manage or change the system (e.g. where someone who has received counselling after a racist attack still has to live and function in a racist society).
- Key networks and systems, such as family, education or peers, may not provide support, challenge or the opportunities to acquire knowledge and learn the skills required for healthy development or to negotiate developmental tasks successfully.
- The interface between the environment and developmental stages may demand skills, knowledge, support and resources that the person does not have (e.g. a single parent who lacks the assertiveness, confidence and financial resources to access adequate pre-school experiences for his or her child).
- The perceived present state of the world and the individual's inability to affect what happens (e.g. futile wars, ecological 'meltdown', global terrorism) may produce alienation, despair, cynicism and loss of hope.

A people-in-systems framework

Given this analysis it is not surprising that Egan is critical of approaches to helping that have tended to privilege an individual-centred focus over a consideration of the socio-cultural settings in which the individual experiences his or her life. As the list of contributing factors above suggests, an understanding of clients and their difficulties needs to happen at several levels, and Egan presents a structure for so doing through his 'people-in-systems' framework (Egan 1984a; Egan and Cowan 1979). This framework involves understanding clients not only as unique and individual people, but also within the context of their lives. Context, as it is used in Egan's writing, consists of a number of dimensions and levels.

First, at a personal level, there is a requirement for counsellors to understand the developmental tasks and stages that face all individuals as they move through the phases of their lives. This lifelong and stage-specific process of development will involve both challenges and necessary losses (Viorst 1987) and may invoke crises and impasses for individuals who lack the knowledge, skills and experience to navigate their way successfully through developmental tasks and opportunities. The developmental life cycle of the individual is mediated by culture and within that culture will, unless disrupted in some way, tend to follow a common pattern. Human development through the life cycle is considered through the eight dimensions of: life stages; key human systems; developmental tasks; developmental resources; basic human support; working knowledge; skills; and developmental crises (Egan and Cowan 1979). These are described in a little more detail below.

Dimensions of human development through the life cycle

1   *Life stages* acknowledges that there is likely to be a certain predictability about the specific age-related tasks and transitions that an individual will move through within their particular society or culture. Counsellors need to understand the culture-specific life stages of their clients.

2   *Key human systems* refers to the need for helpers to understand the broader context of their clients' lives by considering how locations (e.g. family, school, work setting) impact on the individual's life stages in both supportive and challenging ways.

3   *Developmental tasks* are essentially life's challenges; these demand risk taking and the learning of new skills and behaviours in order to be successfully managed.

4   *Developmental resources* are those attributes needed to assist in managing developmental tasks, and comprise, in particular, human support and challenge, working knowledge and skills.

5   *Basic human support* is provided by those who are able to offer empathic understanding of someone's experience from that individual's own frame of reference (e.g. religious elder, teacher, peer group, counsellor).

6   *Working knowledge* refers to a level of informed understanding needed to deal with developmental challenges. Therapists may need to facilitate the development of working knowledge where this is missing (e.g. people who have been sexually

abused as children often have deficiencies in working knowledge about how to negotiate non-abusive and appropriately paced sexual relationships as they move into adulthood).

7   *Skills* refers to the competencies needed to manage the demands and challenges of life stages and transitions (e.g. problem-management skills, self-management skills, interpersonal skills).

8   *Developmental crises* are those 'dividing' points in an individual's life where significant change, for better or worse, is confronted with associated feelings of anxiety, hope, anticipation, upheaval (e.g. leaving home for the first time or facing one's own mortality as the result of a serious illness).

Egan's view of human progression through the life cycle is perhaps best summed up in the following words: 'there is no development without ongoing conditions of challenge and support in the human systems of our lives' (Egan and Cowan 1979: 31).

The impact of personal settings

The second aspect of attention to context requires the therapist to consider how an individual's experience will be influenced by the immediate personal settings of that person's life, for instance extended family, network of friends and colleagues, school, college, care home, place of worship or workplace. Egan and Cowan state this plainly in asserting that 'it is impossible to understand human development merely by focusing on individuals or on what transpires inside them, because the ways in which individuals develop are influenced not only by other individuals but by society as well' (Egan and Cowan 1979: 66).

One way in which therapists need to take account of the personal settings that impact on clients is to consider the roles that different settings require of their clients and the tensions that can arise between conflicting demands within these roles. An example of one such tension frequently encountered by counsellors is that of the unrealistic expectations that clients can place on themselves and which are derived from family or work colleagues. Clients also often experience tensions as they progress through therapy and begin to replace an external locus of evaluation with an internal one. While the client may experience a more authentic and congruent sense of self as a result of this process, partners, children, colleagues and friends may struggle to accommodate the changing person who no longer appears to think, feel and behave in the accustomed manner in which he or she has previously occupied his or her role.

The interaction between the individual and personal settings

Third in our consideration of contextual factors, helpers will need to acknowledge the impact that the interaction between these immediate networks – social, family, community and workplace – will have on the individual. An example here might be a child who has behavioural problems that manifest in school but are found to originate from an abusive family situation.

Egan suggests that one of the most widely experienced precipitating and sustaining factors for people's problems in living is being 'out of community', that is, cut off from those social and familial roles and responsibilities that are self- and other-enhancing. Carr (2004: 113) defines social responsibility as 'the ability to co-operate and contribute constructively to one's social group' and demonstrates that people who have strong social support networks and bonds have 'better physical and mental health, fewer illnesses and less depression, recover more rapidly from physical illness and psychological problems, and have a lower risk of death' (Carr 2004: 218).

If counsellors can help clients to build links between themselves and the personal systems that surround them, they may enable clients to live more rewarding lives in a '*community* of systems rather than a series of disparate subsystems' (Egan and Cowan 1979: 88). The following example from my own counselling practice (included with the client's permission) illustrates this:

> The client came into counselling in the early stages of her recovery from alcohol and heroin addiction. In the process of weekly counselling over two years she came to terms with her experiences of childhood sexual abuse and her consuming and compulsive need to blot these experiences out with alcohol and drugs. Prior to counselling, her day-to-day existence for several years had consisted entirely of working out how to get her next drink or fix of heroin. This had involved her in activities that put her in danger of breaking the law and in

frequent unsafe sex. She had become entirely self-absorbed in this lifestyle and, in the process, had alienated herself from her family and friends.

In parallel with her individual counselling sessions the client regularly attended group meetings of Alcoholics Anonymous (AA) and Narcotics Anonymous (NA) and increasingly involved herself in the running of these groups at local and regional levels. As her guilt over her previous destructive and harmful behaviours softened into remorse, she developed strategies for making some amends for these behaviours, such as becoming a volunteer prison visitor and a support person for others working AA and NA programmes. She re-established regular contact with her immediate family and made a priority of repairing past ruptures with them. At the same time she started to get involved in a number of social- and health-related activities, such as joining an astronomy society and a gym and regularly attending alternative therapy treatments. As her counselling drew to a close she registered for a professional practitioner training in an alternative therapy and declared her intention of joining a church fellowship in order to publicly acknowledge and share with others the joy she experienced in the spiritual dimension of her recovery.

The impact of large institutions

Fourth in Egan's review of contextual factors, it is suggested that the client needs to be viewed and understood within the context of the larger institutions that, directly or indirectly, influence his or her life, for instance government, global alliances, the media and organised religion.

Although these larger systems do not 'enfold' clients in the same immediate way that their personal networks do, they may have a profound effect on the quality and course of a person's life. One way this is often encountered in counselling is with clients who experience themselves as powerless and at the mercy of invisible forces that control their fate (for example, the asylum seeker awaiting the outcome of an application for political refugee status; the client with enduring mental health problems who is turned down for disabled living allowance; or the single parent who is faced with the desperate prospect of having to become homeless before having any hope of being properly re-housed).

Cultural influences

Fifth in considering context, Egan suggests that broader cultural identifications, traditions and assimilations need to be included in the helper's vision to gain as wide a perspective as possible on the client and his or her world. In defining culture as a 'system' at this level, Egan cites Novak's (1979: 40) definition of culture as 'the system of symbols, values, ideas, rituals, practices, and institutions that define the attitudes and daily operations of . . . people, that give substance and meaning to their political and economic activities'.

By their very nature, cultural influences are enduring and pervasive and often exist as unexamined assumptions around which our lives are structured. It is an ethical and professional requirement of counsellors to do what they can to develop culturally sensitive practice and to challenge their own culturally bound assumptions and stereotypes when working with clients who have backgrounds and life experiences different from their own. An exercise to help trainees begin to develop culturally sensitive practice (Exercise 1.2) is included at the end of this chapter.

It will have become apparent from the discussion so far that Egan's view of the person comprises a 'deficit' rather than a pathology model. This means that he views many of the problems that clients bring to counselling as arising from their difficulties in harnessing energy and resources (both internal and external) to realise their best potential. He cites Maslow's oft-quoted assertion that what is usually considered to be 'normal' in psychology 'is really a psychopathology of the average, so undramatic and so widely spread that we don't even notice it ordinarily' (Maslow 1968: 16). Egan considers that unused human potential, because it is more widespread, 'constitutes a more serious social problem than emotional disorders' (Egan 2002a: 151).

In summary, although a unified theory of personality is not presented in Egan's work, he clearly identifies the healthy and functional person as someone who has the necessary knowledge, skills and resources to successfully complete developmental tasks and transitions and to handle upsets and crises (and even view these as opportunities for growth) when they occur along the way. The individual's ability to accomplish life's challenges will be mediated by external factors in the environment and may be enhanced or diminished by these. Thus individuals who are on a low income or are badly housed will have their options in living limited by social and economic constraints; institutional and individual forms of racism will oppress minority clients; and a dysfunctional or neglectful family environment may leave someone an enduring legacy of interpersonal skill and relationship deficits. A natural extension of Egan's attention to the socio-cultural context of counselling has been his development of change agent models and skills within the broader field of organisational change (Egan 1985, 1988a, 1988b, 1993, 1994).

In Chapter 2 I will move on to consider the goals of helping as understood within the skilled helper model before beginning to outline the model itself and highlight the key steps and stages within it. Before starting the next chapter you may wish to review the training exercises that follow and build on the discussion so far.

Exercise 1.1: The use and misuse of power and authority in counselling

Take a few moments to reflect on the following questions. Then work in a small group to explore your responses to the questions with others. Share the time equally between you and allow for a few minutes at the end to debrief your experience of the exercise with the rest of your group.

Think of yourself as a client/helpee:

• How have you experienced the misuse of power when you have been a client or helpee?
• What was your response to this?
• Why do you think you responded in this way?

Think of yourself as a counsellor or helper:

• As a counsellor or helper, when and how might you have misused your power?
• What may have caused you to do that?
• How do you own and/or deny your own power as a counsellor or helper?

Now think about the following questions:

- Who and what do you think has had an influence on the way you respond to power issues as a counsellor/helper and as a client/helpee?
- What do you consider to be some of the legitimate ways counsellors or helpers can exercise their power and authority?
- How might your exploration of these questions inform your own practice as a counsellor/helper?

Tutor: allow time for a whole-group debrief to air thoughts and feelings about the exercise and to bring together any significant learning.

Exercise 1.2: Helping counsellors to develop awareness of their own cultural identification and assumptions

Start with a few minutes of personal reflection to list all the cultures and subcultures you belong to, or might be seen as belonging to by others. Culture here is taken to mean all the aspects of diversity that you own and acknowledge. Culture in this sense extends beyond race or ethnicity to include other dimensions such as religion, class, education, socio-economic status, sexual orientation, mental and physical ability, gender and age.

Discuss your list in a small group and take the time to consider the following questions:

1 What cultural similarities, norms and differences do you notice in your group?
2 How do these impact on your relationships with others in your group?
3 Who do you identify with most in your small group and why?
4 Who are the people who feel more like outsiders in your group? Why do you feel like this?
5 What would need to happen for the outsiders to be able to feel more understood and included in this group?
6 What are the power differentials in your group? Who is seen as holding the most power and why is that?
7 Has anyone in your group felt oppressed or dominated by a culture to which someone else in the group belongs? How do/did you experience that?

Take some time to debrief the exercise within your small group:

- What did you appreciate about the exercise?
- What was difficult?
- What have you learned – about yourself, about others, about counselling/helping?
- What was it like to work together on these issues?

Tutor: allow time for a whole-group debrief to air thoughts and feelings about the exercise and to bring together any significant learning.

Chapter 2

Overview of the skilled helper model 1: stage one

This chapter starts with a consideration of Egan's understanding of the goals of helping and then presents an overview of stage one of the skilled helper model. A number of the key competencies that counsellors need to develop in order to work effectively in this part of the model are outlined. The overview presented in this chapter is in no way intended as a substitute for a detailed study of Egan's original text on the skilled helper. Instead, what is offered here is a summary of the model, in the language and terminology in which I practise and teach it. By implication, this is therefore a personal and partial perspective on the model but one that hopefully will also add to the reader's understanding of the counselling process outlined in *The Skilled Helper*.

A truth that I have learned in my own counselling practice is that time well spent in stage one of the model pays dividends in expediting the work of stages two and three. This learning is reflected in the material that follows in that I have chosen to write more fully about stage one (in this chapter) and rather less about stages two and three (in the next chapter). Case study examples based on real counselling sessions are included in the hope of bringing the process alive for readers. At the end of the chapter are guidelines and an exercise designed to give readers the chance to explore some of the material presented in more depth.

The goals of helping

The following fable (Egan 1984a; Egan and Cowan 1979) provides a potent metaphor for Egan's view of the helping process. Although rather lengthy, it is quoted here in full as I often find myself referring to this fable when teaching the model and attempting to summarise Egan's 'upstream' and proactive approach to counselling.

> A person walking beside a river sees someone drowning. This person jumps in, pulls the victim out, and begins artificial respiration. Then another drowning person calls for help. The rescuer jumps into the water again and pulls the second victim out. This process repeats itself several times until finally, much to the amazement of the bystanders who have gathered to watch his drama, the rescuer, even though screams of yet another victim can be clearly heard from the river, gets up from administering artificial respiration and begins to walk upstream. One of the bystanders calls out: 'Where are you going? Can't you hear the cries of the latest victim?' The rescuer replies: 'You take care of him. I'm going upstream to find out who's pushing all these people in and see whether I can stop it.' He might have added: 'I'm also going to find out why all these people can't swim and see whether I can teach them how'.
>
> (Egan 1984a: 23)

The point of this fable is to highlight the limitations of remedial, 'downstream' approaches to helping that, as Egan asserts, frequently fail to 'strike at the social conditions that spawn individual casualties and to teach those who suffer from oppressive social settings how to cope' (Egan 1984a: 23). A prime culprit here, Egan believes, is the medical model with its tendency to define problems in social living as types of illness that require treatment. The corollary of this is that people are blamed for problems that actually have their primary origin in society – a phenomenon that is colloquially known as 'blaming the victim'.

An alternative view is to consider that much of what is called 'mental illness' may well be a healthy and normal response to a sick system. A summary of Egan's view is that in psychological intervention we should be moving from remediation to prevention – from downstream to upstream forms of helping. In this, Egan's perspective aligns itself with deconstructionist therapists in rejecting therapeutic approaches that treat the individual as the locus of pathology and, as observed by Kaye (1999: 20), thereby divert 'attention from the role played by socio-cultural factors in the genesis of psychological distress'.

Kaye has outlined the key assumptions that underpin the medical model of therapy and these tie in closely with Egan's criticisms of the predominant victim-blaming culture of much psychological intervention. These are:

1   An underlying cause or basis of pathology
2   The location of this cause within individuals and their relationships
3   The diagnosability of the problem
4   Treatability via a specifically designed set of techniques.

(Kaye 1999: 20–21)

Two very significant corollaries of these assumptions that are frequently reflected in therapeutic activity are: (1) exploration and interpretation of the client's story from the therapist's frame of reference; and (2) attempting to engage the client in behaviour change consistent with the therapist's frame or theory. Kaye highlights what he considers to be the major flaws in this conceptualisation and the impact these have on counselling activity in terms that again closely mirror Egan's expressed concerns about therapist-led forms of helping:

> This conceptualization perpetuates the concept of the therapist as having privileged knowledge, a socially accredited expert who can both provide an authoritative true version of a problem and act according to a set of prescribed activities to correct it. In practice this gives rise to a top-down and instrumental therapist-centred activity – one in which the therapist acts instrumentally via dialogue with the 'client's' narrative and behaviour in order to change it rather than working collaboratively together with the 'client' toward new solutions which the 'client' finds fitting.
>
> (Kaye 1999: 21)

Far from viewing counselling as a 'cure-all' for people's problems in living, Egan suggests that the costs and consequences of counselling when weighed against other forms of human and social intervention should be carefully considered. This is illustrated through an analogy used to show that counselling, like other professions, can suffer from 'the law of the instrument'. In the same way that the child who is given a hammer is likely to discover that almost everything needs hammering, so 'helpers, once equipped with the models, methods, and skills of the helping process, can see all human problems as needing their attention' (Egan 2002a: 231). The dangers of operating according to the law of the instrument can be reduced when helpers have clear goals for the helping process that increase the chances of that process being one of minimal, effective intervention.

Egan outlines the two principal goals of helping encompassed by the skilled helper model as:

> Goal 1: Help clients manage their problems in living more effectively and develop unused resources and missed opportunities fully.
> Goal 2: Help clients become better at helping themselves in their everyday lives.
>
> (Egan 2002a: 7–8)

This emphasis on equipping the client to become an effective self-helper has contributed significantly to the popularity of the skilled helper model, particularly in the field of brief counselling. Hudson-Allez (1997: 41) argues that the skilled helper model lends itself well to time-limited therapy because of this essentially pragmatic quality and suggests that it 'is probably the most commonly used model of counselling taught in the UK today' precisely because 'one of its primary goals is to assist clients to become more effective at managing their own lives'. In the service of these two over-riding goals for the helping process, counsellors need to be both skill learners and skill trainers. This is because gaining interpersonal and problem-management skills is considered by Egan to be the solid foundation for human living and optimum growth.

Overview of the skilled helper model

Here again I wish to emphasise that for readers who need to acquire comprehensive knowledge and understanding of the skilled helper model, this chapter and the one that follows are no substitute for a careful study and application of Egan's own current text on the model. In the following sections I give a skeleton outline of the three stages and nine steps of the model but have chosen to concentrate most on those aspects that, in my own experience as a trainer and counsellor, merit further 'unpacking', either because their apparent complexity seems initially to baffle some trainees or because I feel I have adopted a somewhat different 'take' from that of Egan. In so doing I have adopted more of a discursive than a textbook approach to presenting the material and, as a consequence of this, certain elements of the model are examined and explored more fully than are others. I hope that where I may have fallen short on breadth of coverage I have compensated for this by depth of engagement with the elements I have chosen to address.

For the purposes of simplicity and clarity I will present a summary of the three stages as if they are separate and sequential phases of counselling, whereas in reality the stages and steps are many-layered and textured and inevitably interweave and overlap in terms of both process and content. Egan has called this the requirement for a 'trialogue' (York St John counselling summer school 1993) between the three different stages of the model as they interact with one another. Several examples of transcript based on actual counselling sessions are included to illustrate how the therapist and client might experience the model in practice. Figure 2.1 presents an overview of the skilled helper model.

The skilled helper model is a pragmatic framework that shares the 'parsimonious' principle of cognitive behavioural approaches. Egan suggests that we use as little or as much of the model as will benefit the client. Minimum intervention, as already indicated, is considered to be the optimum way of working. Egan (1984a: 25) advises that models of change such as the skilled helper must satisfy two criteria.

1   They must be complex enough to account for the reality they attempt to portray and
2   They must be simple enough to use.

Models that satisfy only the first criterion may be theoretically sound but difficult to apply, whereas those that meet only, or mainly, the second criterion may be overly simplistic and conceptually limited. The skilled helper model is designed to be both complex enough to cover the main aspects of any helping relationship and uncomplicated enough to be easily learned and applied.

Stated in simple terms, the three stages of the skilled helper model are concerned with:

THE SKILLED HELPER MODEL

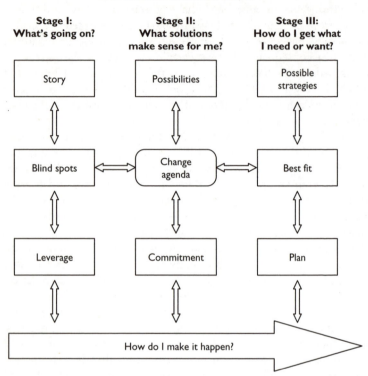

Figure 2.1 Overview of the skilled helper model from *The Skilled Helper: A Problem Management Approach to Helping*, 7th edition, by Egan, © 2002. Reprinted with permission of Wadsworth, a division of Thomson Learning.

1   problem definition
2   goal setting
3   action planning.

Egan has used different terminology in the various editions of *The Skilled Helper* to describe the three stages. In the seventh edition (2002a), these are captioned as follows:

Stage 1: 'What's going on?'
Stage 2: 'What solutions make sense to me?'
Stage 3: 'How do I get what I need or want?'

The terminology is still evolving. In his most recent publication on the skilled helper (Egan 2006) the stages are captioned as follows:

Stage 1: Current picture
Stage 2: Preferred picture
Stage 3: Action plan

In this latest publication Egan uses the term 'interrelated tasks' instead of 'steps' for the subsections within each stage of the model. This is in order to emphasise 'the work that needs to be done in each stage' (Egan 2006: 13).

Underpinning the three stages of the model is an action arrow (see Figure 2.1). This displays the question: 'How do I make it happen?' in the seventh edition of *The Skilled Helper* (Egan 2002a) and the caption 'Action leading to valued outcomes' in *Essentials of Skilled Helping* (Egan 2006). The language of positive psychology describes problem solving as 'the ability to identify social and interpersonal problems, define them in solvable terms and generate and implement effective solutions' (Carr 2004: 113). Close comparisons with Egan's problem-management model are evident here. The action arrow underscores Egan's view that the counsellor should have no dialogue with the client that does not result in some form of action at every step and stage of the model. Indeed, he has suggested that the best predictor of success is what the client does between session one and session two.

One way that I have found that action can become embedded in the process from the outset is by asking clients to summarise where they are up to at the end of a session and then asking: 'Is there anything that would help us to manage this or move it along before the next session?' If the client returns and has not done anything to move things on I can still instil the possibility of change by asking 'If you had thought of acting, what might you have done?' Thus no session, in Egan's view, should end without some action points – although action can take many forms, as discussed below.

The skilled helper model is sometimes criticised for its perceived emphasis on outcomes and action over depth exploration and 'being with' the client. As argued in the next chapter, I consider this criticism to be more apparent than real. Detractors of the model on the grounds that it is 'too action-oriented' may be viewing it through a rather simplistic definition of action. Action, as understood by Egan, is not limited to behavioural change. Action can be understood in terms of *internal* (an inner shift or change in attitude, thinking or feeling) and *external* (observable action in behavioural terms) and as occurring both *in sessions* and *outside sessions*.

Thus a matrix of action can be envisaged to understand the various forms of action that may occur within all steps and stages of the model (see Table 2.1). Internal actions such as insights and shifts in thoughts and feelings can be turned into options for change through the counsellor inviting clients to consider how they might become rooted in real life, either symbolically in the counselling relationship, or in real-life 'experiments'. Here is an example:

The counsellor and client have been thinking together about whether there might be any significance in the fact that the client is always at least five minutes late for her session.

Counsellor: There are so many practical things that can get in the way of you getting here on time and I understand that it would take quite an effort for you to be here for the start of every session. And yet I am conscious of you making do with less than what is available to you every time we start late.

Client: It's hard for me to think about it like that – making do with less. It's actually what I do all the time but I think you are the first person who's ever commented on me being late in that way. Most people make a joke about it.

Counsellor: What is it like for you when I comment on it in that way?

Client: It makes me think about how I always expect to make do with less and that it doesn't matter [starts to look tearful].

Counsellor   [gently]: Does it still not matter?

Client: It matters a bit more now that I'm starting to value myself more. I didn't think you would be bothered,

> but now that I know that you notice when I'm late, it feels like it's going to be harder for me to be late.
>
> Counsellor: I feel like I've given you another problem to deal with [both laugh].
>
> Client: Well, I could try being on time so that you are not sitting waiting for me.
>
> Counsellor: You don't need to be on time for me. If you do come on time, I would like you to come on time for you.
>
> Client: That feels like quite a challenge. I'm not sure if I can do it for me, but I want to try.

Following this interaction the client was hardly ever late for future sessions and indeed displayed anger towards those who delayed her on the rare occasions where she was held up at work and wasn't able to arrive on time. The example perhaps shows how internal actions (shifts in thinking and feeling) can lead to observable changes in behaviour.

Table 2.1 gives a number of examples of the different kinds of internal and external action encompassed by the skilled helper model. The session transcript presented in Chapter 3 (p. 72) gives further examples of the different forms of action identified in Table 2.1.

Stage one: current picture

What's going on?

There are a number of ways of considering the question 'What's going on?' that underpins stage one. When unpacked, this big question is likely to include the following sub-questions, all of which are relevant to the work that will take place in the first stage of the counselling process:

- Why have you come for counselling now?
- What seems to be the essence of what is wrong?
- What are you/we avoiding or overlooking?
- What is *really* going on?

Table 2.1 Different types of action encompassed by the skilled helper model

Internal in-session action	External in-session action
Covert behaviours and changes in thoughts and feelings in the counselling session (may be disclosed or remain undisclosed), such as: • Seeing a situation differently (e.g. from another person's perspective) • Having an insight about something • Making links between past and present (e.g. recognising my mother's critical voice is still in my head) • Experiencing an unfamiliar feeling (e.g. relief, sadness, anger) • Having a body sensation (e.g. feeling sick or light headed)	Observable in-session behaviour such as: • Practising a new skill (e.g. making eye contact; speaking more assertively) • Role playing how to handle a situation • Desensitisation work (e.g. approaching a feared object) • Engaging in relaxation or guided imagery exercises • Saying 'I let you make me feel stupid' instead of 'You make me feel stupid' • Dialogue work (e.g. empty chair or switching chairs) • Crying or laughing
Internal between-session action	**External between-session action**
Covert behaviours and changes in attitudes, thoughts and feelings between counselling sessions, such as: • Making a decision to keep a journal • Imagining what the counsellor might say in certain situations • Deciding I need to adjust my work/life balance • Using relaxing imagery in stressful situations • Using coping self-talk • Repeating silent affirmations • Crying inside	Changes in observable behaviour between counselling sessions, such as: • Keeping a diary of panic attacks • Attending lectures more regularly • Reading self-help literature • Ending a dysfunctional relationship • Cutting down on drinking • Making more time for self-nurturing • Asking questions about the past of family members • Eating something and keeping it down before a counselling session

- What is the potential you are not using that is frustrating you or getting you into difficulties?
- What are the blocks to you using your potential?

This list is not given to suggest that counsellors rattle these particular questions off to the client, more that they need to rest in the helper's awareness and inform his or her listening. By holding such questions in mind it is likely that the counsellor will listen out for the client's resources and for the opportunities he or she might be missing, as much as listening for problems and stuckness.

Although presenting the model in a linear way makes stage one appear to be a beginning stage, the question 'What's going on?' is one that applies throughout the counselling process. Issues that the client brings forward for the counsellor's attention in the beginning phase of therapy often give way as the work proceeds to new and emerging problems, dilemmas and difficulties. 'What's going on?' is a question that is as much applicable to the process as to the content of therapy. It is often as productive (sometimes more so) to consider what might be going on in the relationship between counsellor and client as it is to think about what is going on in terms of the client's issues. 'What is going on between us?' (counsellor and client immediacy) is frequently a more timely and pertinent question than one that is aimed to elicit some aspect of the client's story. Immediacy in the counselling relationship is discussed in more detail in the section on blind spots and new perspectives (1B) below.

Step 1A: story

At the heart of most counselling interactions is the process of helping clients to construct a coherent and meaningful personal narrative or story. In the post-modern, constructionist view of therapy, narrative is a powerful transformative element that enables clients to reinterpret, or re-author, the events of their lives with new and different meanings and realities (Anderson and Goolishian 1992; Epston *et al.* 1992). Egan has been at pains to point out that story is not the same as history. He advises helpers not to encourage endless history telling but to view story-telling as a process of sifting relevant facts from the client's history. Unskilled helpers tend to get mired down in too much history. If we don't know what else to do we simply tend to look for more and more detail, so Egan suggests that we have a constant check-step in mind in the form of a question: 'Is there some kind of movement here?' As already discussed, movement has many subtle and diverse forms that can vary from faint, hardly perceptible ripples to great surges.

Within the skilled helper model stories may consist of both problems and missed opportunities. The importance of active listening is emphasised throughout the model. This emphasis is sometimes missed by those who consider that the model privileges action above understanding and 'being with' the client, whereas in fact Egan has explicitly stated that 'listening is not merely a skill', rather 'it is a rich metaphor for the helping relationship' (Egan 2002a: 75). The counsellor enables the client to tell his or her story through those active listening skills that comprise the building blocks of interpersonal communication: attending (both verbal and non-verbal), listening, reflecting (content, thoughts and feelings), summarising and clarifying.

These communication skills help to convey the key quality of empathy, through which the counsellor expresses understanding and acceptance of the client. Egan is clear that empathy is far more than a set of skills, as his comments on paraphrasing indicate:

> I still avoid such terms as *paraphrasing* and *restatement*. If you are truly empathic, if you listen actively, and if you thoughtfully process what you hear, putting what the client says in its proper context, then you do more than paraphrase or restate. There is something of *you* in your response. A good response is a product of caring and hard work. Good [empathic] highlights are fully human, not mechanical.
>
> (Egan 2002a: 97, original emphasis)

Empathy, while key to understanding the client's world, can only ever be an approximation given that it is 'metaphysically impossible to actually get "inside" the world of another person and experience the world as he or she does' (Egan 2002a: 76). The best attempts at understanding are determined by the willingness of the counsellor to allow the client to have an impact on him- or herself. This is the essence of empathic resonance. 'Real understanding, because it passes through you, should convey some part of you. Parroting doesn't. To avoid parroting, tap into the processing you've been doing as you listened' (Egan 2002a: 115).

To elicit as clear and specific a story as possible, the counsellor encourages clients to tell their story with concrete examples of behaviours (what the clients do and do not do), experiences (what is happening or has happened to them) and feelings (how they feel about their behaviours and experiences). So, rather than talking about feelings in a vacuum, clients are encouraged to relate their emotions to what they experience and do.

It is often productive to help clients turn what they may well describe as entrenched character traits into specific behaviours.

This is because it is behaviours (what clients do and do not do) that often keep them locked into problem situations. Thus while a client may say 'I'm lazy', a more useful way for the counsellor to hear this may well be 'I don't seize opportunity or freedom'. A counsellor who takes such a view might then invite the client to describe behaviours and situations in which she is 'lazy' in order to help her consider the costs and consequences of this way of being. A useful question to begin this process would be 'How do you know that you are lazy?'

In the process of story-telling, the helper enables the client to explore feelings in terms of their nature, frequency and intensity as this will help to uncover the client's emotional range and what underlies this. For example, the client who frequently talks about being angry, but never shows it except for infrequent 'explosions', may believe that anger is unacceptable, dangerous and means being out of control. Faced with such a client the counsellor would do well to encourage gentle enquiry into where and how she learned about anger, and this might then generate a fruitful exploration of previous relationships or childhood experiences. This point is illustrated with a client example later in the section.

The essence of a good counselling intervention consists of an invitation to clients to connect with their internal world. Novice counsellors often allow clients to get away with reporting *on* themselves and their external world when they would do better to help them engage in a reflective process of internal communion *with* the self. As Bugental (1987: 26) proposes, the effective therapist 'is sensitized to note how genuinely his client is present, and he is prepared to devote significant efforts to aiding that client to increased involvement in the work. This focus on presence is a major cornerstone of the therapeutic art'. The fact is that clients often come to counselling with familiar stories that they have recounted many times previously (either to others or in their own minds, through constant rumination). The counsellor's task is to intervene in the repetitive loop of familiar story-telling to enable clients to see and experience their story in new ways.

One way of doing this is to encourage clients to view their response to their difficulties (for example feelings of hopelessness or helplessness) as a problem in itself rather than a reflection of reality. This is akin to the technique used by narrative therapists who help clients to externalise their problems through questioning and reframing (Parker 1999; Payne 2000; White and Epston

1990). This can help to create distance from the problem or crisis and thereby open up the possibility of challenging cognitive distortions and finding alternatives (Leiper and Kent 2001). Clients are encouraged to begin taking responsibility for what it is possible to change in their stories by being invited to talk about what they do or don't do, rather than what is, or has been, done to them. Compare the following two case examples that illustrate this distinction.

Client: I've had another really stressful week at work. My manager has been breathing down my neck like she's watching my every move and trying to catch me out.

Counsellor X: It sounds very difficult. Your stress levels are very high again and the way your manager is behaving is making it worse.

Client: She won't leave me alone to just get on with things and I'm sure it's because she thinks I'm not up to the job.

This is a fairly reasonable, if unexciting, attempt at basic empathy by counsellor X. The client probably feels understood and a bit soothed. We can re-run this scene from a slightly different angle with counsellor Y, as follows:

Client: I've had another really stressful week at work. My manager has been breathing down my neck like she's watching my every move and trying to catch me out.

Counsellor Y: It sounds pretty difficult to feel so stressed again. How do you respond to your manager breathing down your neck like that?

Client: I sort of tighten up and close in on myself. I start feeling that she thinks I'm not up to the job and then I start trying to avoid her.

Counsellor Y: I was just wondering there how much your tightening up and closing in on yourself is linked

	to your feelings that your manager doesn't think you're up to the job – and what else makes you think that?
Client:	I think it's a bit of a vicious cycle that I get into. If I'm a bit stressed and anxious I start to imagine she thinks I'm rubbish at my job. Then I feel bad about myself and sort of start getting all introverted and that makes it worse. I wish I could stop doing it.
Counsellor Y:	Well maybe we can start to look at how you might manage that, now that you are clearer about what you want to stop doing.

Here we can see that counsellor Y's response draws much more useful information from the client who, by her use of 'I' language, is beginning to own her own responses. This opens a way for the counsellor to gently begin to invite her to think about different ways of responding to the situation.

Egan (1998) has captured the balance needed between listening and intervening in stating that counsellors should help clients to tell their story in a way that will make a difference. This accords with the view taken by many narrative therapists that reciting a new story is not enough in itself to make a difference. For change to occur 'new stories must be experienced and lived outside of the four walls of a therapist's office' (Freedman and Combs 1996: 33).

Speaking at one of the York counselling summer schools, Egan made a distinction between interviewing and intervening, which is pertinent here. While interviewing is data gathering, interventions are 'seeing to it that something takes place'. He suggests that helpers should have this question firmly in mind when intervening: 'What can I do to raise the probability that the client will act on his or her behalf?' Another way of putting this is that counsellors should enable clients to tell their stories so that they learn something from so doing.

This sounds both simple and sensible, yet it is advice that is rarely heeded by helpers who allow clients to reproduce endlessly repetitive accounts of their problems and, in so doing, merely reinforce those difficulties. When this happens, what should be a constructive process of dialogue can degenerate into a near monologue by the client. Egan suggests that learning how to forge a dialogue with the client is one of the key competencies helpers need to develop and particularly so in the beginning phase of counselling.

> I find that the helping process goes best when I engage the client in a dialogue rather than give speeches or allow the client to ramble. In a dialogue, the helper's responses can be relatively frequent but should be lean and trim. In trying to be accurate, the beginner is often long winded, especially if he or she waits too long to respond. Again, the question 'What is the core of what this person is saying to me?' can help you make your responses short, concrete, and accurate.
>
> (Egan 2002a: 112)

Take the client mentioned above who has difficulty managing her angry feelings. To begin with in counselling she declared that she never felt angry although very occasionally she 'lost it' in an explosive rage and then felt terrified of seriously hurting herself or her partner. Some interventions the counsellor made at different times that helped her to learn a little more about her anger are given below. These extracts of dialogue are included with the client's permission and her responses are given to show what impact the counsellor's interventions made.

Counsellor: You say you never feel angry and yet we talk about anger a lot here and I don't think it's me who usually brings it up.

Client: Do we? Perhaps it's because it feels a bit safer here. I know I sometimes save things up and bring them here. I wonder if I do that with my anger. I don't *feel* angry, but at least you've noticed I might be talking about it.

Counsellor: Even though you've told me you never get angry, you have used words like 'irritated', 'frustrated' and 'pissed off' today. How close are they to angry?

Client: I don't think of that as being angry. For me, anger is always huge. I suppose I do feel a bit annoyed when people take me for granted, but I'd never say anything in case they rejected me.

Counsellor: If you never feel angry, what do you feel instead?
Client: I think I feel hurt and wounded but I would never show it. The most people see is that I go a bit quiet, but inside I'm trying hard to think it doesn't matter.

Counsellor: What would you be most frightened of if you did feel and express some anger?
Client: [*Starting to look scared and tearful*] Often I get really scared that I might turn out to be just like my mother. If I got angry, that would prove it.

In these examples it is possible to see the client's perspective on her anger opening up and a broader understanding of it emerging. In step 1B, which I will turn to next, this idea of amplifying the client's issue so that it can be seen more accurately and clearly is developed further through the notion of exploring blind spots and new perspectives.

Step 1B: blind spots and new perspectives

In the seventh edition of *The Skilled Helper* this step is called 'blind spots'. In *Essentials of Skilled Helping* (2006) it is called 'new perspectives' and in this publication Egan has noticeably reworked this part of model. The emphasis is more on the 'task' of helping clients reframe their stories and develop new perspectives than on the notion of the helper challenging the client's blind spots. This change in emphasis is in line with Egan's adoption of positive psychology which explicitly promotes a partnership model of helping in which the counsellor becomes the client's 'catalyst for a better future' (Egan 2006: 205).

The idea of exploring blind spots and developing new perspectives blends imperceptibly with the process of story-telling outlined in step 1A in that it means helping clients to tell their story in a way that increases the likelihood that they will do something about the problem or missed opportunity. Essentially, this means introducing manageable (for the client) amounts of challenge into the relationship so that it can support productive conflict in the service of change, rather than just remaining comfortable.

Effective challenge should stimulate, but not overwhelm the client. Again, it is important to emphasise here that this step of the model is *not* about challenging skills *per se* – these only *serve* the process and are not the process itself. Egan describes the role of counsellors here as 'sowers of discord' (Egan 2002a: 176), meaning that the therapist needs to introduce a certain amount of healthy dissonance to encourage the client to move beyond familiar, self-defeating patterns of thinking, feeling and behaviour. This is sometimes referred to in colloquial terms as helping clients move out of their 'comfort zone'.

In this process the counsellor needs to learn both how to honour and how to moderate the client's reluctance to grow. The task then is to find ways of challenging the client's reluctance without creating undue resistance. Egan suggests that we should be intrusive only to the extent that this will help the client. Challenging is by its nature intrusive and resistance can occur wherever clients experience us as adversaries. In managing this delicate balance between unhelpful intrusion and acceptable challenge it is important to remember that defensiveness is not necessarily the same thing as reluctance or resistance. While reluctance and resistance are counter-forces that may impede progress, defensiveness is a value-neutral term with connotations of being careful, guarding against intrusion and self-protection. On highways throughout North America there are signs exhorting motorists to 'Drive defensively!', meaning with caution and consideration for others.

Counsellors need to learn the skills of 'driving defensively' as well as encouraging their clients to do so. In practice this means that it is often more productive for the counsellor, initially at least, to encourage and support the clients' efforts to protect themselves rather than make assaults on the clients' defences. The best way to help trainee counsellors grasp the need for sensitive and respectful responses to clients' apparent reluctance and resistance is to give them opportunities to experience their own. Exercise 2.1 is designed to help trainees develop awareness of their own patterns of resistance together with some guidelines (Guidelines 2.1) for working with reluctant and resistant clients; these are consistent with the values and principles of the skilled helper model.

As well as looking at ways of countering blind spots, this step in the counselling process is also concerned with helping clients develop new perspectives on their problems and missed opportunities. New perspectives arise through dialogue with the counsellor that provides a vehicle for optimum amounts of supportive challenge. Somewhat paradoxically, we need both to respect clients' efforts at self-protection and at the same time actively encourage them to view their defensive strategies as self-limiting devices. Challenging is discussed at some length here as, in my experience as a trainer, I have often seen counselling students fight shy of introducing challenge at an early stage of the counselling process, when it can most usefully begin to bite.

A reluctance to challenge shown by trainees and inexperienced counsellors can be expressed in a number of ways, for instance:

- It doesn't fit with my style of counselling; it seems intrusive.
- If I challenge others I may open myself to being challenged.
- I'm afraid I might get it wrong and hurt others.
- I never know when to challenge.
- When I do it, it seems like a misuse of power.
- I work with the sort of clients who need support rather than challenge.
- If I challenge clients they might get angry with me or not come back.
- I understand that challenging is important but it's hard to get the timing right.
- I prefer to get to the point where the clients can challenge themselves.
- If I challenge clients it might open up issues that they're not ready to face or that I'm not sure I can deal with.
- Our relationship is too new for me to start challenging yet.
- (*To the tutor*) When you challenged me in the training group it wasn't very helpful and I don't want to do that to my clients.

A particular favourite of trainees is to blame the model for their own (understandable) reluctance to get to grips with challenging. This is expressed in laments such as:

- The model doesn't work with the sort of clients/issues I work with.
- I tried to explain it to my client but she couldn't understand the jargon.
- I find stage one useful but stages two and three are too action-oriented for my clients.
- Whenever I talk about preferred scenarios my clients look at me as if I am mad.
- The model gets in the way of the relationship.

- I used it with the client but it didn't seem to help so I've gone back to being person-centred.
- If I try to remember the model I get really confused and lose track of the client.
- I can use it in the training group but it doesn't work the same with real clients.

It is important for students who are learning the skilled helper model to have trainers and supervisors who know and believe in the model to avoid collusive agreement here that it is necessarily the failings of the model rather than the counsellor's reluctance to get to grips with it that are responsible for trainees experiencing difficulties such as these. More about this topic is said in Chapter 5 where issues of training are considered in greater depth.

If someone is to effect change and *do* things differently, they must often begin by *seeing* something differently. This means that the person must be open to being challenged, by both people and events, to develop fresh, more realistic and more creative perspectives on what is currently going on. This is what is meant by uncovering blind spots and two particular variations of the question 'What's going on?' are pertinent to apply to this process. They are:

'What are we overlooking?' and
'Can we uncover what is *really* going on?'

These two questions posit the need to look beyond what is immediately observable and apparent in the client's presenting story to uncover other elements that may be snagging or tripping the client up or keeping her or him mired in current difficulties. Although I am presenting these two questions as part of the step that explicitly deals with blind spots, they have currency throughout the model and merit consideration at every step and stage.

A travesty of the skilled helper model might present the counsellor as moving from supportive listening and empathic responding in step A to a ruthless and relentless confronting of blind spots in step B. Readers will note that the two questions given above are phrased in collaborative terms by the use of 'we'. The best chance of uncovering blind spots will occur if the counsellor encourages a spirit of co-operation. As Egan asserts, 'the skills of challenge are mainly invitational' (Egan 1976: 155).

In similar vein, Jourard (1971: 134) has written about psycho-therapy as an 'invitational process' and has suggested that the client is most likely to accept the invitation 'when the therapist is a role model of uncontrived honesty'. When the therapist is experienced as honest and authentic, the client is more likely to reciprocate. As Jourard says, 'the patient then wants to make himself known and proceeds to do so' and in this 'defenceless state' (*ibid.*) is more open to being influenced by the therapist's interventions. To the extent that the counsellor can harness the energy, interest, hope and goodwill of the client, the less direct challenging she will have to do and the more the client will challenge him- or herself.

The additional competencies needed by the counsellor for effective challenging include:

- *Summarising themes*, e.g. picking up on recurring images or patterns of behaviour.
- *Confronting strengths*, i.e. challenging clients to own their strengths and resources.
- *Using relational self-disclosure* (see Wosket 1999) to enable clients to see things from a different perspective, e.g. offering a contrast of experience: 'You say you hate yourself for crying but I often feel a sense of relief when you can cry, as if at last some of that frozenness inside is starting to melt.'
- *Sensing hidden emotions* through the use of advanced accurate empathy, e.g. 'There's a flatness to the way you are talking, but I sense underneath that you might be feeling a lot of agitation – am I anywhere near the mark?'
- *Giving information* to offer contrasting perceptions of particular events and experiences, e.g. informing clients that in longer-term therapy there is often a point where they will feel worse rather than better and that this is a natural and anticipated part of the process.
- *Using immediacy*: the ability to be honest and congruent with the client in relationship terms, e.g. openly addressing reluctance or resistance.

An axiom frequently voiced in counselling training is that the counsellor needs to earn the right to challenge. Earning the right to challenge begins with demonstrating support and understanding through empathy. So while step 1B is to a large degree about the process of challenging, it is equally concerned with the quality of empathic resonance.

Empathy is the most powerful form of challenge and there is nothing passive about it. On the contrary, empathy is a dynamic process, 'useful to the degree that it helps the client move forward' (Egan 2002a: 108). Empathic responding is both the most subtle and the most incisive form of challenge and as such requires a 'government health warning'. When used inopportunely, empathic challenge can be experienced as threatening, invasive or even brutal. Empathy is so powerful because it is about *being seen*, as the following example perhaps illustrates.

This excerpt of transcript is taken from the first ten minutes of the first session with a new client. Both counsellor and client have been feeling their way into the session and the client has been unsure about where to start and how to continue:

Client: I think I'm kind of missing home. It's so flat round here and I was brought up in the mountains.

Counsellor: It's so different for you here – even the landscape seems alien.

Client: I used to like to walk a lot in the hills . . . I don't know what else to say.

Counsellor: When you said that your eyes changed. You looked away and they softened and I thought you were yearning for something.

Client: [*Starts to cry and hugs herself*] How could you see that so quickly? I am so lonely now and I never used to feel that when I was at home. Even when no-one else was there I could walk in the hills and feel almost like I was part of them. I never felt lonely and now I just feel completely on my own.

To be seen by another as one truly is can be both a liberating and an exposing experience. Empathic counsellors need to take care that they refrain from misusing their power by 'tipping' their clients into feelings that may prove overwhelming or frightening if accessed too early in the therapy. Patterson and Hidore remind us that excesses of ill-timed empathy can indeed be counter-productive:

> At the beginning of therapy an extremely high level of empathy can be threatening and inhibit the communications of clients. Clients may well feel that the counsellor understands them better than they do themselves, which can serve to shift the locus of responsibility away from the client.
>
> (Patterson and Hidore 1997: 79)

Elsewhere they comment that counsellors' responses to clients should be 'calibrated to the client's awareness level' and allow clients 'to hear their own ideas' (Patterson and Hidore 1997: 171). Providing opportunities for clients to hear their own ideas is the basis of self-challenge, as discussed below.

Challenging can legitimately happen from the very start of a therapeutic relationship as long as empathy is present and the counsellor can demonstrate that he or she too is open to being challenged by the client. Indeed, there is evidence to suggest that challenge and confrontation at early stages of a counselling relationship can help to develop a good working alliance and to strengthen a weak alliance (Kivlighan and Schmitz 1992; Tryon and Kane 1993). The obvious way in which counsellors can demonstrate their openness to challenge is to encourage feedback and present opportunities for clients to give this. It may sound a little daunting for the client, who is inevitably in a less powerful position than the counsellor, to be expected to challenge the counsellor. However, I am not talking here about head-on confrontation, more a case of putting out tentative feelers as gentle invitations for collaborative engagement. Here are some examples of phrases and questions that the counsellors might use in a first session to invite feedback and therefore show that they, too, are open to being challenged:

- 'I'm not sure I got that right for you when I said . . .'
- 'Perhaps it was a bit insensitive when I said . . .?'
- 'Maybe I came on a bit strong when I said . . .'
- 'I don't think I quite understood you and I might have sounded a bit critical'
- 'That was a bit clumsy and I'd like you to put me right'

- 'I was stumbling around trying to get a hold on it and you said it much more clearly'
- 'How did you find the session today?'
- 'What felt OK for you and what jarred?'
- 'What have I missed or didn't pick up on very well?'

Counsellors who show that they are open to challenge are more likely to have co-operative and responsive clients when they begin to invite the client to self-challenge. Again, encouraging clients to challenge themselves can happen from the beginning of counselling. Here are some examples of questions and statements that might provide such invitations:

- 'You've probably had that going around in your head for some time. What is it like to hear yourself saying it out loud to me?'
- 'Are you still OK with doing that [behaviour]?'
- 'Are you still comfortable with feeling like that?'
- 'It's something you've relied on in the past that seemed to work – how about now?'
- 'That was the only thing you could do as a child because you were so little and unprotected. Now that you are an adult are there any other options?'
- 'Have you learned anything from that difficult experience?'
- 'Looking back over how that unfolded, is there anything you would like to have done differently?'
- 'You seem to have got that off to a tee – I guess you've had a lot of practice'
- 'You describe that as a familiar pattern you fall into and yet I haven't experienced you like that with me today. How have you managed that?'
- 'What have you managed to do here today that has surprised you or exceeded your expectations of yourself?'
- 'Is there anything you're holding back on that you'd like to say before we finish?'

It is also true that counsellors can find strengths in their clients to challenge from the first session onwards. Challenging the client's strengths is a skill that involves the ability to positively reframe what the client might see as a weakness or limitation. Here are some examples of challenging strengths in a first session:

- 'Even though you found it difficult to look at me when we touched on those feelings that you hate, we managed to stay with them for a few minutes. When you first mentioned them you told me that you "couldn't stand" to feel them.'
- 'Even though you are feeling pretty despondent and have told me that you don't think that anyone can help you, you've taken the time and effort to try to let me know how bad things are for you. That seems to me to indicate that you haven't quite given up on yourself.'
- 'On the one hand you say that you feel useless and weak because you've felt like self-harming all week, on the other hand you are telling me that you haven't self-harmed, even though you wanted to. How do you see those two things fitting together?'
- 'You say that you feel pretty pathetic for coming and crying for an hour. It seems to me that you came really full up with despair and did the first thing that you needed to do for yourself – empty a little of that feeling out.'
- 'You said at the start that you were quite dubious about whether counselling could help you and at the end of our hour together you're still feeling unsure about continuing. It's good to be cautious and I appreciate you taking the time to weigh this up and think about whether it is what you really want.'

The following is an example from counselling practice, based on a real session, and included with the client's permission, which demonstrates the difference that basic empathy or challenge can make. Hopefully it also shows how the counsellor can balance offering supportive challenge with encouraging the client to self-challenge.

Background to the session

The client in this example has been making good progress in her recovery from childhood sexual abuse. She has been working hard at shaking off her sense of being a victim and is becoming stronger, more outgoing and assertive in her personal, professional and social life. For a number of years her partner has had the tendency to 'walk on eggshells' around her. In the past he has unwittingly bought into her view of herself as someone who is fragile and easily damaged emotionally. In this role he has been used to putting her needs before his own and over the years has made Herculean efforts to act in consistently patient and protective ways. With the client's encouragement, he has begun to read some self-help books for partners of survivors of sexual abuse.

At the beginning of her counselling session the client reports on a difficult incident involving her partner's birthday. For ostensibly valid reasons she had not managed to buy him a present and suggested instead that they choose something together on the day. Uncharacteristically, her partner seemed quiet and offhand in response to this suggestion and the client asked him what was wrong. After a bit of prompting he finally admitted to feelings of hurt and disappointment. At this, the client became defensive and fell back on her rational reasons for wanting to wait and choose the present with him. Things escalated into a row and the client's partner blurted out that he was only trying to follow suggestions he had read in the self-help book for partners that advised the importance of sharing negative feelings when they arise instead of suppressing and bottling them up.

There now follow two examples of how the session might begin to unfold [with some commentary given in square brackets]. The first example shows a basic empathic response by the counsellor.

Example 1

Client:	So it's been quite tense between us for the last few days. I think he knows how hurt I'm feeling and that what he did was too much.
Counsellor A:	You're feeling pretty raw and a bit attacked by the sound of it because that was so unlike him and it hit you out of the blue.
Client:	Yes – I'm not ready for that yet and it feels like a step backwards. We're back to those times when

I'd feel hurt for days until he would notice something was up and then sit me down and get me to
talk about it.

Counsellor A: It feels like a backward step and that's pretty
disappointing.

[Here the client may feel understood and supported by the
counsellor but the result is that she settles back into an old,
familiar (and possibly more comfortable) pattern and invites the
counsellor to join her there. In the second example the counsellor makes a more challenging and immediate response to the
client's initial statement.]

Example 2

Client: So it's been quite tense between us for the last
few days. I think he knows how hurt I'm feeling
and that what he did was too much.

Counsellor B: It's strange, because as you were telling me about
that incident I was seeing it a bit differently. I was
thinking what a mark of the progress your relationship is making that it's now robust enough for
him to feel that he can let you know about his
needs and feelings. I guess that was quite a big
step for him to risk telling you he felt hurt. I don't
think he would have done that a few months ago.

[In the event this is the actual response that the counsellor made
in the session, which then proceeded as follows:]

Client: I'm sure he wouldn't have done. I hadn't thought
about it like that – but it still felt a bit much.

Counsellor B: You weren't expecting it. He sort of caught you
off guard and in a way it sounds like you retaliated
by going back to the old pattern of giving him the
cold shoulder so that he gets a dose of what you
are feeling – hurt and attacked. As we've noted

	before, these are old feelings that go way back and belong to the abuse. Is that how you still want to operate now – and go back to him having to walk on eggshells around you?
Client:	No, I don't want to do that any more. He doesn't deserve it. I've realised now that I used to bully him and I don't want to be a bully any more.
Counsellor B:	He's been so patient for such a long time and now he respects you enough to think that the relationship can accommodate more of his needs and feelings. You've come a long way.
Client:	[*becoming tearful*] He *has* been patient and I do want him to share his feelings with me. He's put up with so much. He deserves so much better.
Counsellor B:	And you have been so open to looking at what happened in a different way with me. I feel as if I've been very challenging with you and you weren't at all defensive.
Client:	I didn't feel defensive. I never do here – or hardly ever [*both laugh*]. I don't know why.
Counsellor B:	I wonder if it's because you came to counselling at a time when you were ready to change and do things differently but you still felt a bit stuck in those old patterns. I'm impressed by how quickly you understood what was really going on there.
Client:	Yes, I don't know why I couldn't see it myself – it seems so obvious now.
Counsellor B:	Now that you understand it better is there something that you want to do about it when you leave here?
Client:	Yes, definitely. I want to talk to [partner] about what happened.
Counsellor B:	What do you want to say to him?
Client:	I want to say I'm sorry for acting defensively and tell him that I *do* want him to share his feelings with me. I *am* strong enough for that now, but I

	think I also need him to warn me a bit more when he's going to do it.
Counsellor B:	How could that happen?
Client:	I'll ask him to try to pick a better moment and say there's something we need to talk about first. I'd also like to ask him to show me what he read in the book so that I can understand better what he's trying to do and we can work on it together.
Counsellor B:	You've got a clear idea of what you want to say. When do you think you might do it?
Client:	This weekend. He's coming home tomorrow. I'm going to phone him when I leave here and tell him there's something I'd like to talk to him about so that he knows.

This example also shows how the model might be used in a 'micro' sense in that it is cycled through in one session to deal with an immediate difficulty embedded in a bigger issue that is being worked on long term. Small successes such as this can have a significant cumulative effect on clients and provide the impetus for a spread effect that can make a huge difference to how they feel they are handling the bigger picture.

Step 1C: leverage

The idea of a lever as applying a force to shift or move something is a useful image for this part of the helping process. We use levers to unfasten gates, to prise things open, to change gear when driving and to gain purchase on objects that would otherwise be hard to shift – like heavy weights. All these images fit what the counsellor and client are attempting to achieve in the process here. We are trying to gain a firmer grasp of what will begin to give momentum to forward movement. In essence we are asking the client to choose which issue (or opportunity) *if pursued vigorously* will contribute to the overall management of the problem situation. I tend to use the term *focus* rather than leverage as this is an expression that is more in common usage in my own culture.

In this step of the counselling process we are helping the client to bring more clearly into view for closer attention particular aspects of substantial issues. The general idea behind this is that before we can help to solve a problem we need to know exactly what we are dealing with. This is not necessarily the first thing that the client brings or starts the session with. Clients often present in the initial stages of counselling as 'moving targets' where they shift from one issue to another – not all of which merit equal amounts of attention from the counsellor. A common mistake that inexperienced helpers make is to get involved in issues that clients can manage for themselves. We can think of these as smokescreen issues (whether or not the client is intentionally creating the diversion).

Our time as helpers is not well spent if we are willing to deal with every trivial issue the client brings up. I have been surprised at how often clients will say something like 'Actually there's something more important' or 'I think I know what to do about that' when I take the risk of following the whiff of a possible red herring and ask, 'Is this what you most need my help with?'. This brings in the idea of leverage as an evaluation component (Sugarman 1995). In early versions of the skilled helper model (Egan and Cowan 1979) evaluation was included as a separate fourth stage of the model along with implementation. In later editions, evaluation is embedded in all parts of the model as an ongoing process of quality assurance. Thus the leverage question 'Are we working on the right stuff, in the best way?' applies not only to 1C but to all steps and stages of the problem-management process.

The essential question being asked here is 'What can we work on that has some substance and will get us somewhere?' Egan advises that *working on* is not the same as *working through*, in that a lot of issues brought by clients can be transcended rather than worked through. Again, he suggests that working through every issue can be self-indulgent for both client and counsellor. More about transcending problems is said in the following chapter in relation to stage two.

In helping the client establish and maintain a focus, the particular skills that the counsellor is likely to utilise are:

- probing
- questioning
- summarising
- clarifying.

Contemporary cognitive therapy acknowledges the function of emotion in promoting leverage. 'The emotion contains crucial cognitive elements, providing a therapist with a point of leverage into the whole client experience' (Wills and Sanders 1997: 5). Indeed, Wills and Sanders assert that, contrary to popular belief, cognitive therapy is 'actually all about reaching and working with clients' salient feelings' (1997: 9) but that in cognitive therapy these are considered to be most often accessible through cognitions. Thus what clients think is both a product and a determinant of what they feel. Clients usually come to counselling saying that they want to change what they feel, rather than what they think and it can be important to bear this in mind when helping them establish a focus that will provide some leverage. Some clients, for instance, are better able to answer a question like 'What feelings would you like to work on?' than 'What thoughts would you like to work on?'

I will draw this chapter to a close with a final word about crisis management. Clients not infrequently present for counselling in crisis – at which point the crisis is the obvious immediate focus of the work. In this sense, as Leiper and Kent (2001) point out, it is important to make a distinction between crises that precipitate an initial request for counselling (e.g. a student who is in imminent danger of failing a course requests an urgent appointment with a student counsellor) and crises that occur as part of an ongoing therapeutic relationship (e.g. a client who begins to feel more actively suicidal as depression starts to lift during the course of therapy). In the former situation, the counsellor's response would normally be of a cognitive-behavioural/interventionist/problem-management nature. In the latter it would be important to understand the meaning of the crisis and, perhaps, allow it to run its course.

Before turning to the next chapter, which continues our overview of the skilled helper model, you may wish to review the guidelines and exercise that follow. These are designed to give an experiential feel for some of the theoretical material on working with reluctance and resistance which was covered earlier in the chapter.

Guidelines 2.1: Working with reluctant and resistant clients

Although they may appear similar, it can be important to try to differentiate between reluctance and resistance. The *reluctant* client is one who may wish to do the work, but is cautious, wary, anxious, ambivalent or scared. The *resistant* client may be consciously or unconsciously obstructing the work through defences they have erected in order to protect themselves. In either case, reluctance or resistance should be accepted, supported and understood as normal and healthy in any counselling relationship.

It is helpful for the counsellor to learn to respect and allow resistance and reluctance, rather than regarding them as something to be ignored or demolished, because:

- The client's resistance/reluctance may be telling me something important that I have missed or am not hearing (e.g. my lack of acknowledgement or understanding of cultural differences).
- Resistance/reluctance may be an indirect plea from the client for closer contact.
- Through resistance/reluctance the client may be checking out my willingness to stay with them when they are not being a 'good' client.
- Through showing reluctance/resistance the client may be provoking me to punish or reject them to 'prove' how unlikeable or unimportant they really are.
- It may be the only way the client can say 'No, I don't want this'.
- Resistance/reluctance often provides the key that unlocks more significant material.

I may be able to help my reluctant/resistant client by:

- Asking myself 'What is my client trying to tell me?' and making every effort to understand the meaning of the client's reluctance/resistance.
- Using sensitive and tentative 'hunches' as invitations and in a way that allows the client 'room to manoeuvre' (e.g. 'I imagine that it would be very difficult for you to let me know that you are angry with me for being away last week and yet I would expect you to feel a bit let down, even if it is hard to say').
- Picking up on non-verbal communication and/or inviting non-verbal responses (e.g. 'It seems really hard for you to talk today. I notice that cushion on your lap is getting a hug and I wonder if that's something *you* feel you need today instead of talking').

- Working at the client's pace and not demanding too much, too soon.
- Empathising with the client's feelings and perspective, even when they seem irrational, rather than justifying or explaining my own position. When clients feel truly understood and accepted they are more likely to challenge themselves and shift perspective (e.g. 'It must be so hard to come "knowing" that I would ditch you if you told me about the "big stuff". Yet you've gradually been able to tell me some of the things that are more difficult to talk about – when you've done that have I seemed to want to ditch you?').
- Staying with the resistance and exploring it with the client using immediacy (e.g. 'I seem to be talking more than I usually do today and I think that could be because I sense there's something not quite right between us and I might be trying to put it right by reassuring you').
- Not pushing the client in an attempt to break through the resistance.
- Validating the client's reluctance/resistance as a useful and necessary protective or coping strategy. Giving permission for the client to be ambivalent (e.g. 'I would expect you to be cautious about what you say until you are a bit clearer about whether you really want to be here or not. Is there any way I can help while you are taking the time you need to decide?').
- Offering to work in a flexible way that gives the client some control (e.g. shorter sessions or the rule of thirds: first third of the session settling in, reviewing, preparing for the next part; second third focusing on the more difficult work; last third processing the work that has been done, winding down and preparing to leave).
- Being alert to reluctance/resistance which may manifest through over-talkativeness, compliance, cutting off from feelings, going off on tangents, difficulty in concentrating, playing games, etc.
- Confronting discrepancies, using description rather than accusation. Using statements instead of questions can be less threatening (e.g. 'We've been talking quite a lot about the things you feel you've managed well this week. At the start of the session you also said you had had a really low point and we haven't come back to that yet. I don't want to miss what

has been difficult and I wonder if you might sometimes think that I only want to hear about the good stuff').

- Checking that the client understands the process of counselling and what might happen if they do 'open up'. De-mystifying counselling through giving information in non-technical language.
- Being alert to the client who 'talks about' feelings rather than experiences them.
- Sharing my thinking and ideas aloud (e.g. 'I was wondering about saying to you that I am finding it difficult to come in with what I want to say without interrupting you this week. And I think I have been holding back because I was worried you might take that as a criticism').
- Allowing myself to be vulnerable with the client. Avoiding withdrawing or becoming resistant myself as by so doing I lose all chance of genuine contact and communication with my client.
- Striving to stay in contact as my first priority even though I might find this painful, scary, exposing or confusing.
- Getting thoroughly acquainted with *my* resistant self.

Exercise 2.1: Understanding my own resistance

Resistance often occurs when we are scared or feeling vulnerable. When we are feeling scared we have difficulty being honest and making real contact with another person. We may become defensive or resistant to hide our vulnerability and stay in control. However, hiding our vulnerability only makes us more vulnerable because we then become scared of being found out. On the other hand, if we make the choice not to hide, the potential for real contact is there.

Work in a small group with people you don't know really well or those that you haven't worked with for a while. Allocate the time equally between you and help each other to explore what patterns come into play when you feel scared or vulnerable in relationships:

- What aspects of interpersonal relationships are the most uncomfortable for you and why?

- What stops you from staying in contact in relationships and what do you tend to do instead?
- Talk about what thoughts, feelings, behaviours, sensations and fantasies come into play when you experience these difficulties.
- Where do you think these responses stem from and how do you think you are trying to protect yourself by having these responses?
- In what ways might these difficulties show up in your counselling or helping activities:
  - as the counsellor/helper?
  - as the client/helpee?

Take some time to debrief the experience in your small group:

- What have you learned about your resistant self – as a person and as a counsellor?
- How might your consideration of these questions inform your counselling/helping practice and your understanding of your clients/helpees?
- Is there anything you want to say or to hear from the people in your group before you finish the exercise?

Tutor: allow time for a whole-group debrief to air thoughts and feelings about the exercise and to bring together any significant learning.

Chapter 3

Overview of the skilled helper model 2: stages two and three

This chapter continues to outline the skilled helper model. Stages two and three are explained and illustrated in some detail and attention is also given to the implementation dimension of the problem-management process. Here again clinical vignettes from counselling practice are included to show how the skills and concepts described may be applied to helping situations in an integrative way. The chapter concludes with an exercise and guidelines to promote further understanding and application of the process.

Stage two: preferred picture

What solutions make sense for me?

At one of the York counselling summer schools, Egan gave his view that counselling is all about *solutions*. He suggested that within the framework of the skilled helper model:

- Stage one is about *failed solutions*
- Stage two is about *solutions* as *accomplishments*
- Stage three is about *solutions* as *strategies*

When Egan talks about stage one as being about failed solutions he is saying that the problems that people end up with are often their unsuccessful attempts to deal with underlying issues (an obvious example would be the person who suppresses their feelings of loneliness and isolation through over-use of alcohol and then turns up at an alcohol counselling agency with a drink problem). To unpack this a little further, Egan points out that the word 'solution' has two commonly understood meanings. Solutions may be strategies to solve or handle something (e.g. one solution to short-sightedness may be to buy a pair of spectacles) or they may be end-products or outcomes (e.g. the solution to the question 'What is the meaning of life?' is yet to be determined).

In the seventh edition of *The Skilled Helper* Egan gives stage two of the model the caption: 'What solutions make sense for me?' and in this stage the second meaning given to solutions is the one that we are looking at, i.e. solutions as outcomes and accomplishments. A way that I often describe this to students is to have them think, in travelling terms, of the difference between a *destination* and a *journey*. Using this analogy, stage two can be thought of as the final destination and stage three as the journey consisting of all the ways travellers might use to get from their point of departure to their final destination. I have included a creative exercise (Exercise 3.1) at the end of this chapter to help trainees to experience the difference between stages two and three.

Where people have difficulty managing their problems this is frequently down to their tendency to link problems to actions ('What do I *do* about this?'), rather than linking action to outcomes ('What do I need to do to get what I want?'). An axiom that Egan constantly emphasises in numerous ways is that 'goals, not problems, should drive action' (Egan 2002a: 248). Solutions-as-goals (accomplishments and outcomes) are the subject matter of this stage of the model. Solutions-as-strategies (actions to achieve outcomes) are the subject matter of stage three, which is covered later in this chapter.

Stage two of the skilled helper model is essentially about helping clients turn their attention from examining their current difficulties and missed opportunities to imagining what the future could hold if their difficulties were eased or their opportunities seized. I often think about this stage of the model in terms of the question 'Where's the hope?'. Egan has summarised the work of stage two as helping to free the client from the tyranny of the past. In his latest publication on the model (Egan 2006) the term *preferred scenario* (a term that has tended to irritate jargon-allergic helpers in the UK) is jettisoned in favour of the more user-friendly phrase *preferred picture* to describe this stage of the model.

The steps of stage two can be summed up in three simple questions:

2A: 'What do you want?'
2B: 'What do you *really* want?'
2C: 'Is what you really want what you are willing to pay for?'

Let us look at each of these steps in turn.

Step 2A: possibilities

The simple rationale behind this step of the model is that if clients are helped to explore what they want, they are then in a better position to make decisions. The essence of stage two of the model is about engendering *hope* as counsellors help clients move from 'problem-centred mode to discovery mode' (Egan 2002a: 263). As already noted, clients have tended to live with their problems for some time and often know a great deal about them. What they tend not to know so much about are the possibilities for imagining a better future. The work of stage two is about beginning to see the previously unseen by helping clients gain a clearer view of what they need and want.

Egan suggests that it is often worth moving into stage two sooner rather than later, the justification for this being that when we work with possibilities we are more likely to rekindle hope. Moving into stage two at an early phase of the helping process is also a recommended option where it appears inadvisable to encourage the client to focus too soon on in-depth exploration. Research (Kivlighan 1990) has indicated that, for some clients, focusing prematurely on areas of difficulty that they are not ready to deal with can detract from the formation of a strong working alliance. In discussing the multi-cultural competencies that helpers need to develop, Egan (2006) also makes the point that encouraging clients to focus on what they want may be more culturally sensitive with those clients for whom exploring intimate details of problems or making exposing self-disclosures is alien within their culture of origin.

The additional skills needed by the helper here include those of future-oriented questioning, creative imagining and divergent thinking. The process is one of inviting the client, in as many ways as possible, to imagine a better future. In learning this part of the process, many students (myself included when I was in training) get themselves tied up in knots by asking convoluted questions that can leave the client staring blankly back in response. The one that often seems to come out in a confused way is some version of the question 'What would things look like if they looked better?' I have found this question hard for clients to grasp and sometimes difficult for trainees to ask in a meaningful way. A much simpler question like 'How would you like things to be?' is often a good opener for this part of the counselling process, as long as the counsellor is clear that the 'how' here refers to goal setting and not to action planning.

Having kicked off the process of imagining a better future, it is normally necessary to keep it going by using further probes and prompts. Some examples of the many questions that the helper might use to sustain the process of building a picture of what the client wants are given at the end of the chapter (Guidelines 3.1). A word of caution is necessary here. Egan has been at pains to point out (York summer school 1992) that step 2A is *not* the technology of brainstorming. Rather the human face of 2A is about finding ways to be with another person so that some kind of reasonable hope is engendered.

Egan has emphasised the integrated nature of the model by suggesting that stage one is about developing a set of story-telling competencies that are then used throughout the problem-management process (Sugarman 1995). A useful way of thinking about 2A, then, is that it is about a different kind of story-telling from that of stage one. Here the story is one of possibilities, instead of one about problems and missed opportunities. So rather than helping the client merely to list the elements of their preferred picture, I would use this part of the model to help them flesh out a detailed vision of what they really want.

The suggestions given in the guidelines at the end of this chapter are general in nature for the purposes of illustration. In actual practice they should be tailored to the issues the client has identified and explored in stage one, particularly 1C (leverage). So if we consider again the client mentioned in Chapter 2, who struggles with her anger, her 'preferred scenario' might consist of building a picture of what life might be like without the two extremes of passive suppression and explosive rage. Some prompts and probes the counsellor might use to help her with this are:

- What difference would it make to your life if you were able to manage your anger better than you do now?

- If you were managing your anger better, how would you know? What would have changed?
- If you imagine yourself dealing with anger more effectively in your relationship with your partner, what would you be doing differently?
- Who do you know who manages anger in a better way than you do?
- What does this person do that you would like to see yourself doing?
- If we imagined seeing anger as a spectrum that has a range of feelings, what are some of the feelings that might sit on that continuum between the two extremes of denying it entirely and exploding like a volcano?
- If you imagined yourself starting to feel a bit angry, but still in control, what would that be like?
- If you imagine feeling angry and expressing it differently from the way your mother did when she was angry, what other options are there?
- What are some of the ways you are different from your mother?
- Which of these qualities might you be able to draw on to make sure that you don't react like her when you get angry?

Egan has remarked on a key function of stage two as throwing a searchlight over stage one. If we can encourage clients to move to a position of imagining how their lives might be if their current difficulties were resolved, or at least more manageable, this often helps them to begin to see their problems and concerns in a new and clearer light. The thinking behind this concept is that sometimes clients need to transcend their problems, rather than always sticking with trying to work through them.

Egan has observed that if counsellors and clients constantly work with problems, then their imaginations tend to become dormant or even shrivel up and die. So, as Miller and colleagues have asserted, sometimes 'therapists are more likely to facilitate hope and expectation in their clients when they stop trying to figure out what is wrong with them and how to fix it and focus instead on what is possible and how their clients can obtain it' (1997: 128). If we are able to help clients tap into their creativity and imagination they are more likely to move into transcending mode. Step 2A links particularly with the work done on challenging strengths in step 1B in that focusing on strengths promotes hope and motivates clients to begin marshalling their own resources to initiate change through goal setting.

The following example shows how the counsellor might work to weave some possibilities for a more hopeful future (stage 2A) into aspects of the client's story (stage 1). This is what Egan means when he talks about listening for the echo of hope when clients tell their stories of pain. Note that the stage 1 question 'What's going on?' is explored both in terms of the client's difficulties and also in connection with what is going on between counsellor and client in their immediate relationship. Egan has called this paying attention to both the alpha problem (the problem or opportunities missed as experienced by the client 'out there') and the beta problem (issues and concerns that arise in the counselling relationship and process 'in here').

> The client has come to counselling to resolve issues of childhood sexual abuse. She has lived with these experiences for almost forty years and endures daily the consequences of them. These include low self-esteem, avoidance of people and situations that remind her of the abuse, anxiety, panic attacks, depression, flashbacks and a number of suicide attempts. She is very familiar with these 'symptoms' and can describe them in detail and at great length. What she is less familiar with is imagining what life might be like without them.
>
> Counsellor: I'm beginning to get a sense of how difficult things have been for you and what has brought you to counselling. I just wondered why come now?
>
> Client: My doctor suggested I should come.
>
> Counsellor: So what helped you to act on your doctor's suggestion, because *you* contacted us – your doctor didn't. I think you know that we only take self-referrals.
>
> Client: I don't know really. I just felt so desperate that I'd try anything.
>
> Counsellor: You decided to try because you are sick of feeling so desperate. Kind of like that despair gave you the energy to get here.

Client:	I suppose so, but I just can't imagine getting over this. No-one really does, do they?
Counsellor:	It's hard for you to think that it might be possible to heal and recover from being hurt so badly. What would 'getting over this' mean for you?
Client:	I don't know . . . I just want to be normal and get on with my life.
Counsellor:	People have different ideas of what is 'normal'. I'm not sure what that means to you.
Client:	Well things like a normal social life and sex life . . . you know . . .
Counsellor:	Is that what you mean by 'get on with my life'?
Client:	Yeah . . . and things like having a job and not being so pathetic and scared all the time.
Counsellor:	And what would it mean to you if you had some of those things?
Client:	I wouldn't feel such a freak.
Counsellor:	'Freak' sounds pretty hard on yourself.
Client:	Well I think that's how you must see me. It's how I see myself. All that stuff I've just told you about. Most people aren't like that are they?
Counsellor:	It's hard for you to think I could hear all of that and still think you are OK as a person. What did I do or say that makes you think I see you as a freak?
Client:	Well nothing obvious. But that's your training isn't it? You're not supposed to show what you really feel. You have to pretend you like everyone.
Counsellor:	Ouch! That hit the mark.
Client:	I'm sorry. That wasn't fair . . . I don't think I'm very good at people being nice to me . . . That's just come to me now.
Counsellor:	So is that what you were beginning to feel – that maybe I might care about what has happened to you?
Client:	I always think that people will think I'm disgusting if they know what happened. I suppose that's one of the reasons why I never talk about it.

> *Counsellor:* You've risked talking about it to me here and you were inclined to think I would have that reaction. What do you think now?
>
> *Client:* Well . . . you don't *look* disgusted. And you didn't get up and run out of the room.
>
> *Counsellor:* You're right – I'm still in my chair [*both laugh*]. So could this possibly be somewhere where we might be able to test out if some of what you fear from people is always going to happen?
>
> *Client:* Maybe . . . I hadn't thought about counselling like that.

This extract of dialogue also provides examples of the different kinds of behaviour that can lie on the 'action arrow' both within and outside sessions (as discussed in Chapter 2 and illustrated in Table 2.1, p. 40) in that it shows:

- *Internal action, outside-session*: Deciding to go to doctor; deciding to contact the counselling agency.
- *Internal action, in-session*: Shift in thinking in terms of: (1) insight: 'I don't think I'm very good at people being nice to me'; and (2) different perspective: 'I hadn't thought about counselling like that'.
- *Observable action, outside-session*: Going to the doctor; getting to the counselling appointment.
- *Observable action, in-session*: Taking the risk of disclosing difficult material; beginning to verbalise what a better future might look like.

In this part of the counselling process it can be useful to help clients explore what they want through the notion of 'possible selves' (Egan 2002a: 262), as the counsellor begins to do in the extract above. This aligns with a post-modern perspective in considering that people have the potential to experience a number of different, sequential or even distributed selves throughout their lifetime, rather than being frozen into a fixed self that remains essentially consistent throughout adult life (Andrews 1991; Gergen 1977, 1985, 1996, 1999; McNamee and Gergen 1992; Rappoport *et al.* 1999; Reinharz 1997). Freedman and Combs (1996: 35), for instance, describe how instead of looking for an essential self they work with people to establish 'preferred selves', in order to 'bring forth various experiences of self and to distinguish which of those selves they prefer in which contexts'.

A useful way of helping clients to flesh out their preferred picture can be to help them to imagine how they would like to see their 'preferred selves' in different situations through prompts such as:

- What would you like to be like in that situation?
- Who would you like to be like?
- What would you be doing?
- What would you be thinking?
- What would you be saying to yourself?
- What would you be feeling?
- How would you look?
- How would you behave?
- How would you feel in your body?
- What would be some of your noticeable qualities and charac-teristics?
- What would others notice about you that was different?
- What would you like the outcome of being different to be?

In outlining stage 2A of the skilled helper model, Egan has suggested that in many ways 'outcomes are more important than actions' (Egan 2002a: 261). This is because being clear about what will be in place when things change for the better will determine the appropriate strategies needed to achieve that outcome. Clients can easily slip into what they might *do* rather than what they *want* at this point in the process. When this happens it often helps to ask '*And if you did that, what would it help you to achieve?*' as this brings the focus back to outcomes and to the possibility of estab-lishing clear goals that are more likely to result in purposeful and sustainable action. Here is an example of how this might happen with a client who has been avoiding making an appointment to see her doctor:

Client: If I wasn't such a coward I'd just get off my backside and go for it.

Counsellor: And what might that help you achieve?

Client:	Well for a start, I'd stop just constantly worrying about this lump and get it checked out instead.
Counsellor:	So in terms of what you want, can we add those two things to your list: stop worrying, and have the lump checked out?

In the next section we will look more closely at the process of goal setting as a framework for enabling clients to establish what they want and need in ways that are likely to lead to constructive change.

Step 2B: change agenda

In his work on positive psychology, Carr (2004: 31) has reviewed the link between happiness and goal attainment and drawn attention to existing research that indicates that individuals 'report greater happiness on days when they achieve highly valued goals than on days when they achieve less valued goals'. Goal setting is a crucial part of the problem-management process as it is concerned with redefining those outcomes identified in step 2A in terms of achievable aims.

There are various ways that the counsellor can help the client move from step 2A (imagining a better future) to step 2B (establishing workable goals). Perhaps the most simple way to begin this process is merely to ask the client: 'Out of what we've been looking at, what appeals most to you?' If the client has been writing down or drawing elements of his or her 'preferred picture' (it is normally a good idea to encourage the client to do this), then the counsellor can invite the client to tick or draw a circle around those items that appeal most. It doesn't matter at all at this stage if these appear unrealistic or over-adventurous. Judicious probing by the counsellor can still set the process of realistic goal setting in motion, as in the following example:

Counsellor:	Out of all the things we've looked at, what do *you* most like the look of?
Client:	Just 'being normal', the first thing I wrote down, is still the one that stands out – but that will never happen.
Counsellor:	What do you see as the difference between you and what you call 'normal' people?

Client:	Well, normal people don't feel tired and depressed all the time. They feel like getting up in the morning. They have things to look forward to. They don't just mope round the house all day watching TV and not being bothered to go out.
Counsellor:	There are a couple of things you've said in there that could be things you'd like for yourself, for instance 'I'd like to feel like getting up in the morning' and 'I'd like to have some things to look forward to'. Is that right?
Client:	Of course I would.
Counsellor:	Well, if we were to take a closer look at those, which one would you choose first?
Client:	I suppose feeling like getting up in the morning. Sometimes I just stay in bed till lunchtime and that really makes me feel useless and miserable.

Here we can see a gradual process of shaping happening as the client moves from the vague and amorphous wish to be 'normal' to a specific activity that may be accessible to change through goal setting. A similar process can work with clients who pick something fantastical from a picture of what they would like, in which case the dialogue might go something like this:

Counsellor:	What we can do now is take a look at what you've written down and see what attracts you most.
Client:	If I'm *really* honest the one that appeals most is 'being the first woman on Mars'.
Counsellor:	What were you feeling and thinking when you wrote that down?
Client:	How brilliant it would be just to leave all this crap behind and be somewhere where no-one could bother me or come after me.
Counsellor:	What else appeals about being the first woman on Mars?
Client:	There wouldn't be anyone else to compare myself with. I could do just what I wanted and no-one could criticise me. I could lie back and gaze at the stars all day if that's all I wanted to do. There'd be no pressure and no money worries. There wouldn't be any mirrors or scales so I wouldn't have to worry

about my weight or what I looked like. It would be blissful.

Counsellor: There are so many things that you would like in there and even though we've only been to Mars in our imagination, what would you most like to bring back with you?

Client: That sense of being at ease with myself and not being so bothered what other people think of me.

Here again we can see the possibility of something tangible to work towards gradually unfolding from the client's exploration of her fantasy.

Egan describes a client's goals as constituting his or her 'agenda for change' (Egan 2002a: 29). If, like me, you tend not to talk in the language of 'change agendas' with your clients, you might prefer to think of this part of the model more in terms of helping the client decide what they want to 'achieve', 'change', 'develop', 'find', 'fix', 'manage better', 'turn around', 'do differently', 'resolve', 'sort out' or 'heal' and then helping them turn these hopes and desires into 'do-able' goals.

Egan takes care to point out that goal setting is best approached with a sense of flow and rhythm as the counsellor moves back and forth in the stream of the helping process and uses the client's language to make interventions that sound natural and unforced. Within the ebb and flow of the counselling relationship, the task for the counsellor in step 2B is to work steadily away at helping the client turn vague aims or intentions into achievable objectives. A rough and ready way of approaching goal setting, and one that tends to appeal to trainees and clients alike because of its common sense, ease of recall and simplicity, is the acronym SMART, which stands for:

Specific: concrete, not vague
Measurable: verifiable and quantifiable
Appropriate: substantive and will make a difference
Realistic: workable and achievable
Timed: set in a reasonable time frame.

I would normally make this part of the helping process very explicit with clients in order to approach the task of goal setting in as transparent and collaborative a manner as possible. Here is the sort of thing I might say at the point where the client has identified a desire, aim or intention that they might be prepared to work on. I'll build on the example above of the client who is worried about a suspicious lump she has found on a part of their body.

Counsellor: We've agreed to look at 'having the lump checked out'. If we think about this as a possible goal, what might be useful is to use a few pointers to help us decide if it's going to be a workable goal for you.

If the client agrees to this the counsellor can write the word SMART on a piece of paper and say something like: 'To be of any use, goals need to be workable and this word can help us decide together if your goal is manageable or might need a bit of re-shaping. We can use SMART as a kind of checklist to help us do that. This is what the letters stand for . . .'

I would then use each word as a kind of criterion (although I wouldn't use that word with the client) for evaluating the work-ability of the goal. So I might be asking questions like:

Specific: 'Is "having the lump checked out" specific enough for you to know exactly what you want to happen?' In an example like this it could well be, or it might be that the client says: 'Well I was thinking of asking a friend of mine who used to be a nurse if she thinks there's anything for me to worry about.' The counsellor might need to challenge this by exploring with the client if verbal checking-out with a friend will be enough to put the client's mind at ease and the client may then specify that going to the doctor would be a better option.

Measurable: 'How would you be able to tell that you'd achieved the goal of having the lump checked out?' The client might say: 'Well I'd have had it examined by the doctor and maybe a specialist if she thinks she needs to refer me on.'

Appropriate: 'How much difference will it make to how things are for you at the moment if you get the lump checked out?' The client might respond: 'I'm just worrying about it constantly at the moment. I'm scared of going to the doctor in case it's bad news but then at least I'll find out one way or the other. It's getting to the point where it's worse *not* to know.'

Realistic: 'As a possible goal, how realistic is it to think of you going to the doctor to have the lump checked out?' The client might say: 'Well, there's nothing to stop me except me. I've just got to get up the nerve to pick up the phone and make the appointment. That's the hard bit'. When the client says something like this, it may be helpful to let her know that you intend to get on to looking at how she might 'get up the nerve' in due course, for instance by saying: 'We can look at that hard bit together once we're sure that we're on the right track here.'

Timed: 'When would you want to have had the lump checked out by?' The client may say 'Pretty soon' – which will need shaping up into a more specific time-frame, e.g. 'Can we be a bit more precise than "pretty soon"? to make sure things don't slip too much?'

It is then useful to invite the client to write down or say out loud what her goal now looks like, having worked through this process. This is because it is important that the client, rather than the counsellor, states the definitive goal in order for her to own it as her own. Encouraging the client to say it in 'I' and 'outcome' terms will help here. In the example given above, what started with 'having the lump checked out' might become, in the client's words: 'By the end of next week I will have been to the doctor to have the lump checked out.' A series of simple check steps provided by the SMART criteria can enable client and counsellor to concretise goals while avoiding the danger of getting lost in complex detail and losing sight of the hoped-for outcome.

Step 2C: commitment

At one of the York summer schools (1991) Egan used the following shorthand to summarise the three steps of stage two:

2A = hope
2B = direction
2C = cause

In this step of the model, the client's goals become the cause to which he or she commits him-/herself. Counsellors enable clients to commit to their own causes by helping them move up the scale of levels of involvement, as indicated in Figure 3.1.

Ownership

Commitment

Buy in

Compliance

Obstruction

Figure 3.1 Levels of involvement in goal setting

The counselling relationship becomes instrumental here in enabling clients to commit to their objectives. The counsellor needs to help clients assess competing agendas in their lives (for instance, counter-intention, life events, seemingly unalterable circumstances) by helping them search for incentives that are likely to raise the probability that action will take place. 'What are the things in life that get you going?' is a useful kind of question to ask the client to begin to stimulate this process.

Egan suggests that as part of the course of counselling, step 2C is not so much a separate step, more a further dimension of the goal-setting process. A viable goal must have some kind of appeal for the client. As part of weighing up the odds of choosing to commit to such a goal the counsellor may need to help the client find reasons to stick to it. A useful way of doing this is to ask about 'payoffs', for example 'What would be the payoff for you of saying that you don't want to have sex when you don't feel like it?'

This step of the model is essentially concerned with weighing up the costs and consequences of pursuing goals and using a 'balance sheet' approach as a way of checking out choice and commitment with the client. Egan has pointed out that commitment is not the same as motivation. Rather, commitment is about identifying specific incentives, either external or internal, that keep the client moving forward in pursuing a goal. Internal incentives (finding the pursuit of a course of action rewarding in itself) are usually more powerful and long lasting than external incentives (Carr 2004) so the helper does well to join the client in searching for the former rather than concentrating on the latter.

It may be that committing to a goal has hidden costs in terms of the impact it is likely to have on other people in the client's life and it is important that such costs are recognised and explored. An example here would be where someone decides to pursue a goal of being more assertive that is likely to lead to increased conflict with her partner. Here the counsellor would need to help the client weigh up the 'pros' of getting her needs met more fully with the possible 'cons' of increased disagreements and fall-outs in her relationship.

The step of choosing and committing to goals often shows up as a crunch step if addressed in sufficiently concrete and specific terms.

Consider the difference in specificity between these two examples of a counsellor working with a student who has run into difficulties on his course:

Example 1

Counsellor A: So how do you feel about the idea of discussing your personal concerns with your tutor?

Client: It's probably the best thing in the long run. I think she's in college on Friday and I might try and see her then.

Counsellor A: Great! I'll look forward to hearing how it goes.

Example 2

Counsellor B: So what does your goal look like now that we've done some work on it?

Client (reading from what he has written down after re-shaping it with the help of the counsellor): By 4.30 on Friday I will have talked to my tutor about the personal issues that have got in the way of me attending lectures.

Counsellor B: When you say that out loud now, how does it feel?

Client: It sounds great on paper, but it's really hard to do because I find her so scary and she's bound to be cross.

> *Counsellor B:*   Perhaps we should take a step back then to look
> at how realistic this is. Maybe there's a way we
> could break it down into smaller steps if that feels
> too much.
>
> Counsellor and client then proceed to look at a sub-goal of
> leaving the tutor a note apologising for not attending lectures
> and asking if he could have a tutorial on Friday to discuss some
> personal difficulties.

I hope it is clear from the examples themselves which conversation
would be most likely to result in a meeting between student and
tutor.

Objections are sometimes legitimately raised about the endorse-
ment of the pursuit of individual over collective goals that is explicit or implicit in most Eurocentric and Westernised approaches
to counselling – the skilled helper model included. So here the
counsellor has to be careful not to contaminate the client's process
with his or her own conscious or unconscious bias towards the
reinforcement of predominant cultural norms attached to goal
setting.

The process of goal setting can still be usefully applied to com-
munal or collective contexts, for instance where the client's allegiance to family or cultural expectations prevails over individual
preferences or objectives. Committing to a course of action that
honours a sense of duty is a legitimate goal. For instance, the goal of
keeping the family together may be a high priority for a working-
class, Irish Catholic woman and one that, if accomplished, might
give her more of a sense of achievement and fulfilment than pursuing the individual goal of leaving an unsatisfying relationship.

Stage three: action plan

How do I get what I need or want?

Putting a somewhat different spin on how the term is normally
used, Egan has suggested that counsellors are 'client centred' if
they can enable clients to act in their own self-interest: 'caring
tough love is also client-centered' (Egan 2006). Stage three of the

skilled helper model is essentially about helping clients produce numerous pathways to the achievement of their clearly formulated goals. Put more simply, the central question that the counsellor is asking here is: 'How do we get from a situation you don't like, to one that is better?' In the seventh edition of *The Skilled Helper* Egan has captioned this stage of the model 'How do I get what I need or want?' I often think of this stage in terms of the collaborative question 'How can we move things forward?'

Egan has written about the logic of the problem-management model being embedded in people's consciousness as evidenced by their tendency to find it familiar and easy to grasp. 'At some level of their being they understand the model' (Egan 1984b: 137). I find this particularly true of stage three. If counsellor and client arrive at the point of contemplating action on agreed goals, having thoroughly and carefully prepared for this stage, it often seems that clients gain the momentum and awareness to take the process forward for themselves. An example of how this can happen is given in the following section.

Step 3A: possible strategies

Helping clients to identify possible ways of achieving what they want requires that the counsellor helps them to tap into their imaginal and creative resources (even when they don't think they have any). I am frequently amazed with the great ideas that clients come up with that I could never have thought of for them, which in itself is a good reason for holding back on giving my own advice and suggestions. There follow a couple of real examples to illustrate how just creative and resourceful clients can be in coming up with their own strategies for action.

The first example is of working with a young person who came to counselling with a number of different issues she was attempting to resolve. She was trying to stay off street drugs and moderate her alcohol misuse and self-harming (cutting) behaviour. She suffered from agoraphobia and panic attacks and felt isolated and depressed. She had very little money and no home of her own.

She spent periods of time staying with different relatives, an experience which she found by turns oppressive and chaotic.

For the first several weeks of coming to counselling she could only get to her sessions if she was brought by her older sister, who then waited to take her home again (even though she lived within easy walking distance of the counselling service). The work with this young person lasted several months and mainly involved exploring the reasons behind her presenting symptoms and difficulties and how they were in many ways failed attempts to solve problems stemming from a neglectful childhood. In particular she came to understand that her agoraphobia and panic attacks were self-confirmatory experiences, re-enacting and attesting to the reality (denied by family members) that as a young child she had sometimes been left alone at night while her parents went out drinking. In therapy she was able to describe and reclaim these memories with great clarity, together with the accompanying feelings of terror at the conviction that no-one would come back and find her and that she might die, and the subsequent thought that it must be because she was bad that she was left on her own in the dark.

As she became more able to understand these symptoms and their antecedents, the client became motivated to work towards achieving goals that would relieve her of them. She quickly got the idea of working in incremental steps that could have a stretch and ripple effect and begin to make a real difference to her life. So, for example, she tried having her session knowing her sister had popped out for a cup of tea in a nearby café before coming back at the end of the hour (rather than insisting the sister didn't budge from the waiting room in case she felt like bolting from the session). She was then able to try coming on her own in a taxi as long as her sister put her into it and was at home when she returned. Next she decided she wanted to be able to come entirely on her own to counselling and we began to work explicitly on changing the agoraphobic behaviour.

In one session we spent time on imagining what it would be like for her if she didn't have the agoraphobia and panic attacks any longer (stage 2A of the model) and I thought that in the next session we might be able to move towards establishing some goals. I underestimated her at this point. She came back the following week and announced that the day after her last counselling session she had done several walking circuits of her sister's house and had gradually extended the length of these. For the first time she had also walked to the counselling agency on her own. When I asked her how she had managed to do these things, her reply went something like this:

Client: After we talked last week I knew that I was ready to do this but I didn't want to take on too much at once. I thought about going out and it scared me. Then I told myself that I didn't need to go far. I could just go a little way and if I felt scared or panicky I could come back. Then I had an idea about how to do it. I got Lucky's [sister's dog] lead out and he went crazy, jumping all over me, thinking he was going for a walk. I couldn't disappoint him then, so I took him round the block. It helped having him with me because I kept talking to him and that took my attention off what I was doing. It also felt like I wasn't on my own, even though I only had the dog with me. I sort of felt he could protect me if anything happened – even though he's only little. It felt OK so I did it again the next day and went a bit further. Then I tried it on my own and that was all right too. I felt nervous but I did it and nothing terrible happened. Then I thought I might as well try coming here on my own – so now I've done that too.

This is an example of where full and careful work in stage one of the model can pay dividends when stages two and three are addressed. The exploratory work that we undertook in stage one provided a strong springboard for the later action phases that the client initiated and, in the way that Egan suggests, this client appeared to take to these as if they were familiar and already known. Ideally, as this example illustrates, change should grow organically out of the therapeutic encounter, rather than occurring as a kind of 'add on' at the end of the process.

In the next example the client had a high level of exam anxiety and frequently experienced paralysing levels of stress as he approached his end-of-year exams. These were in danger of completely overwhelming him as his final-year exams loomed. With his counsellor he had been working on realistic goals around arriving only in a nervous (as opposed to terrified) state for his exams and staying calm enough to think and write during the exam itself. Here are some of the strategies that he came up with to help achieve these goals:

1   Leave the radio on low at night tuned to a pleasant music station so that when he couldn't sleep, rather than busying his mind with anxious thoughts, he could listen to music that might help him drift off again.

2   Work hard at replacing negative thoughts with more encouraging and realistic ones as he approached the exam day, e.g. instead of 'Oh my God, I can't do this, I am going to have a panic attack and fail completely' he could practise saying to himself 'I know I'm intelligent and now is a chance to really show all that I've learned'.

3   Arrive just a few minutes before the exam so as not to be hanging around feeling anxious beforehand.

4   Make sure he knew exactly where the room was and how to get to it – by going and having a look a day or two beforehand – so that he wouldn't feel anxious about finding it or think he needed to arrive early in case he couldn't find it.

5   Leave straight after each exam and not hang around for 'post-mortems' that would just feed his anxiety about having done badly.

6   On exam days wear his glasses rather than contact lenses (the client was very short-sighted). Take off his glasses whenever he looked up from his exam paper and around the

room so that the other students would look blurry and he wouldn't have his usual sharp focus on everyone else, heads down, writing calmly and collectedly while he felt blank and stupid.

Counsellors can use their skills of probing and prompting to help clients come up with such a range of useful strategies. The following are a few of the questions that helped this client. They correspond to each of his strategies numbered as above.

1   When you can't sleep what could you do instead that wouldn't increase your anxiety?

Is there anything that has helped you to sleep before that might work again?

Most people find that sometimes they nod off in bed even when they don't mean to. What helps you to nod off?

If you decided that you didn't want to sleep, but you wanted to stay in bed and rest, what might you do instead of sleeping?

2   If you dumped that unhelpful thought and had a new one based on all the work that we have done, what could that new thought be?

If you imagined me walking into the exam room with you and whispering something helpful into your ear, what would it be?

What's the opposite extreme of that horrible negative message that you keep giving yourself? What is the thought that is the most unlike it you can think of?

3   If your panic levels shoot up from 7 to 10 in the time just before the exam, how could you change that time?

If you didn't give yourself that 'rehearsal' time in which to panic and went straight for the final 'performance', what would you do differently?

What's the optimum time to get there to ensure you are not worried about being late but also not to give yourself the time to indulge in the luxury of an extra dose of worrying?

4   What might help you to orientate yourself?

How could you deal with the dread of the unknown and unfamiliar exam room?

Have you ever taken the time to go and have a look at where the exam will be held beforehand? Might that be an idea? (This is an example of what Egan calls the 'prompt and fade' technique, whereby the counsellor offers a suggestion as a form of 'pump priming' but then hands consideration of the suggestion over to the client to invite him or her to evaluate its usefulness.)

5   What do you usually do after an exam? How helpful is that?
    What would it be good for you to do straight after the exam?
    If you were able to cut off from that exam straight away in order to concentrate on preparing well for the next one, what would be the first thing you would need to do?

6   Any 'off-the-wall' ideas that might also help?

Step 3B: best-fit strategies

This part of the model is helpful wherever the client has generated a good range of possible action strategies and needs help with choosing those that will most likely contribute to the outcome(s) he or she is working towards. Sometimes the most attractive options are not the most helpful. Spending an evening alone with a pile of junk food and a good film might provide a temporary solution to boredom and loneliness but is unlikely to have a lasting effect on someone's experience of isolation. Nonetheless, it is important that actions that the client chooses are from their own (not the counsellor's) frame of reference.

The most helpful actions are those that are prudent, directional and wise. Prudent actions are ones that are life-affirming, rather than life-limiting. Egan makes the distinction between two types of action: those that initiate and those that sustain action. In step 2B we looked at a useful acronym, 'SMART', that can assist in setting workable goals. In step 3B, I sometimes use a different acronym 'CRAVE' to help the client check out best-fit strategies to achieve their goals. CRAVE stands for:

Control: Is this strategy in the client's control?
Relevant: Does it address the goal?
Appeal: Is it attractive to the client?
Values: Is it in keeping with the client's values?
Environment: What external resources and constraints might help/ hinder?

When it comes down to it, we are talking about common sense here and this suggests that strategies chosen should be ones that the client is most keen on and that are cost effective and most likely to succeed.

Step 3C: plan

Sometimes a range of strategies such as those listed above by the student with exam anxiety will naturally fall into a plan. At other times, clients might need some help in sequencing their chosen strategies to avoid the danger of random or insufficient action. The value of a plan is that it can provide a structure that empowers the client to get something done in an economical and intentional manner. Actions can then be aimed at specific outcomes rather than being splattered all over the place. A plan takes the strategies and puts them in order so that they are organised in time. This can make time a friend, rather than an enemy, and in this sense changes the culture of action that may have inhibited the client in the past.

A plan takes the strategies identified in step 3B and makes them much more immediate in the life of the client. Asking clients *what* they will do and *when*, *where* and *how* they will do it is often helpful in giving some decent action ideas more precision and a higher likelihood of success. An important check-step question to ask even when a plan seems water-tight is: 'Is there anything you need to do before taking that first step?' This will often highlight a necessary step that, if omitted, is very likely to sabotage a good action plan even before it gets off the starting blocks. For instance, if the client's action plan relies on the presence or actions of another person, it may be that a first step is to check that that person will be in the right place, at the right time and in the right frame of mind to help with the plan.

Action leading to valued outcomes – how do I make it happen?

Underlying the three stages of the model is an 'action arrow' (see Figure 2.1) that brings in the 'fourth' dimension of what Egan has more accurately described as a 'four-dimension model' (Sugarman 1995: 278) than a model with three parts. In the seventh edition of *The Skilled Helper* this arrow is captioned 'How do I make it happen?' In *Essentials of Skilled Helping* the arrow is dubbed

'Action leading to valued outcomes'. The action arrow underpins the whole problem-management process to emphasise that action lies at the heart of change. As Egan points out, 'if clients don't act on their own behalf, change does not take place' (Sugarman 1995).

I have tried to make it clear in what I have written about the model so far that there are many forms of action, both internal and external, that run throughout the process and form part of the action arrow. Implementation is represented visually by this action arrow to show that consideration of how to implement change needs to take place from the beginning of the counselling process and not simply be seen as a grand finale to that process.

To work at its best, implementation needs to be tactical and conceptualised to allow for the unexpected. In this sense, any plans that are made are required to be open to change and adaptation. Effective action within the framework of the skilled helper model is conceived of as an unfolding process. Rather than a series of dramatic lurches, action is a cumulative sequence of constant, incremental change. As Egan advised during a lecture given at one of the York counselling summer schools: 'Don't look for the "big score" because that is getting into drama, not counselling'. The skilled helper attunes his or her antennae to pick up and help amplify the smallest signs of change in the client wherever they occur in the course of counselling.

Egan has also spoken about 'ratcheting in' change. What he means by this became much clearer to me during the course of a holiday I recently took to New England. Mount Washington, the highest mountain in the North Eastern United States, has a remarkable railway, the second steepest in the world. It runs to the top of the mountain on a cog system. The train is able to inch its way to the summit along seemingly impossible inclines, with gradients as steep as 38 per cent in places, because each small cog the train passes on the track acts as a ratchet to hold it in place as it lumbers slowly on up the steep slopes. This train, taking three hours for a round trip, rewards the traveller with one of the most magnificent views in New England. In terms of how action is conceptualised in the skilled helper model, this analogy probably speaks for itself.

Egan suggests that it is useful for counsellor and client to consider three kinds of ratchet at the implementation stage of action planning: before, during and after implementation. If we consider the case of the young person mentioned above who managed to overcome her agoraphobia with the help of her sister's pet, we can see that these three kinds of ratchets were in place:

- Before ratchets: coping self-talk; showing the dog his lead so that he believed a walk was imminent.
- During ratchets: talking to Lucky during the walk; imagining that he could act as a protector.
- After ratchets: going for another walk the following day to reinforce the action; taking a third walk soon after without Lucky for company.

Action, of course, is not always a smooth ride and may be derailed by a number of obstacles. The two gremlins that most frequently cause trouble are *inertia* and *entropy* – leading to what is colloquially known as 'the no-start/fall-apart syndrome'. The counsellor can help clients with inertia (those who have trouble getting going) by encouraging them to concentrate on results rather than the pain of starting. Clients who are likely to fall prey to entropy (failure to sustain action) can be helped to envisage the pitfalls that lie ahead and take these into account in planning action.

Force-field analysis is the term that Egan gives to a process that can be used to help the client develop strategies to counteract the pitfalls involved in taking action. It provides a way of considering with the client the question: 'What will raise the likelihood of this plan starting, continuing and being completed?' The essence of this process is found in the proverb that to be forewarned is to be forearmed. It involves a proactive consideration of what might help and what might hinder intended action, and then thinking of ways to enhance the former and decrease the latter. By so doing, success is more likely to prevail over failure.

The process that the counsellor uses in force-field analysis is to take the client through a series of steps as follows:

1 Help clients to list all the restraining forces (in themselves, in others and in the environment) that might keep them from initiating or sustaining action.
2 Help clients to list all the facilitating forces (in themselves, in others and in the environment) that might help them keep them on track with their intended programme of change.
3 Help clients to identify the forces in each of their lists that seem most significant.

4   Help clients to find ways of reducing significant restraining forces and enhancing significant facilitating forces.

Written in this way, the process may sound rather cumbersome and mechanical. Translated into the language of helping it can become a natural extension of ongoing collaborative work between counsellor and client. The following example shows how the counsellor might work with someone to help them begin to identify and deal with their restraining forces.

The client here has been working on a plan to confront an over-familiar acquaintance and ask him to back off as she is beginning to find his attentions uncomfortable and intrusive. She has decided that next time he phones she wants to tell him that she doesn't want a close friendship at this time and does not want him to call round uninvited or keep phoning when she has told him she is busy.

Counsellor: Sounds like we've got a plan there. How do you feel about it?

Client: I'm good at making plans. I'm just not very good at putting them into practice.

Counsellor: What's likely to get in the way?

Client: I don't like hurting people's feelings and I can easily start to think that I'm not being very nice.

Counsellor: Anything else?

Client: Well, I'm already thinking that maybe it's me that's got the problem and he just wants to be friendly.

Counsellor: It's easy to talk yourself out of it. What did you think when we were exploring the problem a few minutes ago?

Client: Well, I got upset then because I *do* worry about it and every time the phone goes or someone rings the doorbell I think it might be him. I don't like switching my computer on because I know I'll have loads of e-mails from him. And I *do* want all that to stop happening.

> Counsellor: You sound much firmer there when you think about how much this is bothering you. So how do you think you might be able to deal with those doubts you mentioned about not being very nice, or that it's you that's got the problem?
>
> Client: Well, if I don't stop it now, I think it will just get worse. I've tried dropping hints, but he doesn't take them. I suppose I just have to remember that and that I haven't done anything wrong.

Where the counsellor and client take time to undertake preliminary work such as this to prepare for the implementation of a plan they can substantially increase the likelihood that the plan will bear fruit. In the example given above the client did manage to stop this acquaintance pestering her and the 'mop-up' work then involved the counsellor helping her to manage her residual feelings of guilt at having 'rejected' this person.

At this point I have come to the end of this brief presentation of Egan's skilled helper model. In the next chapter I will turn to a consideration of the various critiques and commentaries that have been made of the skilled helper model and say more about how I have adapted my own use of the model to take account of a number of these. I hope that by so doing I will show more clearly how it is possible for helpers to assimilate the skilled helper model into their own integrative or personal style of counselling or helping.

Guidelines 3.1: Questions to help open the process of step 2A

Possibilities for a better future:

- What do you want in your life that you don't have now?
- If you were living your life more fully, what would be different?

- If counselling was working for you, how would you know? What would have changed?
- What is your dream or vision of your life as you'd like it to be?
- What have you lost, or never had, that you'd really like to have now?
- What have you been longing for that has always seemed out of your grasp?
- If you imagine seeing yourself having fun/more relaxed/more confident/having dealt with your guilt . . . etc., what do you see?
- If you looked beyond your old patterns of thinking/feeling/ behaving . . . what would you see?
- If you got rid of those old patterns what would be different?
- For your life to be better, what would you have less of and more of?
- If you imagine relating better to your partner/child/parent . . . what would be different?
- You say you've never thought about what you wanted before. So imagine taking a look at that for the first time – what do you see?
- What is working for you in your life now that you'd like to build on?
- If we were to meet again in five years' time and you were managing better, what would you be telling me about your life that would help me to know this?
- What would your life look like if you didn't have this problem?
- If you were feeling better about yourself, what would you like to be feeling instead of what you feel now?
- What character or person do you admire? What characteristics do they have that you'd like too?
- Can you describe for me the person you'd really like to be?
- If you had changed something so small that only you could sense it, but it still improved your life, what would that thing be?
- When your life in the past was better than it is now, what did that look like?
- You say that you just want to die. What would being dead relieve you of? If you can imagine having this relief *and* staying alive what would have changed?

Exercise 3.1: Creative exercise to experience the difference between stages two and three

Take some paper and crayons/paints and work on your own for 15 minutes.

Remember a favourite holiday and where you went. Draw or paint a picture of it, including all the things that you liked and enjoyed when you got there.

On a separate piece of paper, write or draw how you got to your holiday destination. Include the preparations you made, the means of transport that got you to your destination and the luggage that you took with you. Put down all the people and resources that helped you to get to your holiday, including what you yourself did to help make it happen.

Spend some time with one other person and divide the time equally between you to explore and describe your pictures and writing.

You might like to think about:

- What is the relationship between your two pictures?
- What did it feel like to draw them?
- What was difficult about what you remembered and drew or wrote about?
- What was the best part?

Tutor: allow time for a whole-group debrief to air thoughts and feelings about the exercise and to bring together any significant learning.

The kinds of points that might come up in feedback are:

- You need to know where you are going before knowing what to pack.
- Journeys need a bit of planning.
- Having a clear idea of what it might be like when you get there helps you to know what to take.
- Different kinds of destination need different means of transport.
- Sometimes things don't go to plan and you need to be resourceful and creative to make sure you get to your destination.

- Some journeys take longer and are more complicated than others.
- It's good to have the holiday to look forward to even when it is some way off.

Tutor: it can be helpful to invite trainees to do this exercise without giving any prior input on stages two and three of the skilled helper model. This will encourage them to experience for themselves that having a good idea of what they want and need, and why, can be important in determining the kind of actions they take to achieve those outcomes.

Chapter 4

Critiques and commentaries of the skilled helper model

In this chapter I will attempt to elaborate on specific aspects of the skilled helper model that have been raised in debates and critiques offered by other writers and commentators. I will examine published criticisms of the model, acknowledge those that seem valid and attempt to offer reasoned rebuttals to others, where I feel this is appropriate. The chapter will also address more anecdotal but pervasive criticisms of the model that have been made by students, trainers and practitioners.

A further intention of the chapter is to broaden discussion of the model beyond the current perception of it being a one-author approach and to explore ways of 'translating' various aspects of the model in order to engage with a wide range of perspectives. In so doing, I will discuss in some detail issues relating to the counselling relationship and working alliance whilst using the model. I hope to emphasise the range of relationship styles that can be accommodated within the model and also explore using the skilled helper framework to work with issues located in the past. I will argue that the model offers a sound framework for integrating the past and maximising the benefit to the client of such work. I will also discuss concepts from narrative and post-modern approaches and suggest how these can usefully be integrated into the model.

There is no model of counselling, no matter how comprehensive and well learned, that can make a good counsellor. The skilled helper model is no exception. As a trainer with twenty years' experience of teaching this approach, I have seen some appalling travesties of the model in practice. Among the worst are those where the model is mechanically applied in a directive and super-ficial manner that takes insufficient notice of clients' non-linear and complex experiencing of their difficulties. Egan is at pains to point out that the model's structure constitutes 'principles, not formulas to be followed slavishly' (Egan 2002a: 105). Despite this caveat, students of counselling (and sometimes their teachers) seem at times to adopt the model as if they are painting by numbers, rather than practising the delicate and creative art of therapy.

Consider the following two examples of extracts from the opening portion of the same (imaginary) session with two different counsellors. Both of these counsellors claim to use the skilled helper model.

Extract 1

Counsellor A: We have an hour to talk today. Perhaps you'd like to tell me your story.

Client: Before we start, would you mind telling me something about how you work. My last counsellor was psychodynamic and I wondered if you were the same.

Counsellor A: I work a bit differently to that. I use a problem-management model that is about helping you to deal with your current problems and also helping you develop any opportunities you might be missing. We can talk about it some more now if you like, or as we go along.

Client: OK, that sounds quite straightforward. Well, I suppose what's brought me here is a number of problems. I don't know where to start really. It feels a bit awkward . . .

Counsellor A: How about if we start with the problem that feels most pressing – the one that you feel would make a difference to your life if you were able to manage it better.

Client: Mmmm . . . Well I think it's something about my relationship with my partner. It's not going well at the moment and it seems to be getting worse.

Counsellor A: If your relationship with your partner was getting better instead of getting worse, what would that look like?

Client: I'm not sure what you mean.

Extract 2

Counsellor B: We have an hour today and the time is yours. Where would you like to start?

Client: Before we start, would you mind telling me something about how you work. My last counsellor was psychodynamic and I wondered if you were the same.

Counsellor B: I'm not sure if you are hoping that I might use a similar approach or something different.

Client: I'm not sure myself. I feel a bit uncertain about coming to see a new counsellor. I've been OK for some time and now things just seem to be getting on top of me again.

Counsellor B: Well, in answer to your question about how I work, I would hope that together we might begin to understand how come things are getting on top of you again and then look at how you might start to deal with them a little better. I can tell you more about the process we might use to do that now if you like, or as we go along. It depends on how much you want to hear from me at this point and how much you would like me to hear from you.

Client: I think I was just a bit anxious about getting started and it felt easier to ask you a question than launch straight in about me.

Counsellor B: It can be pretty daunting starting off with a new counsellor and it's bound to take a while for us to settle in.

Client:	I'm feeling a bit better now, although I still don't know where to start – there's so much and it's all really confusing.
Counsellor B:	There's no right or wrong place to start. If you take a moment to scan around all that confusing stuff where does your attention settle?
Client:	It sort of shifts between my relationship with my partner – which isn't going well – and something else that feels more about me.
Counsellor B:	You've named your relationship with your partner there as a difficulty we might look at, but there's also something about you that's more difficult to name, or perhaps may be harder to talk about?
Client:	I *would* like to try to talk about it – it's what I came back into counselling to do I think. It's sort of left over from my last counselling as something I couldn't really deal with then. I thought I might be ready to now, but now that I'm actually here, it seems much harder.
Counsellor B:	There seems to be quite a tension there for you between wanting to explore something that really matters to you and not knowing if, or how, you can.
Client:	It's like I just clam up and I want to run away and I wish I'd never said anything.
Counsellor B:	And yet you haven't run away and you've been able to let me know how you feel and you've had the courage to tell me there's a really sensitive issue here.

Both of these counsellors could be said to be working with the word, if not the spirit of the skilled helper model. Yet if we look at the counselling styles of counsellor A and counsellor B, we might notice some pretty significant differences. Counsellor A wears the model on her sleeve and rubs the client's nose in it at every opportunity. She's impervious to the nuances of the client's words and behaviour and pushes ahead at her own pace, regardless of the client's ambivalence and reluctance and, in consequence, the process quickly stalls. Counsellor B, on the other hand, has the model hovering lightly in the background. He uses it with an almost imperceptible touch to shape his interventions and to gently hold and guide the client who, he has the sense to see, is working hard at the edge of her comfort zone. As a result, the client is telling a much more meaningful story to counsellor B.

Counsellor B gives as much attention to the therapeutic relationship as he does to the content of the client's story. In this he brings a relational approach to the model. He uses lots of empathy and tries to work from the client's frame of reference. He gives the client the opportunity to start wherever she wishes to start (which happens to be with the process rather than content) and again gives her options when he invites her to scan around her issues to find a focus. This section of dialogue illustrates how focusing (leverage) is more usefully seen as a process than a single question. He challenges her strengths towards the end of the extract of dialogue and provides encouragement and affirmation.

In contrast to this, counsellor A works from her own frame of reference and agenda, which seems to be to fit the client to the model at any cost, rather than adapt the model to where the client might be and what she might need. She goes for the simple option of an easily stated problem while counsellor B tentatively touches on an issue that the client finds harder to articulate. With empathy he gently coaxes the issue into the light and helps the client to amplify it without naming it before she is ready. In my experience, many of the criticisms that are made of the skilled helper model are based on the perception that therapists who use the model are more like counsellor A than counsellor B.

It is noticeable that in fact very few commentaries and critiques of the model have been published in the UK. This is striking given that there are hundreds of references to Egan's work scattered throughout counselling and training texts that have been published in the UK over the last 25 years. These clearly attest to the enduring influence of the skilled helper model. Of the published material that does exist, Jenkins (2000) has a produced a largely descriptive chapter on the model in *Integrative and Eclectic Counselling and Psychotherapy* and a brief critique of the model for *Counselling News* (Jenkins 1993). Fetherston (2002) has

published an article critiquing the model from a social constructionist perspective. There is a short, developmental account of
the model in the *Handbook of Counselling and Psychotherapy*
(Wosket 2006). Although there is a discursive chapter (Inskipp and
Johns 1984) on the skilled helper model in the first edition of
Individual Therapy in Britain, no mention of Egan's work is made
in the three subsequent editions. Connor (1994) explores and
evaluates the skilled helper model as a core model in counsellor
training. Nelson-Jones (2002) includes the briefest of critiques of
the skilled helper in his book outlining a 'skilled client' model.
Otherwise, only short descriptive summaries and passing references to Egan's work are evident in critical anthologies of counselling currently available in the UK.

The sections below attempt to engage with the debates and
criticisms raised in published commentaries on the model as well
as with those that are commonly voiced, albeit anecdotally, by
students, trainers and practitioners in the field. For clarity, I have
divided these into themes under the following headings. Each of
these is considered in turn in the sections that follow:

- theoretical and contextual factors
- socio-cultural factors
- structural and stylistic considerations
- the therapeutic relationship
- working with the past and unconscious processes.

Theoretical and contextual factors

The model is too cognitive-behavioural

To suggest that a model may be overly cognitive-behavioural is,
presumably, only a legitimate criticism if cognitive-behavioural
therapies can be shown to be demonstrably flawed and limited *per
se*. As there appears not to be a general consensus that this is the
case, then those who criticise the model on these grounds may
merely be expressing an aversion to cognitive-behavioural therapy.
As a way of countering the criticism that the skilled helper model
is too cognitive-behavioural, I will briefly consider some recent
developments in cognitive-behavioural therapy that indicate that
a number of criticisms frequently levelled at this approach are
outdated.

Certainly it has been acknowledged that early formulations of cognitive and cognitive-behavioural therapies had a number of limitations (Wills and Sanders 1997). Amongst these are: (1) an over-emphasis on thinking; (2) too little attention being paid to the therapeutic relationship; and (3) insufficient acknowledgement of early formative experiences. However, cognitive-behavioural therapy has undergone huge changes in recent years and contemporary formulations provide a more holistic approach that accommodates: (1) working in depth and long term; (2) paying more attention to feelings and emotion; (3) working with transference, countertransference and other dynamics of the therapeutic relationship; and (4) developing non-verbal ways of working including imagery (Wills and Sanders 1997).

The alliance between counsellor and client is now considered by modern exponents of the cognitive-behavioural approach to be centre stage and they may happily draw on psychodynamic concepts, such as attachment theory, in working with the therapeutic relationship (Safran 1990; Safran and Segal 1990). Ways that psychodynamic and relational concepts are now integrated into cognitive therapy and can be incorporated into integrative approaches that draw on cognitive-behavioural theory (such as the skilled helper model) include:

- According a central role to how dysfunctional beliefs about self and others can be disconfirmed through the experience of the therapeutic relationship, e.g. encouraging clients to treat their perceptions of others/the therapist as hypotheses to be tested out in the relationship.
- The use of historical information to activate change (see the section on working with the past; p. 124).
- The therapist acting as a 'secure base' from which the client might experiment with new and different ways of being and acting.
- Focusing on inner experiencing, which requires the therapist to give importance to turning his or her attention inward to track his or her own responses that, in turn, may give useful clues to what the client evokes in others.

Despite these developments, there is still a frequent misperception that cognitive-behavioural therapies are shallow, simplistic approaches that are limited to helping with the regulation and management of surface problems in short-term therapy. In fact, developments in cognitive therapy have brought the approach closer to psychodynamic ways of working, in particular through the notion of working with 'schemata' – deeper levels of core beliefs that are responsible for determining an individual's prevailing self-concept and mode of being in the world (Wills and Sanders 1997).

Cognitive-behavioural therapy is increasingly being acknowledged as an effective treatment for the most challenging of issues (Leahy 2001, 2003), including severe depression (Scott 1992; Segal *et al.* 2001), psychosis (Fowler *et al.* 1995; Kingdon and Turkington 1995; Morrison 2002; Morrison *et al.* 2003; Slade and Haddock 1995), a range of personality disorders (Beck *et al.* 2003; Wills and Sanders 1997), obsessive-compulsive disorders (Clark 2004) and dissociative identity disorder (Fine 1999; Gold *et al.* 2001). Interestingly, in 1995 it was estimated from survey results of members of the British Association for Counselling that one-fifth of respondents defined their counselling approach as cognitive (Palmer and Syzmanska 1995) – a finding that confirms the growing popularity of cognitive-behavioural approaches.

Because of its emphasis on problem solving and action, the model is superficial, lacks depth and is applicable only to short-term counselling for surface issues

This is a criticism that tends to be levelled by those who have not undergone a thorough training in the model and have not learned to use it in a genuinely therapeutic way. In essence the model *is* simple. This is not at all the same as being simplistic. It is also, as noted in Chapter 1, a life-skills model that is designed to be given away. If the model, as Egan advocates, were to be taught as part of adolescent and continuing education this might result in more people being able to engage naturally in preventive problem management and opportunity development. Potentially, this might mean less need for expensive, remedial therapy.

It is not inconceivable that some adherents of the more esoteric and arcane schools of counselling and psychotherapy might have a vested interest in having us believe that therapy has to be a mysterious, complex, long-term, specialist procedure requiring years of highly theoretical and technical training. Perhaps some might secretly fear that to 'give away' the basic processes and techniques of helping may be to give away their power, status and even livelihood.

A common misperception of the skilled helper model is that it is primarily concerned with problem solving. This is an inaccurate perception, as Egan clearly points out: 'The goal of helping is not to *solve* problems but to help the troubled person *manage* them more effectively or even transcend them by taking advantage of new possibilities in life' (Egan 2002a: 6, original emphasis). The approach also acknowledges the value of compromise and that clients have the right to choose *not* to change. Helping clients manage problems is often about helping them cope better and the value of coping should not be underestimated. 'Helping clients cope is one of the best things helpers can do' (*ibid.*: 290) in that it promotes a positive approach to life and its challenges.

It is true that Egan says little about the capacity of the skilled helper framework to accommodate working in depth with deep-seated issues located in the past or with extremes of client experience (trauma and abuse, for example). It has been left to others to articulate its usefulness in these areas. Hall and Lloyd in their seminal (1993) text on working with survivors of child sexual abuse have clearly articulated the usefulness of the skilled helper model with this client group. They recommend the model as 'particularly useful and practical' (1993: 322) for working with abuse survivors because of its emphasis on problem exploration before moving towards solutions coupled with the attention it gives to the importance of building a good therapeutic alliance in order to facilitate the process of counselling.

I recently worked for several years in a voluntary counselling agency where the client group solely comprised women survivors of child sexual abuse and I found the model similarly useful in this context. At initial intake interviews, the vast majority of clients using this service voiced what they wanted from counselling in terms of observable and concrete change. These clients, most of whom could not afford private therapy and so turned to a voluntary agency, did not present for counselling for personal development reasons. They came because they were hurting and their lives were falling apart and they wanted this to change. There is nothing superficial about the work that these clients undertook and for many of them therapy lasted for years, rather than weeks or months.

Even with very distressed clients who may experience a great deal of disturbance I have found the skilled helper model can appeal to parts of the client that are able to function well. The structured framework of the model promotes self-responsibility and can provide a lifeline for clients who habitually feel in chaos and out of control. The model can engage those parts of the client that crave structure, control and safety when other parts more characteristically demonstrate this craving through self-harming behaviours. In this way the model can provide a constructive outlet for energy that can be harnessed to help the client develop more functional problem-management skills.

This process can be seen at work in the following words of a client quoted (with her permission) from her end-of-counselling evaluation form. This young (17-year-old) woman came to counselling having been homeless and at risk from a life on the streets. She frequently misused alcohol and street drugs and was depressed and suicidal. At the end of her counselling, which lasted thirty weeks, she wrote:

> I was at a stage in my life where I felt I wanted to sort through my problems and stop using drugs – grow up basically and admit I needed help. Counselling was a starting point. I know a lot of how I've managed is down to me but my counsellor was outstanding and in a professional, very clever way helped me to learn to think instead of hide! My life has turned around. I have gained my self-respect and confidence back. I am drug free and I've learned to sort through problems and deal with people and consider everyone's feelings.

What is striking about this feedback is that it appears to confirm the notion I have touched on several times in this book, that client factors are an important determinant of successful outcomes. What seems to have been so potent for this client is a combination of her motivation and determination to change *and* the active catalyst provided by the counsellor and the problem-management process offered.

Two years after her counselling finished, I wrote to her asking if she was still willing for me to use some examples from our work together in this book. I had the delightful experience of having a letter back from her to say that she is continuing to do well, now has a wonderful partner and a beautiful baby (photos enclosed).

She referred to her counselling saying, 'If it wasn't for your help during my counselling sessions I don't think I would be here today'. Experiences such as this attest to the enduring influence that a problem-management approach to counselling can have. I am also left with the thought that it would be enlightening to know which aspects of the change process were experienced as most helpful by this client – was it her own motivation to change, the problem-management process or her relationship with her counsellor? Questions such as these are fundamental to research issues involving the skilled helper model, as discussed in Chapter 6.

As a proactive rather than a remedial approach, it is perhaps in its training-as-treatment function that one can most easily see the potential for the model to address substantial issues. For instance, helping clients develop problem-solving skills can be a strong deterrent to suicidal behaviour since this can enable them to obtain the necessary distance from their hopelessness to see it as a problem in itself, rather than a reflection of reality (Lieper and Kent 2001). If clients at risk of suicide are taught problem-solving skills this can encourage them to take responsibility for their feelings and actions. This is illustrated in the words of the initially suicidal young client, quoted above, where she writes about how her counsellor helped her to 'learn to think instead of hide'.

Despite his preference for seeing counselling as a short-term process of minimal intervention, Egan does concede that, as an estimate, between 20 and 30 per cent of clients will require longer-term intervention 'lasting more than 25 sessions' (Egan 2002a: 249). My experience is that the model can provide an appropriate frame and container for long-term, in-depth work, although the skills and experience needed to work with more complex issues will require counsellors to undertake additional specialist professional training and development.

The skilled helper model is a one-person approach that lacks empirical validity and a solid research base attesting to its efficacy

This is a key and fundamental criticism of the skilled helper model and one that merits close scrutiny. To do justice to this topic, I have chosen to discuss it separately and at length in Chapter 6, where issues relating to research and supervision are explored in greater detail.

The model does not have a theory of personality

By their nature, models are more pragmatic than theoretical. A good working model, as defined by Egan, is 'a framework or cognitive map with "delivery" potential' (1984a: 25). As an integrative framework, the skilled helper model does not posit a unified theory of personality, rather it accommodates a number of perspectives on what it is to be human. Although integrative, the model derives from, and is influenced by, a consistent view of the person and this is outlined in some detail in Chapter 1.

The model does not provide a sufficient or in-depth training for helping professionals

In addressing this criticism I would want to assert first that the model is only a template for some helping skills and a process to activate them. Egan does not claim that learning the problem-management process and the skills that drive it constitutes learning all there is to know about how to be an effective therapist. On the contrary, he is at pains to point out that the model and its accompanying skills constitute a starting point and a very small part of counsellor training and development (Egan 2002a).

I would also wish to make the obvious point here that good standards of training rely on the quality of trainers and the curricula they deliver. Poor training in the use of the skilled helper model, when it occurs, is often due to ineffective teaching by trainers who have a limited knowledge and experience of using the model in their own counselling practice and therefore present it in superficial, mechanical, unconvincing and lifeless ways. I get to grips more fully with the issue of the skilled helper as a core training model in the next chapter.

Socio-cultural factors

The model takes insufficient account of cultural differences

Many approaches to counselling and their associated texts have suffered from paying insufficient attention to issues of difference and diversity. The skilled helper model is, arguably, no exception. Certainly its 'masculine' language and perceived emphasis on the pursuit of individual goals within an opportunistic society have done little to dispel the myth that the model is a paternalistic approach that is most applicable to white, middle-class, articulate and well-resourced clients who have the freedom to determine their own lives.

Somewhat paradoxically, then, it is also noteworthy that within the literature on multiculturalism, the model's capacity to incorporate an understanding of society's response to individual difference within its people-in-systems approach has been acknowledged as one of its strengths (Bimrose 1996). It is noticeable that recent editions of the *The Skilled Helper* (1998, 2002a) have dealt more explicitly with developing culturally sensitive helpers and the case examples that are used to show the application of the model are drawn from different cultural and social settings throughout these texts.

It is perhaps significant in relation to the development of Egan's thinking about transcultural issues in helping that his newest publication on the skilled helper model, *Essentials of Skilled Helping* (2006), engages more forcefully with debates on difference and diversity than do his earlier texts. This publication presents an updated, more streamlined, and more compact version of the model designed to appeal particularly to para-professional helpers.

In this text he explores both the professional and ethical requirements for culturally sensitive practice together with the danger of losing sight of individual differences by placing too great a focus on cultural groupings, norms and assumptions. He quotes Patel's view that 'psychotherapy can never be about celebrating racial diversity because it is not about groups; it is about individuals and their infinite complexity'. To achieve a balance, he suggests that helpers need to temper a broad understanding of the 'characteristics, needs, and behaviors of the populations with whom they work' with sensitivity to within-group differences 'in personal assumptions, beliefs, values, norms, and patterns of behavior' (Egan 2006: 34). This publication explicitly acknowledges the importance of cross-cultural sensitivity when applying the model through the inclusion of a companion brochure *Skilled Helping Around the World*, which has been designed to accompany the book.

The skilled helper model has been translated into a number of different European and Asian languages and is taught worldwide (Sugarman 1995). There is therefore some evidence that it is a 'good traveller' and that, with some adaptation to take account of local context and culture, it can have international appeal and efficacy (Coles 1996). Egan does acknowledge that, like any counselling model, it has its limitations and is to a degree culture bound, particularly in its democratic and liberal origins. By saying 'if clients are relatively free and in charge of their lives, then the model becomes a counselling model, based on free choice' (Sugarman 1995: 276), Egan concedes that the model does not offer a universally applicable panacea. This accords with his views on the limitations of counselling *per se*, which are outlined in Chapter 2.

The model is too male oriented with its emphasis on the individual and on goals, tasks and behavioural change. As such it takes insufficient account of social and relational contexts

The language of the skilled helper model may be rather masculine and the process is indubitably action-oriented. Jenkins writes about the peculiarly 'kinetic, muscular quality' of Egan's prose (Jenkins 2000: 167), which can make it seem authority-driven. Exception has been taken to what can be seen as a particularly male, task-oriented emphasis on the pursuit of goals at the expense of a more female understanding of the process of change (Fetherston 2002; Russell 1996, 1999a, 1999b). More recently, from a post-modern perspective, Speedy (2001) has criticised Egan and Cowan's people-in-systems approach as overly Westernised and individualistic in its rather rigid view of 'unique individuals at the centre of their systems' (2001: 33).

I would agree that a drawback of Egan's emphasis on individual, goal-driven accomplishments is that it reflects a tendency to privilege a consistent and unified self above a relational view of the self. My own counselling practice is mainly with adult survivors of child sexual abuse, a number of whom have dissociative identity disorder. Perhaps because of this direct experience of working with individuals with multiple self states, I tend to take the more post-modern view, as advocated by narrative and relational therapists, that a boundaried, unitary view of the self can be limiting and is more of a social and historical construction than an enduring reality.

I believe it is a truer reflection of most people's subjective experience to view the self as multiple or distributed, and as consisting of organised collections of subjective experiences that are in a process of constant flux and change. Safran and Muran (2000: 67) have observed that 'different self-states emerge in different relational contexts' and the process of therapy is frequently concerned with making use of these emergences as the therapist attempts to attune themselves with sensitivity to the different selves that clients bring to sessions.

We might imagine this self-shifting as being on a continuum. At one end exist the most extreme forms of splitting such as those that are apparent in clients with dissociative identity disorder, where there may be a number of apparently discrete and separate identities with no co-consciousness. At the further end of the continuum are the almost imperceptible nuances of shifting selves presented by all clients and which therapists learn to pick up in intuitive ways. Most counsellors will have had the experience of engaging at the start of a session with a smiling, brave-faced client whose laughter, it later becomes apparent, masks a more desperate or despairing self.

It may only be as the counsellor learns to pick up on and amplify subtle clues that these different selves are coaxed into making an appearance. For instance, the therapist may comment on changes in the client's body: 'I notice your smile looking slightly strained' or voice tone: 'All the time that you are telling me that you can cope and will get through this, I think I can hear a slight tremor in your voice'. Some clients talk explicitly about allowing a self that others do not see to emerge during their hour of therapy – like my client who dried her eyes at the end of her session and said, 'By the time I get down the stairs and out of the door I won't even *feel* sad any longer. It's just like I throw a switch and turn the feelings off instantly I leave here so that no one else will ever see this pathetic side of me'.

One of my intentions in writing this book is to de-emphasise the masculine timbre of Egan's work and to provide a more female counter-balance. I hope that this is particularly apparent in the case examples given – both those that show a female counsellor using the model and those that illustrate the use of the model with female clients.

Despite its undeniably goal-oriented approach, the skilled helper model is firmly grounded in a philosophy of helping that is critical of the focus on the individual that is predominant in North American psychology.

Sociocultural systems, which have such a profound effect on the development of individuals, have, with few exceptions, been neglected in favor of a focus on individual behavior. A theoretical view giving primacy to the individual's thoughts, feelings values, and behaviors while disregarding the socio-cultural settings in which these emerge has led to highly individual-centered approaches to helping.

(Egan 1984a: 24)

Egan's people-in-systems approach makes what I consider to be a valid distinction between 'troubles' (personal difficulties located in the individual) and 'issues' resulting from problematic social and economic conditions. In this sense, troubles such as depression and low self-esteem are frequently considered to be derived from issues and stressors located in the socio-cultural environment.

In Chapter 1 I argued that a view of the helping process as firmly located in the systems and settings of a person's life is fundamental to a proper understanding of Egan's work and that he has gone to some lengths to outline his criticisms of approaches to therapy that are primarily individual-centred. Effective helpers, he suggests, 'are more effective if they can put clients and their problems in living in as wide a perspective as possible' (Egan 1984a: 33). In another publication he asserts that 'the idealization of independent individual action is fictional if it ignores system/ systems interaction' (Egan and Cowan 1979: 87).

While most counsellors will not see themselves as agents of social change *per se*, Egan argues that taking this broader perspective 'does increase their ability to be empathic, to become realistic about the social constraints imposed on their clients, and to help their clients face these constraints realistically' (*ibid.*). He goes on to assert that 'it is not enough to understand the "inner workings" of clients and how they go about creating patterns of self-defeating behavior for themselves, as if they lived separate from the forces that mold people within society' (*ibid.*).

Johns (1996) finds that Egan and Cowan's (1979) people-in-systems structure still offers a valuable framework to promote personal development in trainees in relation to the social context of helping. On a personal level, she suggests that trainees can use this framework 'to get a clear picture of the life space which accompanies them to the course, their valuing of it, what they might choose to change, and what, if anything, is sacrosanct'

(Johns 1996: 46). On a professional level, Johns argues that the framework is useful in helping trainees to explore 'the interaction of values, attitudes, perceptions, and pressures amongst the networks of personal settings and someone's wider social and cultural context' (*ibid*.: 48).

Moving on to a consideration of the apparent emphasis on change in Egan's work, I believe this emphasis is legitimate, not only because it features so clearly in my own clinical practice, but also because it is noticeably reflected in the current professional literature. While some detractors of the model may disparage this action-oriented emphasis, a leading publisher of counselling and psychotherapy texts in Britain has recently considered it timely to commission a series of publications on therapeutic change. This series seeks to examine change as the goal of counselling within a range of different therapeutic approaches. Initial publications in the series cover the person-centred approach (McMillan 2004), the psychodynamic approach (Leiper and Maltby 2004) and the rational emotive behavioural approach (Dryden and Neenan 2004). It seems reasonable to assume that further volumes in this series will follow and that this signifies a drift towards acknowledging that demonstrable change is at the heart of the therapeutic process and embraces most, if not all, schools of counselling.

I believe that a particular strength of the skilled helper model is that it can accommodate and encourage different perspectives on client change and development. For counselling to be of value, it must result in some change for the client. To understand this simple statement in its full complexity we may need to enlarge our understanding of what we mean by change. A narrow view of change would see this in terms of behavioural accomplishments or symptom reduction. However, valued outcomes can come in many guises, some so subtle that they demand perceptiveness on the part of the therapist if they are to be coaxed into life rather than risk being extinguished through lack of attention.

It is important that we learn not to judge change merely by our own standards, which may not encompass the fine nuances of another's. For example, significant movement for a client often takes the form of extending the range of feelings that she or he has access to – and not only positive feelings. A client who has previously experienced an undifferentiated state of vague, deadened and indeterminate feelings may be making huge strides in extending his or her emotional range when he or she begins to experience confusion, anxiety, resentment, sadness or frustration. Similarly, important changes in thought processes may be experienced by clients who learn to be more reflective and questioning, rather than indiscriminately accepting of 'the way things are'. Changes such as these need to be acknowledged and validated by the therapist as significant transformations of the self. Here is an example:

> During her first year of therapy I found it impossible to coax a feeling from my client. She was bewildered by any version of the question 'How do you feel?' and would always respond with 'I don't know' or even 'I honestly *don't* know how I feel. I look and there is nothing there'. A year on in our work and my client was able to identify and convey to me a little more of a sense of her internal experience. When asked about feelings she might say 'I'm feeling tired today' or even 'I don't know what's wrong with me, I don't feel right today'. Now we are in our third year of therapy and in a recent session we had a breakthrough. I asked how she was and she replied 'tired'. After a pause she said 'Actually, I think I am more sad than tired today' and she began to cry.

These may seem like minute amounts of change over a long period of time. For my client, who had spent a lifetime doing her best to suppress any and all feelings in order to survive a devastating childhood, this was, and is, colossal change.

Structural and stylistic considerations

The model is mechanical and prescriptive

This is a criticism that is often voiced about the skilled helper model. As the model is not a 'thing' but merely a description of a process (i.e. a systematic sequence of actions directed towards an end) and some skills that serve that process, it cannot of itself have the inherent qualities of being mechanical and prescriptive. I believe that detractors of the model on these grounds are essentially talking about delivery – how the model is applied. As I consider this is largely a matter of how helpers learn to use the model, I have dealt more fully with this topic in Chapters 5 and 6 where I discuss training and supervision issues.

The model is jargon loaded and unintelligible to most clients (and many students)

Several commentators (Frankland and Sanders 1995; Inskipp 1993; Reddy 1987) who use the model have remarked that, in later revisions, it has become too cumbersome, confusing and complex for ease of understanding and application. Reddy perhaps sums up this view when he remarks on preferring the simplicity of the early editions to the later 'turbo-charged' versions of the text. I believe there is some truth in this perspective and one of the incentives for writing this book is my wish to present a clear and uncluttered account of the skilled helper model and its applications to counselling in language that can appeal more directly to a UK audience, particularly trainees and their tutors.

As far as the needs of clients go, like any theory or model of counselling, the skilled helper requires 'translation' if it is to be offered in a client-responsive manner. There is often a necessary and legitimate difference between how something is taught and how it is applied in practice. The clarity, specificity and precision of language needed to convey original counselling concepts in unambiguous and well-defined terms are not always necessary or even desirable when it comes to translating those concepts into therapeutic strategies to use with clients. Egan's books on the skilled helper model are written primarily as training texts for helpers and, as such, have the textbook style, structure and North American vocabulary that characteristically belong to the micro-counselling school of training (Connor 1994; Ivey and Authier 1971). The present text, as indicated in the introduction, is designed to take Egan's work beyond a training handbook and, using a more discursive style, into the broader field of clinical application.

'The book' is not an easy read and does not flow

This criticism is more one of style than substance. Literary perspectives on the skilled helper model are limited by dint of there being only one core text. The model has not been elaborated by other writers and for readers who do not take to Egan's style of writing their aversion may transfer to the model itself. I too find the style of Egan's writing somewhat packed and dense, with little 'breathing space'. What little padding out there is tends to be provided by the numerous client examples, many of which have a peculiarly American feel, which means they do not always appeal to a British audience. I find Egan's work is most palatable when read in small doses that allow time between for digestion and for my own reflective 'unpacking'.

If this can be considered a weakness, there is also perhaps a strength in this style of writing. As *The Skilled Helper* is more like a textbook or manual than a narrative discourse, it can still remain useful after the first reading as a browser to brush up on and consolidate key techniques and strategies. What the text lacks in discursiveness, it gains in accessibility and structure. It is relatively easy to find one's way around the text (aided by an unusually specific and detailed table of contents) and hone in on the skill, technique or part of the process that one is seeking.

The therapeutic relationship

The model pays insufficient attention to reparative elements of the therapeutic relationship

On the one hand, Egan does not hold with the view that the therapeutic relationship is normally sufficient to provide a reparative or change-inducing experience for the client. Indeed, he has even suggested (York St John counselling summer school 1992) that seeing the relationship as the be-all and end-all of counselling can *de*-humanise the process wherever arrogance leads the helper to believe the process is more about 'us' or 'me' than about problem management. On the other hand, Egan has been at pains to point out that the helping process cannot be separated from a meaningful therapeutic alliance. He has observed (summer school 1993) that 'the life of this model takes on reality in the *living relationship* between counsellor and client'. He also accepts that because counselling is in essence a social influence process, then change can come about through the relationship that is being built up between counsellor and client (Sugarman 1995).

I part company to a degree with Egan here as I do believe that, particularly in long-term and in-depth therapy, the relationship, in and of itself, often makes a significant difference to outcomes. Research evidence accumulated over the last fifty years or so confirms that the quality of the therapeutic relationship is an important determinant of therapeutic change and indeed may be the strongest, most robust predictor of successful outcomes (Agnew-Davis 1999). Studies have indicated that the therapeutic alliance may well account for about 33 per cent of change (Lambert 1992; Lambert and Barley 2002; Miller *et al.* 1997), whereas therapeutic techniques may account for only 15 per cent. (The sobering finding for therapists is that the same sources indicate that the remaining 52 per cent of change factors are accounted for more by placebo effects and concurrent changes in the client's world than by any strategies that the therapist intentionally contributes.)

In the light of this evidence, I would want to give more emphasis than Egan does to the therapeutic relationship as an active ingredient of change and to highlight that working with the relationship is often central to the client's progress. I have conveyed my own views on this subject from a variety of angles in another publication on the therapist's use of self (Wosket 1999).

This stance is supported by a number of research studies. Tryon and Kane's (1993) study of the relationship between the working alliance and client termination found, for instance, that by as early as the third session a counsellor's perception of the quality of the working alliance could be sufficiently clear to predict whether the client was likely to discontinue therapy (unilateral termination) or proceed to the agreed finish (mutual termination). This study of ninety-one counsellor and client dyads found that counsellors rated the working alliance as significantly stronger with clients who later terminated mutually than with those who terminated unilaterally.

In their study of fifteen counselling dyads, Kivlighan and Schmitz (1992) found evidence to suggest that attention given to the relationship through challenge and immediacy by the counsellor served to strengthen the working alliance and improve weak alliances. Another study by Kivlighan and Arthur (2000) appears to confirm that counsellor and client agreement about significant session events is an important mediator of change and is related to the strength of the working alliance which, in turn, is enhanced through immediacy.

Taking a more relational approach than Egan would perhaps adopt, I understand therapy as a dialogue of mutual influence

(Aron 1996; Palombo 1987) in which the therapist is as likely as the client to go through change in what is essentially a bi-directional encounter. This approach emphasises a 'two-person psychology' (Friedman 1992; Hycner 1991; Safran and Muran 2000: 30) in which counsellor and client are equally contributing to the character and quality of the interaction, rather than a 'one-person psychology' where the therapist adopts a neutral, observing stance.

In this approach, counsellors are consistently attending to their own contribution to the relationship and using their own responses to the client to inform their interventions (Wosket 1999). As such, therapy is viewed as a process of 'intersubjective negotiation' (Safran and Muran 2000: 34) in which the therapist's skills of immediacy become paramount in dealing with interpersonal issues as they arise between therapist and client and, importantly, throw light on the client's relationships with self and others. The following example illustrates this point.

During the relationship-building stage of counselling I had taken pains to confine my responses mainly to those of a supportive nature with my client, who was ambivalent about counselling and seemed in danger of being easily scared away. With good reason, given her traumatic childhood, she trusted few people and one way that she protected herself from fears of rejection and abandonment was by denying that anyone could really care for her (me included).

As our relationship developed and began to feel more robust, I allowed myself to acknowledge and begin to express the mismatch I was experiencing between my feelings towards her and her determination not to believe that I might care. The therapy had reached a point where this dissonance was stalling progress and, I felt, was preventing us from working at more relational depth.

In the session where I first touched on these feelings I said to her, 'I feel hurt and a bit angry that yet again you are discounting that I might care about you.' The client seemed quite taken aback by this and did not make a direct response in that session. In the next session I referred to what had happened in the previous session and asked her what she felt about it. She replied, 'What you said made a bit of an impact on me and I've thought about it quite a lot. I was quite shocked, especially when you said you were angry with me, as I didn't think counsellors were supposed to say things like that. But it went in and made me think that I *do* discount that people care about me. I want someone to love and care for me uniquely and unconditionally and I tend to deflect any feelings that someone *does* care, because it doesn't feel enough.'

We were able to move on from this interchange into a more challenging phase where, for instance, I could ask her: 'Who else might really care if you let yourself believe that they do?' and she was then willing to name several people in her life who might fit this bill, if she only allowed them to.

This is an example of the kind of therapist confrontation that Pinsof (1995: 64) refers to as 'therapist-induced alliance crises'. Pinsof argues that planned confrontation of this kind can provoke an 'alliance tear and repair episode' (*ibid*.) that is justifiable if it appears that the therapy cannot otherwise usefully progress. These kinds of alliance rupture can serve a useful purpose if successfully resolved as they may serve to powerfully disconfirm some of the client's dysfunctional views about self and others and permit closer collaboration on the tasks and goals of therapy (Safran *et al.* 1990).

The model places a disproportionate emphasis on change at the expense of relationship elements

Close consideration of Egan's work reveals that a great deal of attention is paid to one particular aspect of the therapeutic alliance. This is the working, as opposed to the reparative, relationship. Egan highlights the importance of the working relationship through emphasising a partnership model of helping. 'In the working alliance, helpers and clients are collaborators. Helping is not something that helpers do to clients, rather it is a process that helpers and clients work through together' (Egan 2002a: 43).

Although not viewed as a vehicle for healing, the relationship is seen 'as a forum for relearning' (*ibid.*) and in this sense it has transformative potential. 'Even though helpers don't cure their clients, the relationship itself can be therapeutic. In the working alliance, the relationship itself is often a forum or vehicle for social-emotional learning' (*ibid.*). Re-learning happens through corrective emotional and behavioural experiencing as a result of counsellor modelling and interaction. Through the experience of a supportive and challenging relationship with their therapist clients may learn to view themselves in new and different ways or risk trying out new behaviours in the safety of that relationship. For clients with a history of impoverished prior relationships, a collaborative working alliance with their counsellor that is experienced as a 'just society' (Egan 2002a: 249) may be of enormous therapeutic benefit to the client.

The kind of relationship that Egan advocates as appropriate to the skilled helper model is 'the kind that will contribute best to clients' taking responsibility for themselves' (Egan 1984b: 136) in the service of managing their problems more effectively. This is a view of the therapeutic relationship that builds on Bordin's (1979) well-known conceptualisation of the working alliance as consisting of a balance of technical and relationship factors provided by the three interdependent components of bonds, goals and tasks.

In Bordin's view, the degree of agreement between therapist and client about the goals of counselling (agreed aims and objectives) and the tasks (what the client is required to do to bring about change and the strategies and interventions used by the counsellor) substantially affects the quality of the therapeutic alliance (the bond). Conversely, the quality of the relational bond between client and therapist significantly mediates the level of agreement about goals and tasks. In considering what helps clients to assimilate and accommodate problematic experiences in therapy, Stiles and colleagues (1990: 419) have concluded that 'a strong relationship is required to hold the client's attention on problematic material' and this is a useful way of viewing Egan's perspective on the function and value of a good working alliance.

This is not to say that Egan advocates a 'one size fits all' relationship, and he emphasises the need for helpers to be able to demonstrate 'relationship flexibility' (Egan 2002a: 44), meaning an ability to modulate the relationship differently for each client and at different points in the process. He has described versatility as the main value that drives the model and this includes the helper being versatile in terms of how malleable they can be in the relationship. His thinking here derives in part from the growing body of evidence that suggests that helper and client matching may be a significant determinant of effective outcomes. The professional literature and research in this area is expanding rapidly as this notion gains greater credence (Beutler and Consoli 1993; Callaghan *et al.* 1996; Dolan *et al.* 1993; Dryden 1989; Feltham 1999b; Hardy *et al.* 1998; Kivlighan and Arthur 2000; Lazarus 1993; McLennan 1996; Mahrer 1993; Miller *et al.* 1997; Norcross 1991; Rappaport 1991; Talley *et al.* 1990).

When considering counsellor and client matching, the fundamental question faced by the therapist is: can I be sufficiently flexible to adjust my stance in the relationship and at different points in the therapy to match what my client can best make use of? So, for example, can I move smoothly from the rapport-building stage to the challenging (and change-inducing) phase of counselling in such a way that engages rather than alienates my client?

Counsellor and client matching within the therapeutic alliance covers a broad canvas. Some of the various components of this field of mutual influence can be considered under the dimensions of personal, relational, procedural, contextual and professional as follows. Most of these elements apply equally to both counsellor and client while a few are more the domain of one than the other.

- *Personal dimensions*: gender; age; ethnicity; sexuality; shared experience (e.g. of the counselling issue, of difference, or of culture); predominant mode of interacting with the world (e.g. thinking, feeling, acting); beliefs and values; perceived attractiveness; motivation.
- *Relational dimensions*: affective bonds; cognitive understanding; interpersonal stance (e.g. warm/distant, formal/informal); enduring attachment style (e.g. secure/avoidant); self-disclosure (amount and type).
- *Procedural dimensions*: agreed goals and tasks; agreed focus and way of working; shared understanding of the change process; appropriate pacing; reluctance and resistance; shifting of balance between support/comfort and challenge/dissonance.

- *Contextual dimensions*: length, duration and frequency of therapy; counselling setting; complexity of issues (e.g. nature, severity and longevity); client's past experience of helping professionals; whether self or other referred.
- *Professional dimensions*: training and experience of counsellor; approach or model of counselling used; management of boundaries; knowledge and understanding of the counselling issue; perceived expertness.

It is important that the counsellor learns about working with what Safran and Segal (1990) term the client's typical 'interpersonal pull', which, in turn, can determine the therapist's countertransference responses. The roots of a client's enduring interpersonal style are normally to be found in his or her early attachment experience, as illuminated by the pioneering work of John Bowlby (Bowlby 1969, 1973, 1980; Cassidy and Shaver 1999).

Egan pays scant, if any, attention to attachment theory and patterns of interpersonal relating from a psychodynamic perspective. He does, however, address the dynamics of interpersonal relationships between counsellor and client that are likely to impede progress when he considers dimensions of the helping relationship such as immediacy, reluctance, resistance, inertia, avoidance, procrastination and so on. The predominant stance he takes is to view these phenomena as issues to be managed or glitches to be resolved to ensure the smooth running of the helping process. More about relationship dynamics is said in the next section, where I consider issues of transference and countertransference.

Working with the past and unconscious processes

The model pays insufficient attention to working with the past

There is an outdated view that cognitive-behavioural approaches to counselling cannot accommodate working with the past. As a model that has many cognitive-behavioural elements, the skilled helper is sometimes criticised in this way. Safran and Segal (1990) challenge this notion when they list several of the ways that working with the past within a cognitive framework can facilitate change, and these are summarised here.

1 Exploring events and experiences from the past can help clients understand how they arrived at their prevailing constructions of self, others and the world around them.
2 When clients are helped to understand this, they are more likely to consider that such views are not necessarily fixed and immutable.
3 Helping clients uncover formative historical experiences can assist them with understanding how they may have developed dysfunctional or outmoded responses (thoughts and feelings) as a way of adapting to and attempting to deal with those events and experiences.
4 When clients begin to realise that they adapted in the best way possible at the time to adverse circumstances they can start to develop greater self-acceptance and less guilt and bad feelings about what now seem to be maladaptive patterns of thinking, feeling and doing.
5 Helping clients to gain greater understanding and acceptance of current dysfunctional attitudes and beliefs can enable them to begin to unhook themselves from these and start to make changes.
6 Insight and understanding about the influence of the past on their present difficulties can help clients make sense of their own experience in a way that can begin to activate a sense of mastery, which is one of the most potent 'common factors' promoting change.
7 I would also wish to add that it can be a transformative experience for clients to be invited to consider how their current circumstances and options differ from those that existed at the time of difficult historical events. This can help clients to access internal and external resources that were, or seemed, unavailable to them in the past.

As portrayed in Egan's text, the skilled helper model encompasses work with the past only in so far as this helps the client deal with unresolved issues in the present. Thus the emphasis is on the past as current story rather than the past as history. There is certainly a bias towards the future in Egan's writing and it is possible to glimpse here echoes of his own personal experience. He was brought up in a family with a 'pragmatic approach to life' (Coles 1996: 195); his mother went out to work to support the family when his father died. In so doing, he tells us that she 'seized life as it was, not as it "should have" been' (*ibid.*) and perhaps in these words we can see the beginnings of a view of problem management as opportunity development.

In the same interview, where he also talks about his roots in the priesthood, Egan owns that 'I'm not a past-oriented person . . . I don't reminisce much over the past, I certainly don't spend time regretting what did or did not take place. I guess I'm like my mother in that regard. I prefer to talk about projects in hand and where things are going' (*ibid.*).

In my own experience, I have found that the framework of the skilled helper model can easily accommodate working with issues located in the past. In the work that I do with adult survivors of child sexual abuse there is inevitably a focus on past events and experiences. However, I do not assume that every client needs to work through or revisit the original abuse. I have certainly worked with a number of clients who preferred to concentrate on the effects of the abuse on their lives in the present and then most of the work has been in this area. Where we do revisit the past, the entry point is often stage two of the model, through goal setting. When we begin to talk about what the client wants and needs, this will sometimes be voiced in statements like:

> I want to come to terms with what happened to me in the past.
> I have this vague sense of dread and want to find out what really happened.
> I feel as if I need to tell someone what happened.
> The last thing I really want to do is to talk about it, but it keeps coming into my head and won't go away.

Where the model is useful here is in its plasticity. Counsellors can calibrate their response to the client's level of intention or reluctance and still invite clear goal setting. So, for instance, a sensitive response to the last statement above might be something like: 'You are talking about it in your head already and that's a start. What would you like to happen with what is going on in your head instead of talking out loud about it, if that is not what you want to do right now?'

The model takes insufficient account of unconscious processes, psychological defences and issues of transference and countertransference

It is evident from reading Egan's work that he has something of an aversion for predominantly insight-oriented approaches to counselling. He steers well clear of psychodynamic terminology and concepts and redefines these in the language of his change-oriented approach. Thus, within the framework of the skilled helper model the pain of insight needs to be turned into the gain of action to make a lasting and substantial difference to the client. Egan's view is that if therapists are not oriented towards a process of change, they may find themselves in the invidious position of operating from the 'unsurfaced assumption that insight will ultimately cure' (Egan 2002a: 228) and thereby privileging the theory of the helper over the problems of the client.

In this regard Egan comes close to views on insight and change held by relational therapists. According to relational therapists, insights have no power to bring about desired change in the client's life unless they are 'performative insights' as DeYoung (2003: 4) has termed them. Performative insights are those that the client translates into action and, as I have argued in various parts of this book, actions can be small shifts in thinking, feeling and doing, as well as big change steps.

In relational therapy, performative insights are closely connected to interpersonal, emotional experiences as these are played out in the relationship between counsellor and client. Relational therapists regard change as essentially determined by how therapist and client interact together to construct ideas and meanings and together reflect on these interactions in terms of the client's relational history. As I tend to take a relational slant on the skilled helper model, I am keen to emphasise these intersubjective, dialogical elements of change. Like many relational therapists, I would do this because I too believe DeYoung's (2003: 6) assertion that 'an individual can feel genuine power, agency, and well-being only in the context of healthy interpersonal connection'.

Egan's distaste for psychodynamic terms and concepts appears in large part to be linked to his concerns about the potential misuse of power inherent in helping relationships. He advises caution wherever there is the possibility of a shift in power from the client as expert to the counsellor as expert. Thus in considering non-verbal behaviour he advocates the following: 'In reading non-verbal behavior – *reading* is used here instead of *interpreting* – caution is a must. We listen to clients to understand them, not to dissect them' (Egan 2002a: 84, original emphasis).

Similarly, in discussing the use of advanced empathy, Egan is concerned to point out that this is not at all the same as interpretation because it focuses on what the client is actually saying or appears to be expressing in other ways and therefore is not an attempt to 'psych the client out' (Egan 2002a: 200). He suggests that if called to account, therapists should be able to identify the experiential and behavioural clues upon which their 'hunches' are based and that this should help to prevent them loading their clients with 'interpretations that are more deeply rooted in your favorite psychological theories than in the realities of the client's world' (*ibid.*: 205).

In particular, it seems to be the concept of dark and inaccessible recesses of the human psyche that Egan finds unpalatable, together with the language in which such concepts are discussed in the psychoanalytical literature. Thus he suggests that the use of 'language such as "mental processes outside of awareness"' is preferable to describe defences and 'keeps the unconscious from sounding like some kind of black hole inside us' (Egan 2002a: 171). In thinking about how the concept of the unconscious applies to the skilled helper model it can be helpful to consider the unconscious more as a process than as an entity.

The simple image that is often used to depict the unconscious is that of an iceberg with a definable line between what is visible above and what is hidden beneath the waves. I prefer to think of unconscious material more in terms of a spectrum of levels and phases of awareness than of fixed states. Perhaps a river, shifting between different levels of depth, with some shallow areas and some deeper pools in places is a more fitting image here. This spectrum of awareness will range from areas that the client knows to be there but actively chooses not to acknowledge or explore; to what is just outside awareness and can be coaxed to the surface fairly easily; through layers that are unknown but are in the process of emerging and are likely to appear in due course as the work unfolds; to experiences (memories, feelings, impulses) that are firmly locked away and may only become accessible after long-term in-depth work, if at all.

Despite his cautionary stance on the unconscious, Egan does acknowledge that mental processes that go on outside awareness increasingly have a place in counselling approaches with a cognitive-behavioural emphasis. This shift is evident in the seventh edition of *The Skilled Helper*, where he takes more account of irrational aspects of decision making, of psychological defences, of reluctance and resistance and, more generally throughout each chapter, of the shadow side of counselling. For instance, he considers that it is important for counsellors to understand their own needs, motives and drives to lessen the danger of misuse of power. Power may be misused where helpers allow the process or the model to become more important than the client or where they fail to live by the values they espouse, for example when they allow clients to become dependent on them.

Where Egan appears ready to call a partial truce with the literature on psychological defences is wherever he enters the field of cognitive dissonance theory (Draycott and Dabbs 1998; Festinger 1957; Strong 1968, 1991). Here he finds great usefulness in the idea that people naturally tend to employ any number of avoidant manoeuvres to protect themselves from the discomfort that dissonance brings. *The Skilled Helper* is permeated with examples of how and when this might happen in the counselling process wherever Egan addresses the shadow side of helping. Thus, in considering the notion of blind spots (the targets of challenge) from a constructivist point of view, Egan discusses the many tactics that clients may employ to preserve their own individualistic constructions of reality. These come close to the lists of defences that often appear in the psychodynamic literature, but are expressed in qualitatively different language through phrases such as 'simple unawareness', 'self-deception', 'choosing to stay in the dark' and 'knowing but not caring' (Egan 2002a: 178).

If working with transference and countertransference, at its simplest, is about how to understand and work with what the client projects onto and into the therapist, and what this then evokes in the therapist, then I do think that Egan minimally addresses these phenomena. He would certainly not use psychodynamic terms but through the language of congruence and immediacy he advocates addressing what may be going on between counsellor and client that is unacknowledged or only partially in awareness.

Where I would differ to a degree from Egan here is in my belief that sometimes an extended period of incubation and experiencing of countertransference feelings is more useful than attempts to immediately dissolve or resolve those feelings. Having said this, Egan does concede that restraint may sometimes be a preferred option to allow awareness and understanding of the therapist's responses to develop. Thus he points out that being congruent doesn't mean impulsively blurting out feelings, such as anger or frustration, towards clients. Self-control is a virtue and in such circumstances 'is not phoney because your respect for your client takes precedence over your instinctive reactions. Not dumping your annoyance or anger on your clients through nonverbal behavior is not the same as denying it. Becoming aware of it is the first step in dealing with it' (Egan 2002a: 68).

I would go further than this and wish to suggest that on occasion it is only by allowing ourselves to experience the repeated and enduring nature of such feelings that we can properly allow our clients to work through and understand the origins of these. A premature confrontation may cause immediate suppression or evaporation of what may be (in the language of change) a new skill, feeling or awareness. Clients who have never dared to be angry with anyone in their life, through being haunted by early experiences of retribution whenever they dared to display such feelings, may be working at their growing edge of expressing anger with their counsellor. Indeed, their counsellor may be the only person with whom they feel safe enough to 'practise' their anger.

If the counsellor is not willing to experience the client's anger directed towards him- or herself (unjustified though it may seem) and thereby help to coax it into life, it may easily be extinguished. Take the example of my client who, uncharacteristically, refused to leave at the end of one of her counselling sessions and then flew into an absolute fury with me when I gently insisted that it was time to finish. In the session following this the client spoke about her feelings of disbelief and embarrassment that she had acted in this way, yet was also able to recognise that this was the first time she could remember that she had ever openly shown her angry feelings to anyone else. In this kind of situation an early immediate intervention with the goal of 'clearing the air' may snuff out the client's embryonic skills of being angry – skills that may need much further careful honing in the counselling room before they are ready to be used productively in the world outside.

In the next chapter I turn my attention to the skilled helper model as it applies to the training of counsellors and those using counselling skills. In so doing, I will continue my critical appraisal of the model and attempt to consider its strengths and limitations as a framework used to educate trainees in the skills and processes of helping relationships.

Chapter 5

Using the skilled helper model in training

My aim in this chapter is to pull together some ideas for using the skilled helper model in the training of counsellors and helpers. Here I have attempted more explicitly to offer my own experience as a trainer whose approach is essentially derived from Egan's work. As such, this chapter contains rather more suggestions for exploratory training exercises and guidelines than previous chapters. It is designed to be of practical assistance to those trainers and trainees who have an interest in developing their knowledge and experience of how to apply the model as an integrative, client-responsive framework. At the heart of the chapter lies a conundrum that I hope I have managed to present as a productive paradox, rather than a baffling contradiction. This is the central paradox inherent in any counsellor training programme that aims to help trainee therapists develop the capacity to use an externally imposed model as the vehicle for constructing their own personally determined counselling approach.

The skilled helper model has been hugely influential in the training of counsellors and other helping professionals in the UK over the last three decades (Connor 1994; Hollanders 1999, 2000, 2003; Hollanders and McLeod 1999; Lindon and Lindon 2000). Inskipp (1996:4) asserts that Egan's three-stage systematic model of helping 'has had a great influence on the development of skills training, both within courses for counsellors and in courses of counselling skills for helpers generally', while Jenkins (1993: 26) refers to this influence as 'both massive and indisputable'.

The enduring influence of the model is largely due to its skills-based approach, which enables trainees to understand and apply the helping process in manageable, incremental steps, and to its applicability to a variety of client problems and settings. The model adapts particularly well to a skills-training approach because, as Dryden *et al.* (1995: 87) have pointed out, the sequential teaching of counselling skills can happen in a logical way that mirrors 'the same order as that in which the skills tend to be used with clients'.

In its simplicity and pragmatism the model appeals to those who wish to develop counselling skills to complement an existing role (e.g. managers, nurses and teachers). In its thoroughness it appeals to counselling trainees as a detailed model for the tasks, skills and process of the helping relationship and one that offers a flexible framework that, to borrow a phrase from Andrews (1991: 493), can be used to 'orchestrate disparate methods in a consistent way'. A further perceived attraction of the skilled helper model is its ability to marry humanistic elements of the reparative therapeutic relationship with notions of change inherent in its focus on problem management. Lindon and Lindon (2000: 109) have acknowledged this strength in suggesting that the skilled helper model has the advantage for trainees of presenting an accessible staged approach that clearly charts 'the possible movement in a helping relationship while staying true to the core conditions of empathy, warmth and genuineness'.

As a model used extensively in training, the skilled helper also has its hazards and drawbacks. The most notorious of these is the danger that students of counselling may view the model as an externally imposed and standardised framework, rather than a process to internalise and use in client-responsive, individually determined ways as they strive to achieve their own personal forms of integration. Clients, too, can be rigidly subjected to interventions prescribed by the model without due consideration being given to individual needs and differences. As this is such a key issue in the training of therapists, I have reserved a whole section for discussion of how to use the model in a client-responsive manner later in the chapter.

In starting to look at the skilled helper as a model used in training, I will first consider notions of competency. In particular, I will highlight the necessary balance that students need to acquire between technical competency in their use of the model and the ability to work in personally determined ways that draw on the therapeutic use of self (Baldwin and Satir 1987; Wosket 1999).

In an article about the training and evaluation of psychotherapists, Shaw and Dobson (1988) attempt to delineate what constitutes a competent therapist. Based on their review of studies in the field they conclude that the competent therapist needs the four minimum requirements of:

1   A theoretical or conceptual framework to guide inter-
    actions,
2   A memory of the patient's central issues,
3   The skilful use of intervention techniques to promote the
    desired changes in behavior or the conditions necessary
    for change, and
4   The knowledge of when to apply (and when not to apply)
    these interventions

                                    (Shaw and Dobson 1988: 667)

Additionally, they advise that the therapist should have sufficiently resolved any personal problems and conflicts that might otherwise interfere with judgements and responses towards clients.

In considering the acquisition of therapist competency, Shaw and Dobson (1988) make a useful distinction between 'trait' and 'state' perspectives that is pertinent to the discussion here. My understanding of these terms is that the trait position emphasises the consistent, underlying competency of the therapist. This position views competency as a relatively unchanging construct largely determined by training and experience. The state position, on the other hand, views competency as a variable that changes according to contextual factors such as complexity of client problems, therapist–client matching and flexibility on the part of the therapist. To a degree, the state position emphasises the therapist's ability to make moment-to-moment adjustments and innovative interventions in response to changing client needs.

The next section loosely follows this idea of trait and state. Rather than viewing these positions as essentially dichotomous, I see them as possibly offering a complementary perspective on therapist competency that applies well to the skilled helper model. I believe that skilled helpers need to display both consistency and variability (i.e. both trait and state factors). This, I hope, will become clearer as the chapter unfolds. I will explore a number of elements involved in training students in the skills and process of the skilled helper model (with an emphasis here on trait factors) as well as some of the more personal components of training and development that may govern the therapist's ability to work in innovative, individually determined and client-responsive ways. Here the emphasis will be more on the state position.

Integrative training

The skilled helper is an integrative framework that has been used extensively as the core training model for many introductory, certificate and diploma level counselling courses in the UK and worldwide. Connor (1994) has elaborated the structure, process and content of one such diploma course in detail. Before going on to consider the nature of integrative training and the place of the model within counsellor education it is pertinent first to consider some of the reasons for adopting a core model in training.

Core models in training

The requirement for counselling training courses to have a core model has been vigorously debated over a number of years (Connor 1994; Dryden *et al.* 1995; Feltham 1995, 1996, 1997a, 1997b; Horton 1996; Wheeler 1998). The British Association for Counselling and Psychotherapy requires any counselling or psychotherapy training course applying for accreditation in the UK to demonstrate the adoption of a core model that demonstrably infuses all aspects of the content, methodology and philosophy of the course. Despite continuing criticisms of this requirement, I think there are several compelling reasons why a core model should provide the backbone to any professional counsellor training.

When students are learning new theory and skills, they require a reasonable amount of certainty and consistency in order to be able to take risks and to work creatively. A core model can provide students with an integrated view of the person; an understanding of the determinants of psychological and emotional distress; a clear idea of the operation of the therapeutic process and a repertoire of helping interventions. From a secure base provided by these elements, trainees have a clearly defined pathway towards becoming skilled and reflective practitioners. A core model that instils confidence can be inspirational and as such provides 'an emotional attachment to a system' that can stimulate the 'incentive and motivation to develop it to its full potential' (Safran and Segal 1990: 14).

Having a reliable and familiar framework that is well known and integrated may serve to contain the high levels of anxiety that trainees frequently experience when embarking on work with 'real' clients. Counsellors who are learning to venture out on their own have, in their core model, a safe and trusted 'parent' to return to and look back on whenever they lose their footing and a steadying presence is needed. The 'rationale and ritual' (Frank 1989: 109) afforded by a core model can provide the underpinning (rather like the stabilisers on a child's bicycle) that gives the trainee their initial impetus, confidence and direction until clinical wisdom and experience come to provide a more innate sense of balance and direction.

Adherence to a core model can build confidence in a tangible, generic framework to which the trainee can attribute successful interventions and thereby start to build up a useful bank of precedents that can be referred to in future work. Having a reliable core model can help to maintain the trainee's sense of competence, especially in the face of the mistakes and failures that are an inevitable part of the therapist's learning journey. The disciplined study of one extended philosophy and methodology of counselling can help to avert the danger of the trainee spewing forth a random set of techniques that are driven by desperate efforts to get the client somewhere at any cost.

Owen (1993) has made the point (borne out by my own experience as a trainer) that many therapists are attracted to the profession as a result of having to address their own personal difficulties. They may therefore 'frequently come from a similar, or almost the same, family background and personality pool as their clients' (p. 10). During stressful periods, trainees, in particular, may suffer from the same doubts, anxieties and insecurities as those manifested by their clients. In these moments it may, as Owen remarks, be only 'the overlay of training and positive coping skills that makes any difference between them' (*ibid.*). A sound core theory and model of counselling can provide a lifebelt that, in turbulent times, keeps them afloat and prevents them being dragged under with (or by) the client.

Solid grounding in a core model helps trainees to learn that therapy needs to take its own course, in its own time, and that this will be at a different pace and direction for each client. 'When a therapy model is well articulated and detailed it allows the therapist to feel that he or she is making progress even without seeing symptom improvement' (Jenkins *et al.* 1982: 311). It is important that students of counselling develop the ability to tolerate impasses, resistances, reluctances and apparent backsliding for the meanings and therapeutic potential that they contain and learn to understand that these are an anticipated part of the client's process. Having confidence in their core model can help to prevent panic or uncoordinated impulsive reactions when students are faced with clients who appear to be getting worse rather than better.

A final key advantage of a core model and the theory on which it rests is that it provides the trainee with a professional identity that may well fuel the active placebo element of therapy. This placebo comprises both the therapist's interest and concern in the client and the perceived expertise invested in the counsellor by the client. These ingredients can, in turn, serve to activate the symbolic healing powers of the therapist (Frank 1989).

In summary, then, we might think of a core model as rather like the scaffolding that is put up to sustain the infrastructure of a new building until it is constructed strongly enough to hold itself up. As trainees move from being novices to seasoned practitioners, the scaffolding of the core model will be less relied on as the counsellor comes to graft sufficient aspects of his or her own particular skills, qualities and therapeutic attributes on to his or her own unique infrastructure. As Karasu (1996: 26) suggests, a counsellor's adopted theory 'offers the therapist the foundation for personal conviction as well as professional allegiance – to prevent confused therapists with marginal identities'.

The main disadvantage of developing strict allegiance to a core model is that it can become a strait-jacket for trainees that forces them into certain fixed postures and poses that can feel unnatural or constricting, or which stifle innovation and discovery. Any model of counselling is open to this danger of being used mechanically and in a limiting rather than liberating way. This particular hazard is addressed more thoroughly later in the chapter, where I look at ways to avert the danger of using the skilled helper model in an overly directive and counsellor-led fashion. A further obvious limitation of any core model is that it cannot be entirely comprehensive. As therapists gain experience they will need to develop different specialisms as they come to work with clients from diverse backgrounds, with increasingly complex issues, and in a variety of contexts.

From this discussion it becomes apparent that an essential paradox for trainers to work with is how to promote a healthy and creative scepticism about the counselling model they are promoting while encouraging trainees to have sufficient confidence and personal conviction in that same model to enable them to embark on the daunting journey of accompanying clients in emotional distress with some hope of alleviating their dis-ease.

The skilled helper model as a core model in training

The skilled helper is a particularly useful core model for counselling training because of its flexibility and adaptability. It can be used in a minimalist way as a loose framework for organising the counselling process or as a highly structured and detailed exposition of the therapeutic process with precise interventions for each of its three stages and nine steps. Thus for beginning trainees it provides safety, containment and direction together with a range of techniques and strategies sufficient to answer that nightmare question that can occur for all novices at any stage of the process: 'What do I do *now*?' As trainees advance and develop their own styles and individual strengths, the model becomes one that encourages freedom and offers room for experimentation and improvisation rather than one that imprisons and restricts.

Crucial to the whole issue of training students in the use of the skilled helper model is the notion that integration for counsellors is best viewed as an evolving process (Hollanders 1999; Horton 2000a; Sprull and Benshoff 2000). In coming to grips with this subject Hollanders (1999) has distilled a number of key issues from the literature on eclectic and integrative counselling and considered their implications for the training of integrative therapists. I have summarised and elaborated on a number of these in presenting the points that follow.

- Integration is a *process* to be engaged in rather than a position to be *arrived* at.
- The emphasis can be on the individual practitioner as the integrator, thus allowing for personalised forms of integration.
- Integrative training needs to provide a 'focal point' for students to be able to gain a sense of identity and commitment.

- Integrative training needs to provide criteria for good practice that are commensurate with its integrative model.
- Integrative counselling training needs to address client issues and needs within the context of contemporary culture.
- Integrative training takes time and cannot possibly be undertaken within a single training. Trainers need to take the long view on this. Since the process of integration is a life-long project, training should not attempt the impossible task of producing fully formed integrative practitioners. Instead, its aim should be to educate therapists to *think integratively*. This will equip them to carry the process of integration forward as they become more experienced.
- A credible integrative training course can be structured primarily on existing theoretical models or on the skills and competencies needed for different stages of the counselling process. In the latter case, different theories need to be introduced for the purposes of informed pluralism.
- Integrative training courses must present a coherent theory of personality development consistent with the core training model or framework.
- The credibility of a training course is largely dependent on the credibility of its trainers. Trainers involved in integrative counselling training need themselves to be committed to, and actively engaged in, the process of integration. One bad mistake that is sometimes made by eclectic/integrative courses is to cover a number of different models and theories by bringing in a range of tutors expert in their own espoused orientation and then to hive off the responsibility for integrating these different approaches onto the inexperienced student. This is a recipe for disaster, as such a course is likely to turn out confused, uncertain and under-confident novice counsellors who will inevitably practise in inconsistent and undisciplined ways.
- Integrative training courses need to appoint supervisors who are conversant with, and supportive of, the core integrative framework adopted by the course. They should also have the knowledge, experience and training to supervise trainees and be conversant with the underlying values, objectives and curriculum of the course.
- Integrative training needs to focus attention on research findings as a means of moving across school boundaries. Research

findings should acquaint students with, for instance, evidence of the effectiveness of integrative therapy; the common factors that appear to inform successful outcomes across all schools; and those interventions that have been shown to have particular utility for specific client groups or issues.

These key points can be used at a macro level as a kind of checklist for course designers and tutors starting to plan an integrative counselling training programme. Egan is very clear that a thorough training for professional helpers encompasses far more than learning a practical model of helping, such as the skilled helper. In Chapter 1 of the seventh edition of *The Skilled Helper* he emphasises this in outlining a comprehensive sample curriculum for the fully trained helper centred on the process and skills of the model.

One challenge faced by trainers that will be apparent from the discussion so far is how to help their trainees learn to achieve the optimum balance between working in a consistent, intentional and disciplined manner whilst also engaging with the client in natural, intuitive and spontaneous ways. Dryden (1989: 8) has captured the quality of this optimum balance in stating that 'intuition refers to sensitive judgements that have become internalised and appear, in highly skilled and experienced hands, effortless'. Another way of considering this challenge is to think of the need to encourage students to learn how to improvise creatively with the model in order to 'custom make' their responses to fit different clients and therapeutic situations. In this regard, Hutchins (1989: 54) has pithily observed that 'theory has to be changed to make it work' – an aphorism that applies to any truly client-responsive application of the skilled helper model.

The skilled helper model as a framework for personal integration

In Chapter 1 I took a brief look at developments in integrative and eclectic counselling and attempted to locate the skilled helper model within this field. This section considers how the model may lend itself to being used as the organising framework for a more individually determined way of working.

A number of writers have proposed that the most effective therapists may well be those who take on the challenge of developing a personally integrated and authentic style of counselling (e.g. Fear and Woolfe 1996, 2000; Horton 2000a; Lapworth *et al.* 2001; Skovholt and Rønnestad 1992; Wosket 1999). This approach to integration views the individual practitioner, more than an externally imposed model, as the integrator. This view is validated by research findings that attest to the prevalence of personal over theoretical forms of integration (Hollanders and McLeod 1999; Skovholt and Rønnestad 1992). The approach I have taken throughout this book is to show how the skilled helper model, as a pragmatic and adaptable framework, can provide a useful container within which this process can unfold. It is worth re-stating here what Egan says on the cover of the sixth edition of *The Skilled Helper* about the capacity of the model to help 'develop a solid foundation for forming your own counselling orientation'. The skilled helper framework can provide the fertile soil from which the seeds of the counsellor's own more personalised approach can sprout and flourish.

While evolving counsellors will continue to need an organising framework for their unfolding style well beyond their initial training, the components of their personally integrated approach will eventually encompass far more than that initial training covered. Thus the completion of initial training is more a point of departure than a point of arrival. The therapist's organising framework will need to be sufficiently elastic to encompass many additional elements as their experience grows. The following list (adapted from Page and Wosket 2001) attempts to summarise some of the main elements of a rounded and personalised therapeutic style.

Key elements of a personally integrated therapeutic approach:

1   My image and concept of the person (person view).
2   My image and concept of the world and its phenomena (world view).
3   My personality and way of being in the world and in relationships.
4   My personal values, beliefs and biases.
5   My own personal and cultural history – together with an appreciation of how it may differ from that of others.
6   My understanding of what constitutes psychological disturbance and health.
7   My understanding of the origin and perpetuation of psychological distress.

8   My understanding of the principles of therapeutic change.
9   My understanding of the goals of counselling or therapy.
10 My repertoire of counselling strategies and interventions – and an ability to adjust these to take account of different client populations and counselling contexts.
11 My experience and understanding of my own upbringing and developmental process.
12 My awareness and understanding of my own functional/dysfunctional attributes and how they impact on my work as a therapist.

It is likely that our understanding of many of these elements will be implicit, rather than explicit, and infrequently articulated in the somewhat formal and academic way they are given here. The developing counsellor will be continually reshaping and refining these elements in what is a fluid and dynamic process, rather than having them permanently set in stone. So, for instance, whenever a client asks me how counselling might be able to help them, I am likely to respond in a way that articulates something of my understanding of the principles of therapeutic change (point 8) and my understanding of the goals of counselling (point 9). However, I am also likely to respond in a slightly different manner to each person when asked this question, so that I take account of each unique therapeutic situation and my own changing sense of my professional self.

What knits these various threads together and provides underlying consistency in the way the therapist practises is some form of overarching framework, whether it be an integrative, eclectic or single orientation model. In this respect, and for the purposes of our discussion, the skilled helper (whether tightly or very loosely applied) can be seen to provide the 'glue' that holds together and unites the various individual strands of the therapist's personal approach.

Many of the elements of an integrated counselling approach listed above contain a personal development component. Attending to the personal development of the helper is generally accepted as a crucial aspect of any counsellor training course. Aponte (1982) picks up on this issue of self-development in making the point that 'the ability of the therapist to implement what he [sic] knows does not come automatically with the acquisition of skill'. In order to be able to apply those learned skills, Aponte recommends that 'the training of the *person* of the therapist is necessary, and that such training primarily address assisting the therapist to know himself *in the therapeutic context* and to learn to use his personal attitudes, characteristics and experiences in his work with patients' (1982: 20, original emphases).

Over my years of teaching the skilled helper model I have pieced together a number of training exercises designed to assist students in developing personally authentic styles of counselling that take as much account of who they are as individuals, as of learned theory and skills. Several of these are signposted below and the exercises themselves are given at the end of the chapter. To make better sense of the commentary that comes next, you may wish to turn to the end of the chapter and glance at the exercises before reading the following section.

A personal style of counselling

Exercise 5.1 begins to help students differentiate themselves from one another as counsellors or helpers. It encourages them to start to see that they may have individual styles and ways of working which clients will be able to recognise and appreciate. The exercise can be run with an established group of students (in which case it works well to invite them to say their sentence to the rest of the group, rather than in pairs) or as an introductory exercise for a new group of participants on a training workshop. The exercise can feel exposing and revealing. The first time that I used it was with a group of counselling students in their final year of training, all of whom knew each other very well. Three things struck me as interesting at the time:

1   How each person said something that was very different from everyone else. Although they were all learning the same core theoretical model (the skilled helper), when they spoke more personally about themselves as counsellors everyone said something that differentiated themselves clearly from the others.

2   That most of the group reported something that their clients had said about them, for instance, 'My clients tell me I'm gentle and tentative'. This is a useful reminder that learning about how to work in personally determined ways is first and

foremost about learning from clients – a finding confirmed by research (Skovholt and Rønnstad 1992).

3   Just how nervous many of the students in the group were as they took part in the exercise. Several admitted to finding the exercise very exposing and to feeling anxious. Some reported having experienced physical sensations such as a racing heart and butterflies in the stomach. This was a group who had been together for two years and yet it seemed almost as if they felt it 'wasn't allowed' to have individual differences in style or approach or to identify and acknowledge something person-ally unique about themselves as therapists.

The evolution of the professional self

Skovholt and Rønnstad's respected five-year research study of therapist development, referenced in point 2 above, purported to uncover an 'unlearning' process of 'professional individuation' that occurs for therapists post-training. This unlearning process is central to the discussion here. A natural and spontaneous use of any counselling model will involve both an initial period of coming to grips with the model and a subsequent phase of releasing the self from its grip sufficiently to allow for other learning experiences to shape a more individual way of working.

Skovholt and Rønnstad identified several key stages in this 'evo-lution of the professional self', which are summarised in Figure 5.1. The first phase of development sees the counsellor moving through a learning process consistent with the adoption of a professional persona. Moving on from their initial training, novice counsellors are likely to adopt a style of working that attempts to emulate respected exponents of their espoused approach – whether these are key founders of schools of therapy, influential writers in the field or admired trainers and supervisors. This will overlap with a phase of application wherein the developing counsellor works to consolidate learning and experiences into a consistent and disciplined approach that is likely to remain closely allied to their core training model for some years.

The second stage of authentic professional development consists of the 'unlearning' phase. In this phase, the evolving practitioner engages in further exploration and integration of new and different learning experiences that begin to fashion his or her own person-alised style of working as the original training model begins to

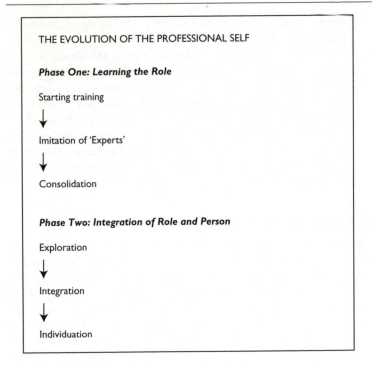

THE EVOLUTION OF THE PROFESSIONAL SELF

Phase One: Learning the Role

Starting training

↓

Imitation of 'Experts'

↓

Consolidation

Phase Two: Integration of Role and Person

Exploration

↓

Integration

↓

Individuation

Figure 5.1 The evolution of the professional self, adapted from Skovholt and Rønnstad (1992)

lessen its hold. This process, which is ongoing and career long, essentially consists of a challenge for therapists to 'individually decide which elements of the professionally imposed rigidity to shed and which elements of the internal self to express' (Skovholt and Rønnstad 1992: 103). The more successful this process is, the more likely it is that the true self of the therapist returns to something approaching pre-training authenticity in which there is a more seamless blend between the personal and the professional selves.

Exercise 5.2, which touches on aspects of this evolution of the professional self, is designed to help students develop an open attitude to feedback from clients. It can assist them in developing their mutuality with clients by exploring how clients can impact on the counsellor. The exercise can help students to begin to recognise the learning potential and therapeutic value of misunderstandings, mistakes, disagreements and conflict in the therapeutic relationship. It can help to instil the notion that these can be welcomed as potentially transformative experiences for both counsellor and client, rather than merely being seen as the client's material to be worked on. Engaging with the questions posed in the exercise can encourage students to recognise that their personal and professional selves can exist together in close proximity and lessen the tendency to split one from the other.

Dyadic feedback

Exercise 5.3 is a simple but powerful exercise that helps students to understand how they experience others in relationship, how others might experience them and how these perceptions are likely to change over time. The exercise can enable students to experience in a real way the psychodynamic concepts of transference, countertransference and projection, from both the giving and receiving end. The prompts provide a constructive way for students to give one another feedback as if they were in the client's role and can help the trainee counsellors to hear and understand how they might be perceived by clients. The exercise can assist trainees to see their interpersonal strengths and areas for development as reflected in feedback from their peers and can therefore provide an impetus for personal change and development.

It is most helpful to run this exercise with a group that has been together long enough for their first impressions of one another to be tempered by ongoing contact. I have frequently used the exercise in the second year of a two-year counselling diploma course as part of a weekend residential. In this setting it can work well as a warm-up exercise that introduces themes such as the therapist's use of self or working with the therapeutic relationship.

Personal and professional profiles

Exercise 5.4 (adapted from Aponte 1982) is designed to help students begin to sift through those aspects of self that they might use or not use as counsellors or helpers as they move towards achieving the closer proximity of personal and professional selves about which Skovholt and Rønnstad write. It helps them to understand that the use of self is as much about withholding aspects of self as it is about displaying their personal characteristics in their encounters with clients.

Typically, when students engage in this exercise they realise that their two lists might well contain overlaps and that certain personal attributes may appear as both assets and liabilities, depending on the context of the client work. The exercise can also help them to question why they tend to hold parts of themselves back when in the counselling 'role' and whether this is always necessary. In this sense the exercise can become one that enhances the growth of congruence in trainees.

The exercises above are included in this chapter to highlight the importance of instilling in trainees the notion that effective therapeutic relationships start with the use of self within a supportive and challenging working alliance, and *not* with the formulaic application of a model or theory. In sections that follow I will present a number of training exercises and guidelines that are more geared towards enabling students to learn and apply the steps and stages of the skilled helper model. In so doing, I will take a microview of training that confines itself to the skills and process of the model, whilst acknowledging that this clearly presents a very partial and incomplete account of what would be involved in a comprehensive and integrated programme for the training and development of the fully rounded therapeutic practitioner.

Training skilled helpers

For each edition of *The Skilled Helper*, Egan has produced a companion training manual full of interactive exercises designed to help the learner of the model develop both the skills of counselling and the skills of reflective practice. In the seventh edition of the book Egan is again at pains to assert that he is not advocating a technique-driven approach to helping: 'The skills are not just bits of helping technology but rather creative and humane ways of helpers being with clients in their efforts to better their lives' (Egan 2002b: 1).

The popularity of the skilled helper model with trainers may well have been enhanced by Egan's development of a coherent training process to accompany the model that sets out a clear sequence of steps from understanding to application (paralleling the sequential unfolding of the counselling process). The elements of this sequence are:

1 Cognitive understanding (input).
2 Clarification (questions and discussion).
3 Modelling (live by tutors or viewed on video-tape).
4 Written exercises (from the manual or other sources).
5 Practice (skills practice in small groups).
6 Feedback (self, peer and tutor evaluation).
7 Evaluating the learning experience (debriefing and reflecting on the process).
8 Supervised client work (applying the model in the work setting).

Members of the training team of the York St John annual counselling summer schools, which ran for over a decade starting in the mid-1980s, embellished and developed a number of the elements of this training process into useful guidelines and teaching materials for trainers of counsellors and helpers (Connor *et al.* 1989).

It is beyond the scope of this general chapter to reproduce much of this useful material here. What I have provided at the end of this chapter are some guidelines for students and tutors relating particularly to item 5 above, which is skills practice in small groups. I have selected this one aspect of the training process for closer scrutiny because the intensive, ongoing experience of skills practice, feedback and debriefing within the roles of counsellor, client and observer is both central and crucial to effective experiential learning of the skilled helper model. Indeed, Connor (1994: 149) has argued that 'skills practice in small groups is at the heart of training in both microcounselling and problem management approaches'. Supervised skills practice with peer and tutor feedback is substantially enhanced by the use of audio and video recording as this adds the additional element of self-feedback where trainees can review tapes of their work either on their own, in the peer training group, or with a tutor.

I hope that these guidelines may be of use to trainers and students alike. On the training courses I am involved with, skills practice is made as realistic as possible by the requirement that when students are in the client role they bring real issues and do not engage in role play. The following section provides commentary on the guidelines, which are reproduced in full at the end of the chapter. These cover role responsibilities in training groups, how to give constructive peer feedback and suggestions for issues which trainees might bring to training groups when in the role of the client. It will probably make more sense to refer to the material at the end of this chapter before reading the following section.

Training in triads: role responsibilities

It is important that trainees have clear and specific guidelines about the purpose and function of skills training groups and what is expected of them within each role they occupy. An optimum number for skills groups is three, to give trainees the chance to move regularly between the roles of counsellor, client and observer.

In addition to giving students the written guidelines reproduced at the end of the chapter (Guidelines 5.1), I explain the function and purpose of skills training groups in discussion with them and emphasise the following key points:

- The main purpose of skills groups is training not treatment.
- The emphasis is on skills practice and not on problem solving.
- Because of this, the emphasis is on the process of counselling, rather than the content of the client's 'story'.
- The key learning role in the group is that of counsellor and the roles undertaken by others are for the purpose of facilitating the counsellor's learning.
- Competence in the expression of therapeutic warmth and understanding is key to the effective use of skills.
- When in the counselling role, trainees are encouraged to take responsibility for their own learning by being explicit about what they would like to practise and have feedback on.
- Because this is training, both counsellor and client should expect that the process may be interrupted by the trainer intervening on occasion to offer feedback, modelling, support and challenge.
- When this happens, the student can expect the trainer to intervene in a sensitive manner with constructive feedback and open questions in a way that encourages the trainee to continue productively with his or her skills practice.
- When in the role of client, trainees are asked to talk about genuine issues that: are current rather than resolved; they are prepared to be open about; that have an emotional component but are not too overwhelming.

Giving and receiving constructive feedback and
suggestions for client issues to bring to training
groups

These guidelines (Guidelines 5.2 and 5.3) extrapolate from the
general points outlined above in relation to the two key aspects of:
(1) giving and receiving feedback; and (2) choosing issues to work
on when in the client role in training groups. Giving students
written guidelines such as these can help to demystify the training
process and provide useful prompts to keep their learning focused
and intentional. In the next section of this chapter I will consider a
number of issues related to helping trainees apply the skilled helper
model to work with clients. This dovetails with point 8 of the
training process (supervised client work) outlined in the previous
section.

Client-responsive use of the skilled helper model

Here I will come back to a frequently voiced criticism of the
skilled helper model that has been touched on already in this and
previous chapters. This is the notion that the model is mechanical
and prescriptive. As this issue is fundamental to the way that
trainees learn to apply and adapt the model, I have chosen to
examine it here as an aspect of training.

It is certainly true that the skilled helper model (like any other
approach) can be imposed on the client in a heavy-handed and
mechanical fashion. A tendency to employ the model in a cumbersome manner naturally and understandably occurs in trainees as
they start to get to grips with remembering and applying the stages
and tasks. Beyond training, mechanistic use of the model tends to
occur when it is utilised by practitioners who have a crude and
simplistic grasp of the steps and stages and who apply these in a
rigidly linear fashion (as does 'counsellor A' at the beginning of
Chapter 4). However, I would argue that this is fundamentally a
failing in the practitioner, not the model. Ineffective helpers, as
Egan states, are wont to 'drag clients through the model even
though that is not what clients need' (Egan 2002a: 39). This
merely demonstrates misuse of power and excessive control by the
counsellor that compromises the true spirit of the model.

Egan advises that 'effective models effectively used are liberating rather than controlling' (*ibid.*). Building on this argument, he is careful to emphasise that formulaic responses to clients are unhelpful and not to be encouraged in trainees: 'you must discard formulas and use your own language – words that are yours rather than words from a textbook' (*ibid*: 102). The skilled helper model continues to appeal as an initial training model because it combines the strengths of being theoretically consistent, containing and pragmatic with the advantages of being open to exploratory and creative ways of working that are individually determined by the practitioner.

A measure of the model's adaptability is that it can be applied in a relational way (DeYoung 2003) where the counsellor's priority is to tune into the client's experience and needs. Indeed, there is evidence to suggest that a significant number of counsellors move on from their original training approach to a way of practising that is more integrative or eclectic precisely in order to better meet the perceived needs of their clients (Hollanders and McLeod 1999).

At all times the model needs to be given a 'human face' (Egan 2002a: 341) in order not to stupefy and alienate clients. Essentially, this means that each counsellor needs to personalise and translate the model into his or her own natural style of working. Competent use of the model also requires that counsellors take proper account of the client's preferred style of learning and 'being helped'. I have had clients who seem gleefully to embrace the specific sequencing of actions that the model can offer and who find tangible relief in its clear, step-by-step problem-management process. Others have baulked at the notion of committing to any sequencing of the work and with such clients I have needed to be far more 'laid back' and unobtrusive in my management of the process to give them enough 'slack' (Egan 2002a: 343).

One seasoned client, a veteran of several years of unproductive therapy with a variety of counsellors, arrived for a first session with me firmly announcing that she did *not* want her counsellor to use *any* counselling jargon, techniques or creative methods of working and that included anything that smacked of goal setting and action planning. Yet I was still able to apply the model to our work in the simplest of language that consisted of gently keeping her on track with what she wanted, where she wanted to go and what would need to occur to make that happen. At the end of two years of counselling to address issues of childhood sexual abuse she said that the two things she had found most helpful were, first, how real and natural she had found me to be as a counsellor and, second, how persistent I had been in keeping her 'on track' and not letting her 'off the hook'.

Often, the model needs to recede into the background in order for the counsellor and client to work with what is 'experientially alive' (Safran and Segal 1990: 126) between them. It is crucial that students learn from the outset of training that this should always take precedence over applying the problem-management process.

In essence, the model is principally useful in providing the necessary connective tissue between moments of meaningful inter-personal dialogue between counsellor and client. The model might then be brought in to give impetus and momentum when the client is 'on a roll' and ready to move towards goal setting or action planning. With the client mentioned above, the first year of therapy consisted mainly of me trying my best to stay in contact with her in a real way. Once that was established and the client felt she could trust me and rely on me not to trick (or be tricked) or abandon her, she began to act quickly on her own behalf to resolve long-standing issues and to develop new and productive relationships. The skilled helper model then provided the shape and direction in which this process could unfold.

The model can also act as an essential aid to kick-starting a process that has stalled, for instance where the client is ready to move forward but lacks the knowledge or skill to proceed. This occurred with one client who came to a place of resolution with her experience of childhood abuse after three years of therapy.

She wished to make changes in body image as a result of her increased self-esteem. Having tried many crash diets in the past that always proved unsuccessful, she felt at a loss to know how to lose weight and become physically healthier. Work in the second and third stages of the model helped her to identify and implement a 'preferred picture' that was expanded to encompass life-style changes that did not involve dieting. She changed her eating habits gradually to accommodate healthier options that meant she was still able to eat things she liked without going hungry. She joined a gym and a ramblers association to gain regular, gentle exercise. She began to go for massages and other alternative physical therapy treatments that helped her to feel more aware of, and kinder towards her body. She lost weight gradually and steadily and felt increasingly fitter and healthier. There were no dramatic changes, but those that happened were sustainable and neither were there any dramatic lapses back to square one.

It is true that the model is overtly directive in its *process*, while at the same time it is designed to enable counsellor and client to negotiate that direction together. In skilled hands it is minimally directive of *content* and it is imperative that trainers give priority to helping trainees grasp this fundamental difference. In this sense, the model is effectively client centred – even radically client centred to use Egan's term:

> Helpers need to become radically client centred. Client-centred helping means that the needs of the client, not the models and methods of the helper, constitute the starting point and guide for helping.
>
> (Egan 2002a: 39)

Because Egan's particular use of the term 'client centred' can be confusing for those more familiar with applying the concept to person-centred counselling (as pointed out by Feltham 1999b), I have preferred to adopt the term 'client responsive' throughout this book. I believe this captures the essence of what Egan means when he talks about placing the client, rather than the helper's preferred model, at the heart of the counselling process.

Hopefully, this is something that experienced counsellors routinely do, but trainees can also be encouraged to think explicitly about adopting client-responsive interventions. As Howard (1986: 72) has observed, most therapists 'recognize the importance of tailoring their ministrations to the idiosyncrasies of the client . . . in order to achieve maximal effectiveness'. This is essentially a deconstructionist view (Karasu 1996; Parker 1999; Spinelli 1994), which places the uniqueness of each client and the centrality of the relationship, rather than established theory or technique, at the heart of the counselling process. Hobson (1985: 203) states a profound truth very simply when he says 'my job is to learn how to relate to this particular person'.

The notion of adopting a client-responsive stance to helping is the *sine qua non* of post-modern and deconstructionist approaches to therapy. Duncan, Solovey and Rusk (1992), for instance, have argued that any global model or theory of counselling is insufficiently comprehensive to take account of the infinite complexities of the range of cases that a therapist will encounter. They have proposed instead an approach to psychotherapy that disavows allegiance to any macro theory in favour of a 'client-directed' orientation that takes 'the client's frame of reference as the guiding theory for intervention' (Duncan *et al.* 1992: 8).

Within this paradigm, Duncan and colleagues propose that therapists take account, first and foremost, of the 'informal theory of the client' (1992: 20) in formulating treatment procedures – informal theory being the client's own subjective notions about the causes and attributions of his or her problems, which are grounded in the client's own meaning system. They argue that therapists should regard the client's informal theory as 'hierarchically superior to the formal theory of the therapist' (1992: 21) and be prepared to select strategies and interventions that are most congruent with this. An advantage of the skilled helper model is that offering a choice of stages and tasks in which to locate the work at any given time gives it a particular facility for accommodating the client's preferred way of working. The example that follows later in this section illustrates the model's potential for taking account of the client's informal theory.

Proposals that therapists should be prepared to negotiate in a flexible way about the approach to be used with individual clients are borne out by research into clients' accounts of resistance in therapy (Rennie 1994). Findings from Rennie's study indicate that unless therapists take the initiative to invite their clients to collaborate openly with them over treatment plans, clients are likely to defer to the power of the counsellor and go along with whatever he or she suggests, even when they have reservations about this.

Resistance is then likely to occur, with clients expressing their lack of cooperation covertly, rather than overtly, often through defensive manoeuvres that undermine the therapist's intentionality and a constructive working alliance.

A view of therapy as collaboration places the client at the centre of his or her own process of change and sees him or her as having the expert knowledge of the problem and what will best alleviate it. If we care to ask them, in my experience many clients have a clear idea of what they want and don't want from therapy, particularly if they have had an unfortunate previous experience of counselling that has been of the 'you'll get what I've been trained to give you' variety.

In their extensive review of findings in this area, Miller and colleagues (1997) have argued convincingly that research consistently reveals 'the client is the single, most potent contributor to outcome in psychotherapy' and 'the chief agent of change' (1997: 25). They contend that, set against the part played by the client's contribution to outcome, the therapist's use of models, theories and techniques pales almost into insignificance. Their view on therapeutic technique is straightforwardly and simply that it 'provides clinicians with something akin to a magnifying glass that brings together, focuses, and concentrates the forces of change, narrows them to a point in place and time, and causes them to ignite into action' (1997: 184). On occasion, taking a client-responsive approach may mean that we forgo the role of expert technician in favour of allowing clients to demonstrate the expertise that they themselves have in authoring their own process of change and development.

I am therefore proposing that the counsellor should start with a preparedness to come alongside the client, affirm an understanding of the client's situation and let this dictate the course and nature of the work. Clients are more likely to shift perspective and re-attribute meanings in the course of therapy when their initial viewpoint has been confirmed and validated by their therapist rather than disregarded or even attacked. The following example from my own experience illustrates how this process may unfold.

I saw a young woman with a cancer phobia who adamantly announced in her first counselling session that she did not want to talk about her past because a previous counsellor had 'made' her do this and it hadn't helped. Instead of this, she asserted that what she wanted from me was some help with dealing with her obsessive thoughts and anxieties in the here and now. I negotiated with her to use a cognitive-behavioural approach, within the framework of the skilled helper model, to address these symptoms. In the language of the model we started in stage two by looking at what it would be like if she were able to slightly lessen the obsessive-compulsive thoughts and behaviours. We set one or two small, manageable goals to help her begin to break into the fixed pattern and identified some ways that she could practise doing this.

After a few sessions (and I admit rather to my surprise) her obsessive-compulsive symptoms appeared to subside quite rapidly. Unfortunately, the cancer phobia was then almost immediately replaced with a new phobia that proved equally troublesome to my client. At this point, and of her own volition, she began hesitantly to talk about her childhood and her experience of inadequate mothering. She easily took flight from this painful topic and I recall having to tread very cautiously as she started to explore her feelings of hurt, humiliation and rejection.

Eventually, and for herself, the client came to realise that the phobic fears were a hook to try to provoke her mother's concern and attract her undivided attention. Her worst fears were that she would die a lingering and painful death and, when I gently asked her about the 'attraction' of these fantasies, she told me that in them her mother rushed to her death bed and asked her forgiveness for having neglected her so badly. So, eventually, she allowed me to go where the previous counsellor had accurately presumed the main work resided. Perhaps the difference was that I waited for her to lead me there rather than imposing the pace and direction of the work and in the meantime demonstrated my willingness to be with her in a different place, even though this turned out not to be the place where the core work lay.

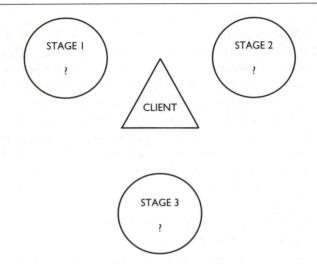

Figure 5.2 Client-responsive use of the skilled helper model

The point that I may perhaps be in danger of labouring here is that the starting place for using the model is where the client is and what the client needs. This is represented simply in Figure 5.2. If a client happens to experience his or her counselling as prescriptive, this is not because the model is fundamentally flawed in this respect, but more likely because the therapist is not offering the model in the collaborative and facilitative manner in which it is designed to be used.

When used effectively, the skilled helper is a model that flows from the inside, not one that is imposed from the outside. It is something that, as helpers, we draw out of people, not impose on them. In their 'client-directed' model of therapy, Duncan and colleagues (1992) advocate a minimalist approach to psychotherapy that provides 'just enough structure and guidance to help clinicians tolerate the uncertainty of face-to-face meetings with people in pain' (pp. 251–252). In my view, this is the best way to consider the skilled helper model – as a framework that has currency for both novice and experienced practitioners, when used with a light and tender touch.

For all the reasons discussed in this chapter, I have continued to find the skilled helper model relevant and useful as a framework and container for my own work in the years that have followed since my initial training as a counsellor. Inskipp (1993) has remarked on the enduring quality of the model (particularly stage one skills) as having 'integrity', which ensures it remains an important influence in her work as a trainer and supervisor. I share her opinion and for me the integrity of the model is most evident in its simplicity and flexibility, which makes it almost infinitely adaptable to the variety of clients and issues I work with. Because it doesn't constrict me, I feel I have grown with it, rather than out of it. In the next chapter I will move on from a focus on training to consider some ways in which the skilled helper model applies to the supervision of counsellors and helpers.

Exercise 5.1: My personal style of counselling

Describe yourself as a counsellor, or helper, to someone else in the group. Choose someone who you don't know well or haven't worked with for a while and introduce yourself by using *one* sentence only to start with. *Don't* use the name of a particular counselling approach, model or school. Instead, say something about *your own* individual helping style or attributes. This may be something that comes from feedback you have had from a client or person with whom you have been in a helping relationship and that feels as if it fits.

Tutor: it might be helpful for students to give them an example here of something a client has said that has helped them to learn something about their own style of counselling.

Take 15 minutes for this so that you have some thinking as well as talking time. After swapping your initial sentences, elaborate on them if you wish to. Be aware of what you are feeling and thinking as you do the exercise and, after introducing yourselves in pairs, debrief what the experience was like.

Tutor: in an established group, students can be invited to share their sentences with the whole group, rather than in pairs. Debrief the exercise in the whole group. Students can be encouraged to say what was interesting, useful and difficult about engaging in the exercise. Give some discussion time to explore what the exercise has raised about personal styles of counselling.

Exercise 5.2: The evolution of the professional self

Take a few moments (about five minutes) to write down on a piece of paper anything you can recall that a client or person with whom you have been in a helping relationship has said to you, or shown to you, that has told you (or might tell you) something useful about yourself as a counsellor or helper. Don't censor yourself – just allow things to surface, even if it is just one word or a vague sense of something, and write (or draw) whatever comes. You can decide later how much of this you are willing to share with others.

Before you draw a line under your list, can you add anything that has been more difficult for you to hear from your clients/helpees? These may be things that you have dismissed, rejected or 'forgotten'. Perhaps at the time you interpreted them as the client's resistance, defensiveness or transference – as their 'stuff' rather than yours.

Spend some time in a group of three sharing your responses to the following questions. Rather than having a group discussion, take turns so that each person has time to consider these questions while the rest of the group helps to facilitate their exploration. Use the last few minutes to debrief together how you found the experience of doing the exercise and working together on it:

1   What are some key things that you have learned from clients or those with whom you have worked in a helping relationship:
   a   About yourself as a person?
   b   About yourself as a counsellor or helper?
   c   About how to engage in the counselling/helping process?
2   How have any of these things helped to shape you as a counsellor/helper?
3   If you allowed yourself to hear the more difficult feedback not as critical, but as a gift and an opportunity for development, what might you learn that could help you develop further as a counsellor/helper?

Tutor: allow time for a whole-group debrief to air thoughts and feelings about the exercise and to bring together any significant learning.

Exercise 5.3: Dyadic feedback exercise

Work in pairs for 30 minutes. Decide who will be **A** and who is **B**. **A** talks first while **B** listens. **A** uses the sentence stems below to give feedback to **B** and adds whatever she or he feels fits to the end of each of these stems. After **A** has finished talking, **B** shares any immediate responses she or he has to what **A** has said and can ask for clarification if necessary. After ten minutes, swap roles so that **B** gives feedback to **A** using the same sentence stems. Again, give **A** the opportunity to respond and seek clarification.

Spend the last ten minutes debriefing and processing the exercise together. What was it like to share this feedback? What was easy and what was difficult to say or hear? What thoughts and feelings did the exercise evoke in you? What have you learned about yourself, each other and your relationship as a result?

Sentence stems:
- When I first met you I experienced you as . . .
- I experience you now as . . .
- If I was your client I would appreciate . . .
- If I was your client I might like more of . . .

Tutor: the exercise can be run as one cycle in pairs or it can form an extensive experiential exercise with a number of cycles where all members of a group have the opportunity to give feedback to one another in pairs. Allow time to debrief the exercise in the whole group. Give students the opportunity to say how they experienced the exercise and what they have learned from it. One helpful question to ask is 'How might you apply the exercise or any learning from it to your work with clients?'

Exercise 5.4: Personal and professional profiles

Take a blank piece of paper and divide it into two by making a vertical line down the middle. Now take five minutes to write a fairly quick and spontaneous profile of how you see yourself as a counsellor or helper in relation to two particular aspects of self. Take whatever comes first without censoring it and try to respond from a feelings as well as a head level. You will be able to decide later what you wish to share with others and what you would prefer to keep to yourself.

1   On the left-hand side of the page, make a list of your personal assets that you feel might be helpful for you to draw on in your counselling or helping practice.
2   On the right-hand side of the page, make a list of those personal attributes or characteristics that you suspect may interfere with your effectiveness as a counsellor or helper.

Take one hour in a group of four to debrief the exercise. Share the time equally between you, so that you each have about fifteen minutes to explore and reflect on your lists and then take a few minutes at the end to debrief as a group. When taking turns you might like to consider:

•   Aspects of myself I think I might usefully bring more fully into my personal style of working;
•   Aspects of myself I may need to be watchful of in order that they don't intrude unhelpfully into my counselling work.

Tutor: allow time for a whole group debrief to air thoughts and feelings about the exercise and to bring together any significant learning.

Guidelines 5.1: Training in triads: role responsibilities

Counsellor

•   Pay attention to building and maintaining a good therapeutic relationship.
•   Practise skills appropriate to the model and to the client.
•   Listen to feedback and seek clarification to assist your understanding.
•   Try to improve and build on the skills practised.

Questions for consideration and exploration:

•   How do I feel about the interaction?
•   What did I do well?

- What did I find difficult?
- What could I do differently to improve and develop?

Client

- Be genuine and use appropriate self-disclosure.
- Bring real issues (right level), not role-play.
- Remember your responsibility to aid skills development.
- Attend to how you are reacting and be willing to disclose this.
- Prepare to assist in feedback.

Areas for feedback:

- I felt . . .
- You helped when . . .
- I felt uncomfortable when . . .
- I would have liked less of . . .
- I would have liked more of . . .

Observer

- Manage the time.
- Attend and listen.
- Look for specific elements of skills practice based on specified learning objectives.
- Feedback to counsellor (*not* client) using feedback that is:
  - specific and accurate (take notes)
  - based on process, rather than content
  - clear
  - supportive
  - constructive
  - balanced – strengths and areas for development
  - owned as your own personal view.

Areas for feedback:

- You said . . .
- You looked . . .
- You did . . .

- I wondered if you missed . . .
- It seemed helpful to the client when you . . .

Feedback sequence

Counsellor (has first opportunity to say what he or she has learned, did well and would do differently)
↓
Client (gives clear examples of impact that counsellor's interventions made)
↓
Observer (adds to previous feedback. Does not take over, become longwinded or go back into content)

Role of trainer/tutor

- Ensures counsellor is clear about what he or she wishes to practise and have feedback on.
- Ensures skills practice starts.
- Ensures each person is participating and knows his or her role.
- Ensures timing is clear and well managed.
- May intervene to:
  - highlight strengths
  - prevent mistakes being practised
  - help with alternatives or to assist counsellor to get back on track
  - model skills and process (briefly).

Guidelines 5.2: Giving and receiving constructive feedback

Constructive feedback

- Promotes self-awareness and increases options.
- Includes critical as well as positive feedback, both given with skill and sensitivity.

Destructive feedback

- Is given in an insensitive and unskilled manner.

- Leaves the recipient feeling bad and deflated with nothing on which to build improvements.

Giving feedback

1 Be specific rather than generalise: 'You asked three closed questions in a row and only got yes or no answers each time', rather than 'You ask too many questions'.
2 Refer to observed behaviour rather than personal characteristics: 'I noticed you had your hands tightly clasped', rather than 'You seem like a very tense person'.
3 Be descriptive rather than evaluative: 'When you asked that challenging question your client sat back in the chair and looked away', rather than 'You were too challenging and your client couldn't take it'.
4 Share ideas or information rather than give advice: 'I remember finding it useful when the tutor told us it isn't very helpful to ask two questions in a row and I noticed that in one place you asked four questions one after the other', rather than 'You shouldn't ask so many questions'.
5 Offer alternatives in a tentative rather than dogmatic manner: 'I wondered if you might have used more reflective responses to help your client feel understood', rather than 'There weren't enough paraphrases and summaries'.
6 Point out the advantages (to the helper and/or the client) of doing something differently: 'If you held back on giving advice perhaps you wouldn't feel that you were being so directive and the client could take more responsibility for coming up with her own strategies'.
7 Highlight strengths and areas for development: 'Your client relaxed and smiled more as the session progressed, which showed you were able to build good rapport. Given that the relationship seemed strong, I wondered if you might have offered one or two challenges'.
8 If a contract exists, stay within the boundaries, e.g. do not go back into the content of the client's story; stick to time.
9 Think about what your feedback says about you, e.g. if you find it easy to highlight strengths and difficult to offer constructive criticism.
10 Provide the amount of feedback the receiver is able to manage. Beware of overwhelm.

Receiving feedback

- Listen with an open mind rather than immediately rejecting, justifying or arguing.
- Check that you have understood correctly and ask for clarification if you need it.
- Ask for specific feedback you may want and did not get.
- Decide what you will do as a result of the feedback.

Guidelines 5.3: Suggestions for client issues to bring to training groups

1　Something I wonder about myself.
2　Sometimes I think people see me as . . .
3　The ways in which I doubt myself.
4　A part of myself I would like to develop.
5　An undeveloped part of my life.
6　The kinds of difficulties I have in relationships.
7　What saps my confidence.
8　Something I am hoping to achieve.
9　Something I've lost or regret.
10　Something I'm putting off doing or saying.
11　How I'd like to see myself in a year's time.
12　How I feel about getting older.
13　Something I find stressful.
14　My expectations of myself.
15　How this course is changing me.
16　The impact this course is having on my friends or family.
17　What I get impatient about.
18　How I let others take advantage of me.
19　A relationship I'd like to improve.
20　Some unfinished business I have.
21　Something I'm starting to wonder about myself.
22　Something I might take to my personal development group.
23　A person I'd like to spend more time with.
24　Ways I put myself down.
25　How others see me.
26　An important value or belief I hold.
27　A change I'd like to make to my lifestyle.
28　Something I've always wanted and never had.
29　Ways in which I try to get my needs met indirectly.

30 What it's like for me when I feel misunderstood.
31 How I deal with criticism.
32 How I feel about myself as a counsellor/helper.
33 What it's like for me in the group.
34 How I feel about myself physically.
35 Something I wish I had the courage to say or do.

Chapter 6

Research, supervision and the skilled helper model

This chapter considers the skilled helper model as it applies to aspects of research and supervision. I will engage with the critical debate about the perceived lack of research activity relating to the model before exploring how the skilled helper framework can be adapted to the supervision of counsellors and those using counselling skills. In the section on supervision, as in the previous chapter on training, the emphasis is on practical application and I have again included a number of training exercises developed, in this case, from my experience of training supervisors.

Thus far in the book the emphasis has been on looking at how the skilled helper model can act as an integrating framework to hold together different ways of working as a counsellor or helper. To a degree, I have broken this mould in the second part of the chapter and taken a rather different slant on integration and the model. In this section, an integrative model of supervision – the cyclical model – is presented. This is derived in part from the skilled helper model of counselling. I have attempted to show how elements of the skilled helper model can be incorporated into this integrative framework and used to develop the skills and process of supervising counsellors and other helping professionals.

In turning first to research matters, I come back to the frequently expressed criticism that was alluded to in Chapter 4, namely that the skilled helper model is a one-person approach that lacks empirical validity and a solid research base attesting to its efficacy.

Certainly, the skilled helper model has suffered from being seen as a single-authored approach. This is evident in the number of references to 'Egan's' or 'the Egan' model that occur in both the literature and anecdotal accounts. Yet Egan himself has written 'beware the person of one book' (Egan 2002a: 15) and has taken care to convey that *The Skilled Helper* 'is not, and cannot be "all you need to know about helping"' (*ibid.*). He has stated that the model is a generic one that he has developed and refined – not invented (Coles 1996; Sugarman 1995). In line with this, he emphasises that the 'logic' of the problem-solving process is universal and 'embedded in human consciousness' (Egan 2002a: 36) and argues that this is the main reason why it is so readily adaptable to different cultural contexts. Elsewhere, he has referred to it as a 'folk' model in that versions of it can be found in 'early philosophical writings and in the very bones of people' (Egan 1984b: 135). He further asserts that the model has an advantage in belonging to no school of helping and therefore avoids the limitations that often go with school-specific approaches, notably 'overconcern with the writings and helping style of the founder of the school and a reluctance to assimilate other useful approaches into the theory and methodologies of the school' (*ibid.*).

In the light of these comments, there is a certain irony in the fact that Egan has come to be inseparably identified with the problem-management process outlined in his *Skilled Helper* books. He has explicitly stated that he does 'not want to be seen as a guru' (personal communication) and has commented about the model that 'I don't see it as an ego trip: it is not "The Egan Model". I simply have my version of it' (Sugarman 1995: 276). He sums up his attitude to helping in very 'un-guru' like words that emphasise the anti-elitist nature of his approach: 'I try to draw up commonsense frameworks that can help people understand and do more effectively the kinds of things they say they want to do in the first place' (Coles 1996: 196).

Rather than considering the skilled helper model to be his own closed property, Egan has written about it as offering a system that is 'open to being corroborated, complemented and challenged by any other approach, model or school of helping' (Egan 2002a: 38). He places the client at the heart of the model in asserting that 'the needs of clients, not the egos of model builders, must remain central to the helping process' (*ibid.*). A strength of the model and one to which I feel drawn as a humanistic practitioner is its non-exploitive and empowering philosophy.

If we turn now to criticisms about the model's lack of a solid research base, we find that Egan has expressed some enlightening views that help us to understand why this research is lacking. In a published interview (Sugarman 1995), Egan has discussed his perspective on research and the skilled helper model. While not seeing himself as a primary researcher, Egan describes himself as a 'translator' of 'research that makes a difference' (*ibid.*: 280). By this, he means that the model and the skills that drive it have been developed from published research into what is 'effective and efficient' (*ibid.*) in counselling. Safran and Muran (2000) have written about the development of stage-process models of counselling in a way that explains how this process of 'translation' may occur:

> Stage-process models are schemas that have been empirically developed to distill recurring patterns of change that take place across cases . . . The psychotherapy process can be seen as a sequence of recurring stages that take place in identifiable patterns. By identifying these stages and modeling patterns of transition between them, researchers have developed maps that can sensitize clinicians to sequential patterns that are likely to occur. The goal is not to offer rigidly prescriptive models, but rather to help clinicians develop pattern-recognition abilities that can facilitate the intervention process.
>
> (Safran and Muran 2000: 140)

If we think about the skilled helper model in the light of these observations, we can see that Egan has developed a process for counselling that makes use of sequential patterns in problem management that have been empirically validated by researchers, as cited throughout the various editions of *The Skilled Helper*.

One finding from research that is relevant to cite here is the discovery that, in valid outcome studies, it may not be possible to separate an approach from the therapist using that approach (Shapiro *et al.* 1989), in the same way that the skill of a surgeon does not depend on the quality of her or his instruments but more on how she or he wields them (Strupp 1986). The model has been used as the basis for researching client change in longer-term counselling (Jinks 1999) and in this study it appeared that relationship factors contributing to client change could not be divorced from skills factors such as probing and challenging. This study reinforces the argument that integrative approaches such as the skilled helper model may not be accessible to empirical research in the same way as a therapeutic approach with strictly definable techniques. To attempt to treat the model itself as an independent variable runs the risk of reifying it. The model is not a set of treatment techniques that exists in any useful way independently of the practitioner who uses it.

Although not the main focus of research itself, the skilled helper model has certainly influenced approaches to research. Throughout the chapters in this book I have highlighted the client-responsive nature of the skilled helper model, and this aspect has been drawn upon in the development of research approaches to evaluating the client's experience of counselling (Jinks 1999; Sutton 1989). Sutton (1989: 47) considers the model to have a 'strong theoretical and evaluative base' and she has developed it into a 'goal-attainment' approach for outcome evaluation that is client centred and can be adapted to any theory of counselling.

As part of the preparation for this book I set up a pilot research project with a mental health charity for which, at that time, I was doing some voluntary counselling. The initial intention of this study was to use a widely respected and validated problem-solving inventory (PSI) (Heppner 1988; Heppner and Baker 1997) with clients at the beginning and end of their counselling. My purpose was to attempt to measure changes in clients' perceived problem-solving skills across a number of dimensions that might then be mapped onto aspects of the skilled helper model. By so doing, I hoped to explore the degree to which a counsellor using the model might enable clients to achieve Egan's second goal of helping, which is to 'help clients become better at helping themselves in their everyday lives' (Egan 2002a: 7–8).

I soon began to encounter difficulties in attempting to measure change in this way. Apparently conflicting evidence from early results seemed to show that a number of other variables were at play, making my seemingly straightforward task far less so. The main difficulty I came up against was that of obtaining reliable measures of change from the self-reporting of clients who completed the quantitative questionnaires. Egan himself has drawn attention to the two elements of researching clients' problem-solving abilities that can sometimes come into conflict with one another (Sugarman 1995). These are the demonstrable problem-solving abilities of clients (as evidenced by how well they are managing problem situations in their lives) as set against their own subjective perception of those abilities. I soon discovered that the two are not necessarily the same thing.

Initially, I was puzzled that good outcomes reported by clients in their evaluation forms returned to the agency were not always borne out by quantitative analysis of their completed questionnaires. On the basis of data derived only from their pre- and post-counselling questionnaires, some clients rated their problem-solving skills as poorer at the end of counselling than they had been at the start of counselling. The tentative conclusion I came to is that some clients in the sample may have thought they were better at problem solving at the start of counselling than they actually were.

Students of counselling are very familiar with the well-known cycle of learning that goes through the four phases of: (1) unconscious incompetence $\rightarrow$ (2) conscious incompetence $\rightarrow$ (3) conscious competence $\rightarrow$ (4) unconscious competence, and there may be parallels to this process in counselling that is predominantly concerned with learning problem-management skills. In short, I may have been coming up against a measure of unconscious incompetence in some of my clients' perceptions of their problem-solving skills at the start of counselling. Thus it is possible that those clients who expressed a diminished view of their problem-solving capabilities at the end of counselling (as recorded on their completed questionnaires) may have done so as a result of increases in self-awareness gained *through* counselling. In this case, questionnaires completed at the end of counselling may have given a truer and more accurate reflection of their problem-solving skills than those completed at the outset of counselling.

Most of the clients who took part in the pilot study had chronic and enduring mental health problems and all of them had lives constrained by social and economic disadvantage. The difference in questionnaire results between the start and end of counselling might in part have been because these clients had developed greater awareness of the origins and extent of their difficulties, which in some cases were considerable. Of course, this is pure conjecture on my part and I have no way of knowing if my assumptions are correct. It is certainly possible that these clients merely gained less from their counselling than they reported in their sessions and on their evaluation forms.

It might seem unnecessary and a little perverse to put an account of a 'failed' piece of research into this chapter. I wanted to do this for reasons of congruence and to present the learning gained from the difficulties I encountered in trying to establish this project. I think my experience here may also throw some light on why there is such a dearth of studies attempting to evaluate the skilled helper model as an independent variable in outcome research.

Whereas the therapeutic efficacy of the skilled helper model itself remains untested in this sense, and while the possibility of so doing remains questionable, this does not mean that the model lacks a coherent and valid research base. Egan has laid out the bedrock of research on which the various components of the model are founded. For instance, in the seventh edition of *The Skilled Helper*, he has drawn extensively on research in the area of what is becoming more popularly known as the field of 'positive psychology' (Argyle 2001; Aspinwall and Staudinger 2003; Carr 2004; Snyder and Lopez 2002). In previous editions of the model he has been careful to show how many of its elements have been developed from research into problem solving, cognitive dissonance theory, social learning, self-efficacy and motivation.

Despite the difficulties involved in researching the skilled helper model, outlined above and revealed in my own attempts, I believe that a number of viable research channels remain open. Perhaps the most interesting one is suggested by the client example given in Chapter 4 on page 108 (this client also took part in the pilot research project) and which might be phrased by the following question: 'Where clients experience successful and enduring outcomes to their counselling, how much of this success is attributable to aspects of the model and how much to other factors such as the quality of the therapeutic relationship; concurrent changes in the client's world; placebo elements such as hope, expectation, motivation and the perceived expertness of the counsellor?' Other research questions relating to the skilled helper model that appeal to my own interests are:

• With what kinds of clients, with which issues and in what contexts does the model seem most applicable?
• Do clients to whom the model is explicitly explained appear to benefit from this explanation in the form of enhanced collaboration in the counselling process?
• To what extent and in what ways do experienced practitioners adapt and improvise the model as a framework for their own personal styles of integration?

I have begun to gather a little data on this last question and this is presented in Chapter 7, where nine seasoned counsellors who are also trainers share their experiences of integrating the model into their own approaches to teaching, counselling and supervision. In the remainder of this chapter I will turn from research to another professional field and consider what the skilled helper model of counselling has to offer to the theory and practice of supervision.

What is supervision and why have it?

It might be useful to start this section by clarifying terms and saying what I mean by supervision as it is commonly understood in the UK. In the context of counselling and helping relationships, clinical supervision is a structured and formal collaborative arrangement whereby a helping practitioner reflects regularly on his or her work with clients or helpees with someone who is experienced both as a practitioner and a supervisor.

The aim of supervision is to safeguard clients and promote the efficacy of the therapeutic work. Clinical supervision is *not* training, personal counselling or line management, although it may contain elements of these. It has three main functions, which are to *support*, *develop* and *monitor* the supervisee and the work that she or he is undertaking with clients. Supervision is a process that aims both to maintain adequate professional and ethical standards of practice and to provide a method of consultative support to encourage the ongoing development and learning of the practitioner.

Whilst the importance of supervision for trainees is largely undisputed, there are those who question the value of mandatory supervision for trained and experienced practitioners. In the UK, counsellors are mandated by their main professional association, the British Association for Counselling and Psychotherapy (BACP), to have ongoing, career-long supervision. To be accredited by BACP, the current minimum requirement is for the counsellor to have 1.5 hours of supervision per month. Recently, this requirement has been challenged (Feltham 1999a; Lawton and Feltham 2000), particularly as it applies to qualified and experienced practitioners. In summary, the main arguments against career-long, mandatory supervision are:

- A lack of research evidence to show that supervision makes counsellors more effective.
- Mandatory supervision for qualified practitioners may give out the message that counselling is a profession that needs constant surveillance.

- The requirement for mandatory supervision infantilises the more senior and experienced members of the counselling profession.
- Practitioners may find supervision more effective if they seek it voluntarily and only when they feel the need.
- Where counsellors are obliged to have a set amount of supervision at regular intervals, the danger exists that the activity will degenerate into empty ritual.
- Supervision is supposed to safeguard the welfare of clients, yet relies largely on second-hand reporting of issues by counsellors. Unscrupulous practitioners may simply censor what they bring to supervision and use supervision as a smokescreen to endorse bad practice.

Despite these objections, I believe that supervision can remain a vital aspect of ongoing professional development for qualified and experienced practitioners in the helping professions (and not just counsellors and psychotherapists). In a recent training workshop with experienced clinical psychologists, participants identified the supervision of qualified staff as having the following functions:

- Providing ongoing professional development: enhancing knowledge, self-awareness and competence.
- Helping with the translation of theory into practice.
- Helping to develop the 'internal supervisor' of the experienced practitioner.
- Providing a safe forum for the working through of ethical dilemmas.
- Providing a quality-assurance mechanism – for both therapist and client.
- Offering a balance of challenge and support that can help to reinvigorate practice.
- Providing a forum for the development of new skills and awareness when working in new and more challenging areas of clinical practice.
- Offering a creative space for reflection and insight.
- Providing a place where transcultural issues and other aspects of working with difference and diversity can be raised and talked through.

- Providing opportunities to deal with organisational tensions and interpersonal issues in confidence and with an objective consultant.
- Providing a place for debriefing difficult or distressing work with clients.
- Helping prevent 'leakage' of confidential client material, e.g. to family, friends, colleagues.
- Providing accountability, e.g. evidence of having sought professional consultancy to deal with high-risk situations.
- Providing consultative support for any supervision work undertaken by the practitioner.

The points raised above suggest that supervision can continue to have a vital containing and enabling function for practitioners post-training. In support of this argument, research indicates that experienced therapists do indeed value ongoing supervision for its potential to help with personal and professional growth issues that are activated by their work with clients (Winter and Holloway 1991).

In the last chapter, I argued for the importance of encouraging students who are learning to use the skilled helper model to develop awareness of their own helping characteristics and to use these to mediate their application of helping skills and process. Supervision, undertaken either one-to-one or in a small group is, arguably, the most potentially useful forum for ongoing learning about how to use the self within a counselling model. This is so because supervision provides the best opportunity to focus on the *person* of the therapist through the close exploration and analysis of how the counsellor interacts with clients (Wosket 1999). Supervision stimulates reflection and insight, promotes autonomous practice and develops the internal supervisor (Casement 1985), all of which can significantly influence the counsellor's ability to use a counselling model in innovative and personally determined ways.

The skilled helper model as an aid to reflective practice

Before turning to a closer examination of the process and skills of supervision *per se*, it is useful to consider a number of different ways that the skilled helper model can be used to think about the counselling process. This will help us to move from considering the model simply as a framework for making direct counselling interventions to seeing its flexibility as a tool for developing reflective practice (Schön 1983).

When used as a framework for organising and reflecting on the process of therapy, the skilled helper model can be employed in a number of ways. Used as an orientating device (what Egan sometimes refers to as a 'browser') as opposed to a linear treatment plan, it can be adapted as follows:

As a case management model

Egan proposes (Sugarman 1995: 276) a number of questions that can be used in supervision to assess the best course of action for a client, even when that person might not be a suitable candidate for the skilled helper model as a counselling process (for example where the client is too disturbed or distressed to function autonomously). These essentially follow the problem-management steps of the model:

1 What are the issues around this client?
2 What might be best for this client?
3 What methods of intervention can we use?
4 How do we implement them most efficiently and effectively in the service and needs of this client?

In this way the model can be used as a diagnostic tool to address the question 'What does this client need?'

To get back on track after a derailment

It can be very helpful wherever the counsellor feels confused or adrift in the process to ask: 'Where am I in the model?' If the model, as we advise, is shared with the client this can become a joint question, e.g. 'Where do you think we are in the model and where do we need to be?' Attention to this question will often reveal what has gone askew in the process, for instance that counsellor and client are attempting to do stage three work on action strategies without having clearly identified any realistic, client-owned goals.

With the client to review and evaluate how counselling is going

Here counsellor and client would use the model in a collaborative dialogue to assess where they are up to in the work (stage one); where they want to be heading in future work (stage two) and how to begin moving in that direction (stage three).

To enhance intentionality (direction and purpose)

Here the counsellor can reflect on his or her work with a client by asking a 'stage two' question such as: 'If counselling with this client was going better, what might be happening that isn't happening now?' If we take the example of working with a client where the counsellor feels the process has stalled, answers that could come up might include:

- I'd be more interested in the client and not so bored.
- I'd feel able to challenge her more rather than feel so worn down by her despair and hopelessness.
- Ideally, I'd find a way of helping her to challenge herself.
- I'd look forward to her coming to sessions.
- There would be some laughter in our meetings.

This 'preferred picture' could then provide a springboard for the counsellor to consider what he or she might be missing or avoiding (blind spots) and what might be realistic goals for the therapy. The counsellor might, for instance, realise that he or she has been guarding against acknowledging a belief that the client thinks he or she is not up to much as a counsellor. It might then be possible to start to shape up a goal around being more congruent with the client.

As a framework to help refocus the work when it has lost energy or momentum

Here the counsellor might ask the client a 'leverage' question, such as: 'How might what we are working on at the moment make a difference?' Depending on the answer arrived at, counsellor and client may recognise a need to shift focus, perhaps to an emerging or underlying concern (e.g. where the client says, 'I think I tend to obsess about my noisy neighbours because it's something concrete to focus on that keeps that vague sense of dread I often feel in the background'). On the other hand, the question may help them proceed with more clarity about the presenting issue (e.g. the client might say, 'I know I seem to be going round in circles a lot of the time, but gradually the threads are becoming clearer').

One reason why it is important for supervisors who are supervising students of the skilled helper model to be conversant with the model themselves is that they can then use the terminology and process of the skilled helper to 'model the model' for their supervisees. This not only helps trainees further familiarise themselves with the skills and process, it also gives them the opportunity to experience what it is like to be on the receiving end of someone using the model – thereby hopefully developing their understanding of the client's perspective. As an example of this, we might consider the notion of blind spots (step 1B) – something that comes up very often in supervision.

Of course it is not only clients who have their blind spots. Counsellors and helpers have them in abundance too. One blind spot that frequently crops up for trainee counsellors is to blame the client for obstructions that occur, rather than taking responsibility for their own deficits in skill, awareness or sensitivity. Clients are often blamed by their counsellors (and not just by trainee counsellors) for being: uncooperative, not 'psychologically minded', defensive or unmotivated, poor attenders, bad time-keepers, unwilling to talk about feelings, unable to focus, not willing to move into stage two, not allowing the counsellor to get a word in edgeways and so forth. A fruitful approach for the supervisor to adopt here is to encourage the counsellor to take some responsibility for these glitches instead of merely reproaching the client.

One way to do this is for the supervisor to encourage the supervisee to reframe the client's obstructive behaviour or attitude as evidencing an outcome, skill or strategy that the counsellor has yet to achieve. For example, the supervisor might suggest that the supervisee tries saying, 'I haven't yet managed to help my client develop a focus' instead of 'The client won't stay focused', or 'I'm not as good yet as I'd like to be in creating a dialogue with my client' instead of 'He never lets me get a word in edgeways'. This approach provides a constructive alternative to pathologising the client and allows the supervisee to practise reframing problems as opportunities to be developed or as solutions still to be achieved. Following on from this, the supervisor can use the processes of stages two and three of the model to ask facilitative questions such as: 'What would you like to achieve in this situation?', 'Is that realistic?' and 'What are some of the ways that could happen?'

If we extrapolate from this strategy into a way of supervising that more fully utilises the framework of the skilled helper model, we can do this by looking at the example of how a supervisor might help a supervisee to explore a client's apparent resistance to what the counsellor is trying to offer. In so doing I will map the stages of the skilled helper model onto this exploration, although this is more a device to illustrate the process than something that I would normally do in such an explicit fashion in an actual supervision session.

Stage 1

Here the supervisor helps the supervisee (a trainee counsellor) to identify all the different forms of resistance that seem to be contributing to the road block (both the client's and the counsellor's). A sample list might include:

- Client's resistances (as perceived by the counsellor):
  - The client always says 'I don't know' when I ask her what she would like to talk about.
  - She always says 'I can't remember what we talked about last time' when I ask if there is anything that she'd like to pick up on from the last session.
  - She avoids eye contact.
  - She often says 'I don't understand what you're getting at' when I ask her anything slightly challenging.
  - There are lots of silences or she only gives brief, non-committal responses to my questions.
  - She keeps changing the subject whenever we get onto something that makes her the slightest bit uncomfortable.
- Counsellor's resistances (as revealed when the supervisor invites him to talk about what impact the client has on him):
  - I always feel tired in sessions.
  - I let her ramble and feel like I can't be bothered.
  - I don't look forward to seeing her.

- I often think she'd be better off with a more experienced counsellor.
- I don't think there's much chance that she'll ever change.

Having helped the supervisee unpack his experience of resistance with this client, the supervisor might bring in a challenging question (stage 1B) by asking, 'What do you notice about your list?' In response the counsellor might say, 'I seem to be asking her lots of questions and not getting many answers' or 'When I look at my list I seem to have written this person off and that's not a very nice feeling'.

Stage 2

Here the supervisor begins to invite the supervisee to consider how he would like things to look if the counselling was going better. She might ask: 'What would it look like if some of this resistance was sorted out?' With some encouragement by the supervisor not to blame the client, the supervisee might come up with the following list:

- I'd look forward to her coming.
- I wouldn't get bored in the sessions (supervisor asks, 'What would you feel instead?' and supervisee replies, 'Engaged').
- I would believe I might be able to help her.
- I would believe she's capable of change.
- I wouldn't ask so many questions (supervisor asks, 'What would you be doing instead?' and supervisee replies, 'I'd be making more reflections and empathic responses').
- I'd be tolerating the silences better.
- I'd be providing her with more invitations to respond.
- I'd be holding her attention better.
- I'd have a better understanding of what is going on for her.
- I'd be thinking I'm an OK counsellor instead of a rubbish one.

Stage 3

Here the supervisor helps the supervisee to explore some strategies to achieve what he would like to see happening if he were managing the resistance better. Possible strategies that they might come up with could include:

- Focusing on something I like about her in sessions (supervisor asks, 'Like what?' and supervisee replies, 'Her quirky sense of humour that occasionally pops up').
- Going out for a breath of fresh air to refresh myself before she comes.
- Reminding myself that you have said that you believe she is a suitable client for me to be seeing.
- If I ask her a question try to make sure my next intervention is a tentative statement or reflection rather than another question.
- Try starting the session by letting her know what has stayed with me from our last session, rather than always asking her.
- Offering more tentative hunches about what I imagine might be going on for her in the silences and then allowing her the space to respond.
- Reminding myself that whether she decides to make changes or not is her choice and not my responsibility.

By taking trainees through processes such as this, supervisors can encourage their supervisees, even when relatively inexperienced, to begin to develop as resourceful and autonomous practitioners who may well find themselves more able to find a way through their difficulties than they had imagined when first bringing them to supervision.

An integrative approach to supervision

Elements of the skilled helper model, such as those outlined above, can be usefully incorporated into a broader integrative approach to supervision. The cyclical model of supervision (Page and Wosket 2001) is one such framework that comprehensively addresses the tasks and process of supervision. This model of supervision, which has been directly influenced by the skilled helper model of counselling, is summarised below for readers who are interested in developing their use of the skilled helper into a systematic framework for the practice of supervision.

   The effective use of a supervision model or framework, as with good use of any counselling approach, is rooted in a sound grasp of communication and interpersonal skills. In his most recent publication on the skilled helper model Egan (2006) emphasises the importance of good communication skills within a therapeutic dialogue by positioning the learning of these skills separately and

outside the model itself. In this publication chapters on the therapeutic dialogue comprise more than half the book.

An equal emphasis on the importance of practising good communication skills is warranted in supervision. Occasionally, practitioners who make the transition from counsellor to supervisor
seem, in the process of making that transition, mysteriously to lose
many of their basic and vital skills of attending and listening. At
worst they seem to believe that they have to become purveyors of
wise thoughts and wordy advice, rather than collaborative meaning makers in mutual dialogue with their supervisees. Supervision
interventions, like counselling interventions, are essentially simple
words used in a timely and sensitive manner. The key communication skills of supervision are:

Supervision skills

- Attending
- Listening
- Paraphrasing
- Reflecting
- Summarising
- Open questions
- Probes and prompts
- Immediacy
- Information giving
- Confrontation
- Sharing hunches and possibilities

Supervisors who use their communication skills effectively aim for
an optimum balance between support and challenge. Unpacked
further in the form of interventions that might be used in supervision, the skills outlined above translate into the following
competencies:

Supervision interventions

Active listening

- Giving full attention (verbal and non-verbal)
- Using encouragers and minimal prompts ('Right', 'OK', 'I see',
  'I'm with you', 'Can you say a bit more?')

Paraphrasing (content and process)

- You've been working hard to establish a good working alliance with this client.
- You've been trying to work out what's going on in the relationship with your client at the moment and it's a real puzzle.

Reflecting

- Key words: 'frustrated . . .?', 'overwhelmed . . .?'
- Feelings: 'You sound quite despairing when you talk about the difficulties that this client is experiencing.'
- Thoughts: 'You're wondering if you are missing something here that the client is trying to tell you.'
- Behaviours (reported, observable and non-verbal): 'You forgot the client's appointment which is a very unusual thing for you to do'; 'In this part of the tape the client almost sounds as if she is trying to pick a fight with you'; 'You're frowning and you seem quite angry as you talk about this client.'

Summarising (themes, issues, key points)

'You've been finding the work with this client very challenging over the last few meetings. He presses lots of your own buttons, which leaves you feeling de-skilled and unsure of how to proceed. Now you're quite anxious about the next appointment and beginning to feel unsure about whether you can help him. Have I got that right?'

Open questions, probes and prompts

- What is your empathy like with this client?
- What made you say that to the client?
- With hindsight, would you do anything differently?
- Can you say a little more about the anxiety you feel when you are waiting for the client to arrive?
- This is a delicate issue, but I'm wondering if there's a bit of sexual tension in the air between you and the client.

Immediacy (you and me talk)

'I've suddenly noticed that I seem to be giving you lots of advice here. I'm not sure about how I got drawn into that – perhaps it comes from feeling a bit protective towards you and wanting to reassure you. How are you experiencing what's happening between us at the moment?'

Information giving (used sparsely and judiciously)

'It's quite common for clients to feel worse before they feel better – it happens a lot with my own clients when we are doing longer-term work. Often it's because the clients feel safe enough to start letting go of their defences and begin facing up to what's really going on. Could this be what is happening with your client?'

Confrontation (using description, not accusation)

'You told me at the start of our session that you would like my help with some difficult feelings that come up for you in your work with this client. I notice that time is getting on and we haven't come back to that yet.'

Sharing hunches and possibilities (tentatively and economically)

'You've mentioned a couple of times that the client is very attractive and then moved on to something else. I might have this wrong, but my attention keeps coming back to this and I'm beginning to wonder if it might be useful, but maybe a bit uncomfortable, to look at what it's like for you to be working with such an attractive client.'

If these are some of the key skills and interventions that underpin effective supervision, the question arises as to how they can be used in an intentional and purposeful manner to address the tasks and functions of supervision, as outlined at the start of this chapter. I will attempt to address this question through presenting an outline of the integrative, cyclical model of supervision, which, as I have said, is in part derived from the skilled helper model of counselling. This chapter allows for only a brief overview of the model and readers are referred to the core text – *Supervising the Counsellor: A Cyclical Model* (Page and Wosket 2001) for a fuller account. In particular, doing justice to the important ethical components of supervision is beyond the scope of this chapter. These are fully covered in the abovementioned publication.

As the present text is first and foremost about the skilled helper model, I will take a particular slant on the cyclical model of supervision here and attempt to show how the different steps and stages of the skilled helper model can be incorporated into this supervision model to provide a flexible framework for the supervision process.

A key and fundamental difference between the skilled helper model of counselling and the cyclical model of supervision is that the emphasis in the former is on a problem-management process, while in the latter the emphasis is primarily exploratory. As Page and Wosket (2001: 42) assert, 'Supervision, to be effective, must be exploratory. It may also be action-oriented, but this is not always necessary in order for it to be effective.' This difference in emphasis is reflected in the shape and structure of the cyclical model and will become apparent as we run through the five main stages. An overview of the model is given in Figure 6.1.

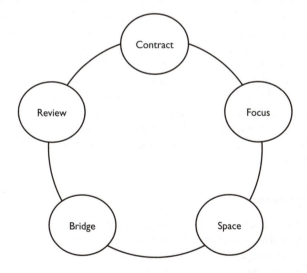

Figure 6.1 The cyclical model of supervision

Although presented here as a sequential model, this is merely for ease of articulation. In reality the model can be accessed at any point within the five stages. Rather than adhering scrupulously to it at all times, students of supervision are encouraged to familiarise themselves with the model and then hold it loosely in mind, to be called forth as and when it might be useful to give shape and movement to the supervision process. Like the skilled helper model, it can be applied to a single session or used to shape the process of work over a series of sessions. A summary of the five stages of the model, with examples of how aspects of the skilled helper model may be incorporated into it, follows. In these sections the focus is mainly on one-to-one supervision, although the model also adapts readily to group supervision (see Page and Wosket 2001).

Stage 1: contract

The supervision process, as with any good counselling arrangement, needs to begin with a contract that establishes groundrules for the work and relationship and ensures that the process gets off to a good start. The supervision contract is important in establishing a secure foundation, which can provide safety and containment for the exploratory work that will follow.

Both supervisor and supervisee are more likely to be honest, open and vulnerable with one another and to take creative risks if a clear and firm contract is in place to support and sustain the supervisory work and relationship. The supervision contract is likely to encompass some, or all, of the following elements: establishing boundaries and confidentiality; discussing time, place, duration and frequency of meetings; agreeing fees and how these will be paid; agreeing on which professional codes of ethics and practice will govern the work; being explicit about accountability, e.g. when, if and how the supervisor is required to report back to an employer or training institution.

Stage 2: focus

The focus in supervision is normally what the supervisee chooses to bring to the attention of the supervisor. The supervisor may then help the supervisee to shape and clarify the focus or, unusually, she may intervene in a more directive manner to alter the focus if she feels strongly that a different issue requires attention.

For instance, this might happen where there appears to be some danger to the supervisee, a client or another person and this is not being addressed by the supervisee. Focusing in supervision has many similarities with the notion of leverage as set out in stage 1C of the skilled helper model of counselling.

Supervisees' issues can be wide ranging. In counselling supervision they need to be related in some way to the work with clients in order to preserve the purpose and function of supervision and to prevent it straying into and becoming lost in associated activities such as training or counselling. Here are some examples of issues which supervisees might bring to supervision:

- a feeling of floundering or being out of depth
- a difficulty in holding a boundary
- a sense of stuckness or impasse
- a difficulty with transitions or endings
- a rupture in the counselling relationship
- strong feelings, e.g. of embarrassment, fear, shame, despair or sexual arousal
- an organisational issue
- a concern about working in a culturally sensitive manner
- feelings of stress or impending burnout
- lack of motivation or appetite for the work
- a sense of over-functioning for the client or of being overwhelmed by him or her
- awareness of transference or countertransference issues
- personal 'crumple buttons' that are being pushed by the client work
- a sense of achievement or success.

One danger in searching for a focus is that too much supervision time may be given over to protracted presentation of background material and case history, thereby cutting back on the more valuable space for exploration and the working through of current issues. Questions such as the following can be useful whenever supervisees are in danger of talking too much about (and thereby objectifying) the client, rather than focusing on their own immediate supervision needs:

- What is your dilemma with your client?
- Could you try putting your issue in one sentence?

- What is the main concern you are bringing to supervision today?

An exercise on focusing in supervision is given at the end of the chapter (Exercise 6.1).

Although supervision is not counselling or psychotherapy, on occasion supervisees will need to take to supervision personal issues that are impacting on their work with clients. I have found that holding the stages of the skilled helper model in mind is helpful in negotiating with my supervisees how we will deal with such issues.

Normally I find that confining my responses to those that would legitimately keep us within stage one of the model is both containing and respectful. In other words, I try to give my supervisee space to tell me about the personal issues that may be affecting his or her work while I attempt to listen with empathy and understanding. Often this is all that is needed – my supervisee has the chance to off-load and we can then move on to consider his or her work with clients whilst taking into account how those personal concerns may have some bearing on that work. I don't attempt to 'work through' personal issues with my supervisees. If they need further help, we would discuss how this might happen, for instance by accessing some counselling support or taking time out from their counselling practice to attend to self-care (Henderson 2001).

Stage 3: space

The exploratory space lies at the heart of the supervision process. It is the place where the counsellor or helper is held, supported, challenged and affirmed in his or her work. Space is where movement and insight can occur as a result of the collaborative exploratory work undertaken by supervisor and supervisee. It is also the place where 'not knowing' and confusion are accepted and tolerated in the belief that time and attention given to the supervisee are beneficial to the ongoing work with clients, even when a comfortable resolution of issues may not be achieved. The key aspects of working within the supervision space are:

- *Collaboration*: working together in a co-operative relationship.

- *Investigation*: exploring possibilities and following hunches, stray thoughts, images, feelings and associations that may throw light on what is occurring in the work with clients.
- *Challenge*: providing supportive challenges and, ideally, helping the supervisee to self-challenge in order to open up blind spots and new perspectives.
- *Containment*: helping the supervisee and thereby his or her client(s) to feel supported and held.
- *Affirmation*: helping the supervisee to feel valued and restored in his or her work.

In many ways, this part of the supervision process parallels steps 1A and 1B of the skilled helper model. Essentially, the task for the supervisor is to help the supervisee tell the story of his or her work with the client in a supportive and challenging manner that brings new perspectives and insights to that work.

There are a number of ways in which the counsellor and supervisor can reflect together on the interaction between therapist and client within the supervision space. The playing of audio or video tapes of client work (which should always and only be done with the client's informed consent) can assist this process and ensure that due attention is paid to the experience of the counsellor within the relationship as well as to the experience of the client. The bringing of tapes to supervision can be especially useful in the supervision of trainees as they provide concrete and recent examples of work that is actually taking place with clients and can enable the supervisor to give specific feedback based on behavioural observations. Specific and detailed feedback of this kind (see the section on review below) is fairer and likely to be more palatable to supervisees than feedback that is experienced merely as the supervisor's 'expert' opinion.

When recordings of client work are used in supervision, supervisors should encourage their supervisees to play excerpts of tapes that leave them with questions about themselves and their practice, for instance: 'I suddenly went completely blank here – I couldn't even remember the client's name for a few moments and I've no idea why' or 'I'm really confused about what was going on here. I thought we were getting along fine and then suddenly the client seemed to turn on me and I felt like I'd done something awful to her'. Attention paid to such significant events usually heralds the greatest learning for the supervisee as the ensuing discussion and exploration with the supervisor can often uncover significant interpersonal dynamics that may turn out to be the key determinants of the counselling session.

Written analyses of counselling interactions undertaken by students in a counselling practice file or log are another source of invaluable learning about the counselling relationship and process. As Egan has observed (Coles 1996), the act of writing about counselling can serve as a form of self-supervision. Writing reviews of their counselling sessions can encourage students to engage in disciplined reflection and systematic enquiry into the detail of their therapeutic interactions. It can be particularly enlightening for students to consider, as part of their reflective writing, the impact the client is having on them personally as well as the impact they feel they are having on the client. Supervisees can be encouraged to bring to supervision extracts from their written case studies, or short transcripts of dialogue between counsellor and client for further examination with their supervisor. The exercises at the end of this chapter can be useful in helping supervisees learn to consider and work with the interpersonal dynamics of counselling and supervision.

The supervision space also affords a place for intuitive and creative approaches that can draw on the symbolic power of objects, images and artwork. The supervisee may, for example, be invited to handle and place stones or shells, which in some way are chosen to represent the client and his or her systemic background. Role-play or two-chair work may be introduced to encourage the supervisee to engage in visual and active forms of supervision. A creative exercise (adapted from Ishiyama 1988) using artwork and imagery that can be used in group supervision, or adapted to one-to-one work with an individual supervisor, is included at the end of the chapter (Exercise 6.2).

It is important that this part of the supervision process is preserved as a place for opening up and exploring possibilities, issues and dilemmas, rather than attempting to resolve them. Getting caught up at this stage in problem solving or action planning can stem the creative flow of the exploratory work and prevent important new material from surfacing and coming into awareness.

It is often through the dynamics of the supervision relationship that unsurfaced material belonging to the supervisee's work with clients becomes accessible for examination. In supervision this is known as the 'reflection', 'mirroring' or 'parallel process' (Calligor

1984; Doehrman 1976; Mattinson 1977; Searles 1955). An exercise for exploring the psychodynamics of supervision (developed from an idea by Steve Page) is given at the end of the chapter (Exercise 6.3). The following example from a training situation shows how identifying a parallel process can help to resolve a supervision dilemma.

The supervisor in this vignette is a trainee. She is an experienced psychodynamic therapist who is learning to become a supervisor. Understandably, her initial model for supervision practice is closely wedded to her therapeutic model and therefore focuses keenly on the unconscious communication that may be going on between the therapist and the client. Here is the first scenario:

This trainee supervisor is supervising a counsellor who works in a student counselling service. They are discussing his (the counsellor's) difficulties with a client who attends irregularly. He says about his client:

Supervisee: She misses scheduled sessions and doesn't come regularly to booked appointments. Instead, she turns up nearly every week for the emergency slot I always offer on Friday afternoons, when anyone can come. If the slot is busy I may only be able to see her for ten minutes. I try to book her in for regular, ongoing appointments, which she agrees to, and then doesn't turn up for.

The supervisor makes several tentative attempts to get the supervisee (who does not share her therapeutic orientation) to identify the unconscious communication that may be going on between himself and the client. The supervisee doesn't seem to understand what she is getting at and she makes one last-ditch attempt to get her point across. She says:

Supervisor: I want you to see that your client is letting you know that it is difficult for her to come regularly and

> that you might be expecting something of her that
> she can't manage at this time.
>
> The supervisee replies, somewhat defensively:
>
> Supervisee: I didn't think I was expecting her to do anything she
> can't manage. I don't think she feels pressurised by
> me.

The process of supervision stalls here. The supervisor's interpretation misses the mark and the supervisee feels the need to explain and defend his position.

> Now let's re-run this with a second scenario.
>   The trainer has intervened at this point and encouraged the trainee supervisor to pay attention to his own responses and bring these into the interaction using immediacy. The supervisor has another go while the supervisee presents his issue again.
>   So, again, the supervisee says about his client:
>
> Supervisee: As I was saying, she misses most of her scheduled
> sessions and only turns up to a few of them. But she
> turns up nearly every week for the emergency slot
> on Friday afternoons, which is open to anyone.
> Sometimes I can only see her for ten minutes if
> we're busy then. So I've tried to book her in for
> regular weekly appointments. She readily agrees to
> these and then doesn't turn up so we're back to
> square one.
>
> Again the supervisor initially responds by making several tentative attempts to get the supervisee to identify the unconscious communication that may be going on between himself and the client. The supervisee, as before, doesn't understand what she is

getting at. This time though, instead of pushing her own interpretation, the supervisor says:

Supervisor: I feel as if I am trying hard to get you to see something from my perspective and it's not working. I don't know if this throws any light on what is happening between you and your client.

This time the supervisee says:

Supervisee: That made me think that maybe *she* is trying to tell me something that I'm not hearing.

The supervisor then asks:

Supervisor: And what might that be?
Supervisee: That perhaps it's too hard for her to come for regular fifty-minute appointments at the moment, but that she wants to stay connected.

In the first scenario we can see that the supervisor is intent on getting her interpretation across and works in thinking mode. In the second scenario she works from her own embodied responses – her feelings of frustration, of feeling unheard and misunderstood. From her own felt sense of the dynamic between herself and the supervisee she develops a congruent and immediate response that – and this is the key thing – is heard by the supervisee as an invitation to do *his own* thinking. There are clearly parallels in this example with immediacy as discussed in Chapter 2 in relation to the skilled helper model of counselling. Here again, the point is emphasised that optimum forms of challenge are invitational rather than adversarial and that the supervisor's skills of immediacy serve to stimulate the supervisee's ability and willingness to self-challenge.

The following list provides suggestions for the kind of exploratory open questions, probes and prompts that can be useful for supervisees to consider when reflecting on a particular counselling session or piece of work within the supervision space. They include some examples of interventions that might help to identify a parallel process. The questions can either be asked by a supervisor or used in self-supervision, for instance as reflective questions used in written analyses for a counselling practice file or journal.

1   Attention to process and skills:
    –   What strategies and interventions have you used?
    –   What were you trying to achieve?
    –   Why were you trying to achieve this?
    –   What was the effect on the client?
    –   With hindsight, what would you do differently?
    –   What do you think you might be missing or overlooking?
    –   Where were you in the (skilled helper) model?
    –   Is this where the client needs to be?
2   Attention to relationship:
    –   What is happening between you and the client?
    –   What stops you from saying that to the client?
    –   What impact is the client having on you?
    –   How would you describe your relationship with the client at the moment? (Try finding an image or metaphor)
    –   What changes have happened in the relationship?
    –   What changes would you like to see happening?
    –   How intact is the relationship?
    –   What needs to happen for you to have better contact with the client?
3   Attention to underlying dynamics and parallel processes:
    –   What is happening between us (i.e. supervisor and supervisee)?
    –   Any parallels with the client in terms of thoughts, feelings, experiences?
    –   Does what is going on between us tell us anything about what may be going on between you and the client?
    –   How does the client make you feel?
    –   What does the client say or do that makes you feel like this?
    –   What does the client want from you and what sort of feeling is s/he trying to arouse in you to get it?
    –   Can you bring any of this out into the open with the client?
    –   What effect might this have on the client, the work, or the relationship?

Supervisors of students who are learning the skilled helper model of counselling can bring aspects of the model more explicitly into the supervision space. This helps trainees to become more familiar with the language and process of the model and how it might be used in a helping relationship. In this way, supervisors can encourage students to reflect on their counselling or helping sessions using prompts explicitly derived from the three stages of the model, as in the sample questions that follow. Again these are probes and prompts that can be used in self-supervision or form the basis of interventions used by the supervisor.

- Stage 1:
  - What was going on – for me, for my client?
  - What were my client's presenting/emerging issues?
  - What was around that wasn't spoken about?
  - What was the focus of the session? Did this shift or change?
- Stage 2:
  - What do I think were the client's goals for the session?
  - What were my goals?
  - Were these achieved?
  - If not, what changed or got in the way?
- Stage 3:
  - If I were to run this session again, what would I do differently?
  - How would this relate to the client's goals and my goals?
  - What do I hope to achieve next time I see the client?
  - What might help me to do this and what might get in the way?
- Evaluation questions:
  - What have I learned from the session: about me, about the client, about counselling?
  - What do I want to take to my external supervisor for further help and exploration?

Stage 4: bridge

The bridge stage of the supervision model deals with applying learning from supervision to the ongoing work with clients. It is in the goal-setting and action-planning components of this stage of the supervision process that the influence of the skilled helper model is perhaps most clearly apparent. A useful question for the supervisor to ask at this point in the process is: 'What would you like to do with what we have covered today?' This open question may generate any number of responses. Often, the supervisee will take the opportunity to sift through what has been discussed to sort out what seems useful to have in mind when next seeing the client or when next grappling with the issue presented. Sometimes, supervisees will welcome further help from the supervisor to assist them in working out a possible way forward. In this case the following elements may come into play:

- *Goal setting*: identifying what aims may be workable and realistic. These will be the supervisee's goals and they may consist of: (1) objectives to take the work with the client forward; or (2) the supervisee's goals for his or her own learning and development.
- *Information giving*: where the supervisor may offer to share her own ideas and experience, perhaps giving suggestions for trying a different technique or recommending some reading.
- *Action planning*: where, having identified a goal, the supervisor and supervisee together brainstorm a range of strategies for achieving the goal and from these create a tentative action plan that allows for the unexpected.
- *Considering the client's perspective*: here the supervisor encourages the supervisee to imagine how any change might affect the client. Goals and action plans may then be reviewed following consideration of their likely impact on the client. An exercise to help supervisees and trainee supervisors experience the importance of considering the client's perspective is included at the end of the chapter (Exercise 6.4).

A number of parallels with stages two and three of the skilled helper model are evident in these elements where the supervisor may invoke a more intentional way of intervening to encourage the supervisee to move the process of the work with the client forward. The following list of probes and prompts offers some suggestions for how the supervisor might intervene at this stage of the process (or again they can be used in self-supervision):

- What do you see as the focus and direction of future work?
- Why do you see it heading that way?

- What, if anything, do you want to change?
- How might you do that?
- What are your reasons for considering change?
- What might be the effect on the client of making this change?
- In what ways might you need to review your plan?
- What do you need to develop or learn to do better?
- How might you begin to do this?

Stage 5: review

The review stage of the supervision process is about evaluation – both formative and summative. Again, here there are echoes of the skilled helper model of counselling in that evaluation is considered to be an integral and embedded component of the process rather than an 'add-on'. If the supervisee is a trainee, reviewing may also have an assessment function. Ongoing review and evaluation are important and sometimes neglected aspects of supervision. They occur best through *mutual* feedback where the supervisee is encouraged to give feedback to the supervisor, as well as vice versa. Feedback that happens regularly as an integral part of the supervision process helps to develop the relationship between supervisor and supervisee and enhance the efficacy of the work. Feedback has a number of important functions, some of which are to:

- highlight what is going well and progress that has been made
- indicate where there are weaknesses or omissions to be addressed
- challenge blind spots or uncover missed opportunities
- develop and deepen the supervision relationship
- clear the air through releasing pent up feelings
- clarify misunderstandings and check assumptions
- provide an opportunity for the sharing of appreciations.

The ability to give feedback in supervision which is likely to be welcomed and well received requires the skills of empathy, assertiveness and good timing. Feedback will be most acceptable to the recipient when it is:

- *Balanced*: positive with negative.
- *Constructive*: helps the recipient to see what he or she might do differently, and the benefits of that.

- *Specific*: given using concrete examples based on behavioural observations.
- *Managed with good timing*: given when the other person is likely to be most receptive and open to hearing it.
- *Given regularly*: not saved up and 'dumped' in a punitive or accusatory manner.

An exercise to enable supervisors to evaluate their own strengths and areas for development in giving and receiving feedback is included at the end of the chapter (Exercise 6.5). Mutual constructive feedback in supervision will often lead to re-contracting or adjustments being made to the initial contract. In this way, it closes the circle and recycles back to the first stage of the supervision model. Review and re-contracting can thus become the starting point for a new cycle.

Having considered how the skilled helper model of counselling can influence approaches to supervision, the next (and final) chapter presents a round-table of perspectives on further developments and applications of the model. A number of experienced practitioners trained in the skilled helper model reflect on the various ways in which they have adapted the model in their own practice – as trainers, supervisors and counsellors.

Exercise 6.1: Finding a focus in supervision

This exercise is undertaken in a whole-group setting and can be used with trainee counsellors or trainee supervisors.

Allow a client (or supervisee) to come to mind who you might take to supervision. Take a blank piece of paper and write down one sentence that begins: 'My dilemma with my client is . . .'

Keep the sentence short and take care to own your dilemma rather than blaming the client (e.g. instead of 'My client tries to avoid my challenges by using flattery', write 'I can get seduced by her flattery into being over-nice and not challenging her').

Group members then read their sentences out loud. They are asked only to read the sentence and not to expand further on the issue. The trainer then invites them to say how they experienced the exercise. Typically, the following responses may come out:

- Writing one sentence really helped to clarify the issue for me.

- It was helpful to be asked to own the dilemma as I have been stuck on seeing it as the client's problem.
- Putting the dilemma into one sentence cut out all the background that I would normally take to supervision.
- Now I feel as if I have taken some responsibility for the issue and it's become something that the client and I can work on together.
- Something really shifted when I wrote the sentence. Now that I can see the issue more clearly I'm beginning to see what I might be able to do to resolve it.

Exercise 6.2: Exploring the psychodynamics of supervision

This exercise is in two parts. The first part involves some personal reflection and the second consists of sharing those reflections in a small group. The following instructions are given to the whole group (which can be a group of supervisors or supervisees):

Part 1

Take a blank piece of paper. Allow a client (or supervisee) to come into your awareness.

Don't force anything. Take the first person who comes – allow someone to choose you.

Now place a word or a symbol that arises from your awareness of that person in the middle of the page. Put down whatever comes, even if it doesn't seem to have any connection. (If nothing comes, place a mark or word that represents 'nothing' on your paper.)

Now take three minutes to free associate around that person and the word, symbol or image you have placed on the paper. Write down or draw around it any words, images, pictures, shapes that come to mind. Don't censor them and note the feelings that arise for you as you do this.

Part 2

Now take some time to work in a group of three or four. Divide the time equally so that the group focuses on one person at a time and helps that person to explore what is on his or her paper and talk about his or her client or supervisee.

When facilitating each other's exploration, ask open questions to help the person presenting to discover his or her own meaning and insight. Share your own tentative hunches, feelings and responses in a minimal and respectful way, as these might help to pick up on any parallel processes that are around. *Don't* impinge on the person's work through making interpretations.

Tutor: allow participants a few minutes to debrief the exercise in their small groups before giving time to the whole group to make sense of the experience.

Exercise 6.3: Visual case processing in supervision, using metaphors and drawings

This exercise is in four parts and is designed to be run in a group (although it can also be adapted to individual supervision). In the first three parts supervisees work on their own to build a picture of their experience of a recent counselling session that they would like to explore in supervision. They can write and/or draw in response to the sentence stems given in parts one and two. In part three they are explicitly asked to draw a picture of the counselling session. Here it can be helpful to encourage participants to draw with their non-dominant hand. This gives people who are concerned about their ability to draw permission to produce a 'bad' drawing. Using the non-dominant hand can also help to bypass a censoring part of the self and encourage artwork that is freer and more spontaneous.

It is important that supervisees complete the stages in the sequence in which they are given, and that they finish each one before they move on to reading the instructions for the next. This is because the exercise is designed to encourage a gradual unfolding and deepening of exploration and insight.

Part 1

Reflect on a specific counselling or counselling skills session by completing the following six sentence stems:

1 What I see as the client's main concern was . . .
2 The way the client interacted with me was . . .
3 What I was trying to do in this session was . . .

4   What I felt or thought about myself as a counsellor during this
    session was . . .
5   The way this session went was . . .
6   What I think the client gained from this session was . . .

Part 2

Now allow yourself to reflect further on the work with your client
by describing a metaphor, image or symbol in answer to each of
the following four prompts:

1   The way I perceive the client with his or her concerns may be
    represented by this metaphor or image:

    _____

    _____

2   The way the client responded towards me and felt towards me
    during the session may be represented by this metaphor or
    image:

    _____

    _____

3   The way I conducted myself during this session may be
    represented by this metaphor or image:

    _____

    _____

4   The way the session went may be represented by this meta-
    phor or image:

    _____

    _____

Part 3

Please draw or paint freely this session on a separate piece of
paper, drawing upon the thoughts and images generated in the
previous stages if you wish. It is not at all important how aesthetic
your drawing is. What is most important is to express accurately
how you experienced yourself, your client and the session. Artistic
qualities are not relevant here at all. Feel free to include abstract

symbols, words, phrases or sentences in your drawing. Please make sure you include the following elements in your picture:

1 Yourself as counsellor/helper and as person.
2 The client and his or her concerns.
3 Your relationship with the client (i.e. how you and the client related to each other).
4 How the session went.
5 Where the work (process and relationship) is going.

Part 4

Share as much as you feel comfortable with about your drawing, your images and your reflections with a small peer group (or with your supervisor), who will help you to explore and process your perceptions further.

You may wish to make additions or changes to your drawing as you gain further insight and understanding in relation to the client work presented.

Tutor: allow at least twenty minutes for each person to present their work in a small group, facilitated by their peers. Give time for debriefing the experience in the small working groups before a plenary session in which the whole group is invited to give feedback on how they experienced the exercise and what they learned from it.

Exercise 6.4: Considering the client's perspective

This exercise is designed to give supervisees greater understanding of what it might be like for the client to experience the impact of any changes they are thinking of making as a result of discussing the client in supervision. It works best when introduced at the bridge stage of the supervision process (as outlined in the cyclical model of supervision) and following on from exploratory work undertaken in the supervision space.

The exercise is undertaken in a group of three where participants rotate between the roles of supervisee (**A**), supervisor (**B**) and observer (**C**). The supervisor (**B**) directs the process and the observer (C) gives observations and feedback at suitable points during and at the end of each cycle.

Two chairs are placed opposite one another and the supervisee (A) sits in one of them, facing the other. The directions which the supervisor (B) gives to the supervisee (A) are as follows:

B: Think of an intervention you might want to make to your client – perhaps as a result of the supervision you have had . . . Now imagine that your client is sitting in the empty chair facing you. Take the time you need to really imagine him or her there . . . Now say out loud to the client what you would like to say. This is an experiment so it is OK to start with saying the 'unspeakable' – the thing that you would never actually say, but that you often feel or think.

The supervisee (A) then speaks to the 'client' in the empty chair.

The supervisor then directs the supervisee as follows:

B: Now move across to the empty chair and 'become' your client. Take the time you need to really imagine being the client – how that person would look, his or her posture, the way he or she would sit . . . Now, as the client, imagine receiving the intervention that has just been spoken to you by your counsellor . . . What impact does it have? What do you think and feel? How would you respond?

The supervisor (B) then directs the supervisee (A) to move away from the two chairs to a position where he or she can view both of them and says:

B: Now re-run that interaction in your mind and imagine it happening in front of you. Watch what the counsellor says and how the client responds . . . What does it look like and sound like? How do you feel about it? Do you want to try it differently?

The observer (C) may offer some observations and feedback at this point based on what he or she noticed about the interaction between the supervisee and the 'client'.

This cycle may need to be re-run several times before the supervisee finds a way to express what he or she wants to say to the client in a respectful and constructive manner such that the client will be able to hear and respond.

Participants then swap roles until each of the three has had the chance to experience each role.

Tutor: allow sufficient time for the participants to debrief the exercise (which can be powerful) in their small group before feeding back their learning and experience in a whole-group plenary.

Exercise 6.5: Giving feedback in supervision – a self-inventory

Please rate your strengths and areas of development in giving feedback according to the following rating scale:

1 = very good or good; 2 = adequate; 3 = needs attention

How good are you at:

1 . . . 2 . . . 3 . . .   Contracting: raising issues about how and when to give and receive feedback at the contracting stage of supervision.

1 . . . 2 . . . 3 . . .   Helping supervisees to understand the benefits of giving and receiving feedback.

1 . . . 2 . . . 3 . . .   Building immediacy and congruence into the relationship from the beginning.

1 . . . 2 . . . 3 . . .   Ensuring that regular feedback is built into the process, preferably at every supervision session.

1 . . . 2 . . . 3 . . .   Enabling and encouraging supervisees to give *you* feedback.

1 . . . 2 . . . 3 . . .   Being descriptive rather than judgemental or evaluative in the way that you give feedback.

1 . . . 2 . . . 3 . . . Ensuring that the relationship remains intact by giving priority to repairing ruptures when they occur.

1 . . . 2 . . . 3 . . . Using (appropriate) self-disclosure (e.g. sharing your vulnerability or fallibility with supervisees).

1 . . . 2 . . . 3 . . . Offering feedback that is tentative and open to negotiation.

1 . . . 2 . . . 3 . . . Offering a balance of positive and negative feedback.

1 . . . 2 . . . 3 . . . Taking account of issues of power and difference in giving feedback.

1 . . . 2 . . . 3 . . . Not letting small opportunities for giving cumulative feedback slip by.

1 . . . 2 . . . 3 . . . Being concrete and specific in the way that you offer feedback.

1 . . . 2 . . . 3 . . . Earning the right to challenge by demonstrating your own openness to challenge and feedback.

Other components:

1 . . . 2 . . . 3 . . . _____

1 . . . 2 . . . 3 . . . _____

Chapter 7

Developments and applications of the skilled helper model: a round-table of views

This chapter is included to offer a range of contemporary perspectives on the skilled helper model as it is currently understood and practised in the UK. It gives an insight into some of the creative ways that the model is being used as a framework for integrative practice and in the education and supervision of helpers. The contributors to this chapter all use the skilled helper model in their teaching, counselling and supervisory roles. The pieces were written independently of each other and the authors were invited to make their contributions before seeing the material in other chapters. They were given a very wide brief and invited to write freely about their experience of the skilled helper model and any aspects of particular interest to them. Therefore the insights and experience they have chosen to share are individual and personal and are not directly influenced by my own perspectives and slant on the model. Nonetheless, it is interesting to see these writers wrestling in a very real and experiential way with the kinds of challenges, tensions and rewards of working with the model that are highlighted and explored in preceding chapters.

The shape of this chapter loosely follows the unfolding of themes as they are sequenced in the previous chapters. Thus the first contribution is by a trainer whose attention is drawn to the emphasis on positive psychology in the model, while the second writer chooses to discuss post-modern and relational perspectives on the model. There then follow contributions from practitioners who share something of their evolving experience of adapting the model to shape their own integrative styles of working, first as counsellors and subsequently as facilitators of others learning the model. The chapter concludes with sections that have a sharper focus on supervision and training contexts, and which include a number of useful examples of how the skilled helper model can be taught and how it can be used in supervision. As the material presented speaks clearly and with conviction for itself, I have merely organised the various passages around a few subheadings and provided an endnote.

A model of wellness: the skilled helper as a precursor of the positive psychology movement

My belief is that in its emphasis on client resources, the original concept of the skilled helper model prefigured the positive psychology movement by some twenty years. Its author is sometimes taken to task for an apparent unwillingness to plumb the depths of individual pathology, yet I would argue that the emphasis and strength of the model have never been in that dimension. This is an approach that *does* ask the question: 'What is going wrong?' – and then goes on to ask not just: 'What can be hoped for?' but, crucially, 'What resources are available to help those hopes be realised?'

Positive psychology, in its different manifestations, attempts to turn the tide of pathologising the human condition by focusing on salutogenic models and the movement towards better health. It can reasonably be argued that, from the genesis of humanistic, cognitive and behavioural approaches to psychotherapy, the profession has had access to strands that de-emphasise poor mental functioning and move conceptually away from the notion of a person's imprisonment in past experience. The existential influences on psychotherapy exercised a levelling effect: we are all bound by the same limits.

Viewed in these terms, anxiety, the fear of freedom and of death, and the desire to escape responsibility are part of our shared humanity – not to be read as the aetiology of an individual's sickness. Thus, for over half a century counsellors and psychotherapists have had access to theory and practice that, whilst accepting the individual experience of mental anguish and distress, acknowledge it as a variant of the human condition and by this very acknowledgement make space for routes to more successful accommodation to that condition.

How this accommodation is viewed as happening varies according to the different theories and models of counselling and psychotherapy. In Rogerian terms, this implies an improvement in the operation of self-judgement. Similarly, though by employing different therapeutic channels, cognitive therapy clears the way for a more productive exercise of evaluations of self, events, others and the world at large. In behavioural work, the distressing event or situation can be worked with by applying skills and competences which may seem, at the outset, to lie beyond or at the limits of the individual's capacity.

The additional step taken by such authors as Seligman and Csikszentmihalyi (2000), Keyes (2002), Ryff (1989) and Ryff and Keyes (1995) – and Egan may be counted a precursor – is to conceptualise the person not in terms of deficits but as a composite of resources that are underused or neglected. Rogers would have concurred that the person has all the potential for self-healing – change the environment and the healing should take place 'of itself'.

The counsellor working with the skilled helper model needs the same groundedness, the same awareness of the pain that living can bring, the same openness to the individual experience of that pain, as counsellors working within any other therapeutic approach. At the same time, Egan's writing and the structure of his therapeutic framework communicate the conviction that every individual carries within them a potential that has not been realised. Even, and especially, when clients have little sense of new possibilities for themselves, the counsellor must have access to that awareness.

For the counsellor to use the types of intervention proposed in stages two and three of the skilled helper model presupposes the existence in the therapy room of the quality of hopefulness. There is ample evidence of the links between enhanced coping strategies and an optimistic or hopeful cognitive set (Salovey et al. 2000). For example, the theory underlying placebo therapy is that the raising of the level of hopefulness can have a discernible positive impact on health. Some connection with a sense of hopefulness can be demonstrated as intrinsic to the search for improved mental and emotional functioning, as indeed it is to the maintenance of good health (Taylor et al. 2000). Whilst a positive mindset may be elusive to the client – or awakened only with great difficulty – it is a candle that must be kept alight in the counsellor. Supervision, however it is accessed, may need to be used to sustain that belief in the possibility that some elements of positive movement in the client may be realised.

For us to enquire into a possible re-ordering of the person's world or of his or her relationship to that world assumes the existence in the client of the resource of imagination. At some level, we are anticipating the existence of creative skills in that person: a measure of openness to new experience, of flexibility, of divergent thinking (see Carr 2004). We assume that the person will, at some point, and however dimly, have the ability to perceive the possibility of inhabiting an altered self.

To pursue the second stage of the model and to ask whether the goal of change is grounded in reality involves the client in a process of critical self-evaluation. At this point in the therapeutic process, the client needs access not just to a connection with consensual reality (in which 'realistic' options can be distinguished from manifest fantasy), but to a cognitive and emotional competence that allows her to discriminate between safe and unsafe, what is doable and out of reach, likely and improbable. She is appraising her own resources and resourcefulness to attain objectives that may well take her beyond what she has achieved in her life thus far. Here again, the process of the therapy is constructed on an expressed or implied consent between counsellor and client that resources exist which can now or at some point be brought into play.

The skilled helper model reflects the philosophy to be found in the positive psychology movement. The interest of the counsellor is to enquire into the version of wellness that the client desires, and to support her some way along the road to the achievement of that condition. The supervisor working to the skilled helper framework needs to communicate a similar spirit of well-grounded hopefulness. As well as assisting the counsellor to understand her perception of and responses to the client's distress, the supervisor should be prepared to offer the stage two questions: 'Where is the client headed?', 'What is she or he hoping for from all of this?'. What follows, then, is to support the counsellor in elaborating her understanding of what resources clients have and may be helped to engage, in the pursuit of a better, more satisfying way of living this part of their lives.

Shapeshifter: narrative, social constructionist and feminist perspectives on the skilled helper model

My first experience of the skilled helper model came in the late 1980s as a student on a certificate course in counselling that embraced the model as a frame for helping practice. On the one hand, the model offered a map through which to explore challenging personal and relational territory, whilst on the other it was a source of succour – a place of safety and security when faced with chaos and conflict. As a beginning counsellor this was powerful medicine. In many respects, as a practitioner, I proceeded to 'grow up' with the evolving editions of the *Skilled Helper Model*, mirroring its 'shapeshifting' over the years and subsequent versions to its current embodiment (Egan 2002a).

As someone who has facilitated students' learning about Egan's skilled helper work, I love to witness the celebratory experiences when the content and processes of the model finally fall into place in their minds and practices – I almost said 'hearts and minds' here, remembering the many students who have initially resisted, only to then learn to love its flexibility and soundness as a relational map.

What is this resistance to the model? One example is my own early difficulties, based on early negative encounters with arithmetic. An ambivalent teacher–pupil relationship and a resulting defensive block against learning were in later years projected onto Egan and his model – hardly conducive to effective and creative learning! Thankfully, with perseverance, this block dispersed. Crucially, along the way I had the good fortune to encounter practitioners and trainers who brought the model alive for me in meaningful and creative ways – including Egan himself, on one of his UK seminars in the early 1990s.

Over time I integrated the model and its ideas into my humanistic-based practice. This capacity to 'shapeshift' and integrate into different approaches to helping practice is one of the model's key strengths. Unsurprisingly, I am not alone in adapting it in this way. For example, Winslade and Monk's social constructionist narrative counselling places the skilled helper at its core (Winslade and Monk 1999, 2000). Like the skilled helper model, in Winslade's approach the client's capacity to mobilise his or her life and relational skills is central to the helping and change process. Relational responsibility within the helping relationship, in ways similar to the skilled helper model, is shared between client and practitioner – a development that is also resonant with Gergen's interpretation of socially constructive and collaborative helping (Gergen 1994a, 1994b, 1997, 1999; Gergen and Gergen 2003; Gergen and Kaye 1992).

The tone of this piece so far has been largely positive yet, undoubtedly, a significant challenge for those new to the model is its denseness and complexity. Whilst life itself is a paradoxical relationship between complexity and simplicity (and the model certainly reflects this), for learners this can be daunting and hinder the learning experience. Some learners never pass stage one of the model, finding this phase most aptly fits with their view of helping as a story-telling activity. Others stay with the dynamic, action-oriented stage three, regarding the helper–client encounter as a means to an end, thereby using it akin to a cognitive-behavioural or coaching approach.

Although the model is often regarded as being cognitive-behaviourist in origin, Egan bases his thinking firmly within a humanistic paradigm. In many respects, he is one of the original integrative theorists and practitioners. His work acknowledges the significant role of the working alliance between helper and client, seeing it as a collaborative venture in which the helper's key task is to facilitate the client's ability to access and utilise the model's capacity as a change 'tool'. When the helping process works well, the model then becomes the client's personal and relational resources.

Although there is no space here to provide a detailed critique of the skilled helper model, it is interesting to speculate briefly on how, say, feminist informed practice might view the model. In relation to helping, feminist ideas have significantly informed our understanding of the power dynamic in the helper–client relationship and work (see, for example, Chaplin 1988; Gabriel 2005; Gilligan 1982; Russell 1999a, 1999b; Sherwin 2001). As noted above, and in its favour, the skilled helper model promotes a relationship characterised by collaboration and mutuality, whereby the therapist/helper imparts the principles and practices of the model, so that the client can make it his or her own. In relation to the lived reality of the power dynamic in the helping work and relationship, this can go some way to militate against the helper being regarded as 'expert'. To this end, the model resonates with social constructionist and feminist-informed practice, where mutuality and collaborative work are valued.

Despite its utility and being embedded in a range of helping approaches, little published research exists as to the model's validity or reliability as a helping approach. Although it incorporates within its theoretical base thinking and practice that are substantiated by empirical research evidence (e.g. cognitive behavioural therapy and positive psychology), we need to examine further its claims as an effective helping agent.

In the hands of a skilful and aware practitioner, the skilled helper model can be fleshed into life in creative and productive ways, across a range of helping, social and cultural contexts. In addition, given its flexibility and capacity for integrative practice, the model is well placed to thrive in the current UK helping field, where there is a fast-growing market for coaching and mentoring. Unashamedly, the skilled helper model offers accessible, tangible and proactive tools for this type of work. My interpretation of the model continues to evolve. Currently, I especially value its capacity to accommodate and embrace both chaos and control – an ability that is fundamental to work in a helping field that is subject, as ever, to powerful social and cultural forces.

Moving from loss to hope: the skilled helper model as an integrative framework for bereavement counselling

The emotionally charged area of bereavement work is not one that would instinctively lend itself to a skills-based approach. None-theless, I have found the skilled helper model to be both flexible and containing enough to work effectively in this demanding area, allowing integration of different concepts according to client need.

Much work has been done in establishing a pattern for the grieving process and the similarities across different types of loss. The attachment history of the individual (Bowlby 1988) is often key, along with predisposing factors such as cause of death and social context for the bereaved person. A generally accepted way of looking at grief is to use the stages of mourning as described by Parkes or Worden (Parkes 1996; Worden 1991). Although the process of mourning has a range of experiences and emotional responses that are often common, it is a very individual response. Therefore, people come into counselling with very varied issues, from the totally practical to the intensely emotional.

Whilst attachment theory acts as a construct for understanding the basis of the grief response and there are explanations for the process of grief that allow us to evaluate and understand what is happening for the client, there remains the question in counselling of how to help someone move through this process and what is the best way to do this. One useful way I have found to think about this is expressed well by Horton as 'utilising some overarching framework or higher-order or transtheoretical concept that provides internal consistency whilst at the same time allowing for the assimilation of explanatory concepts and/or methods from other schools or approaches' (2002a: 284).

My early counselling work was with bereaved clients and, having trained in the skilled helper model a few years ago, my learning from the different needs of each client in this area led me towards an integrative way of working. Since then I have continued exploring a range of different theories of counselling and psychotherapy with an interest in how people actually apply different concepts to the process with the client rather than academic descriptions. Integration seems to address the necessary diversity and breadth of the work whilst holding the relationship at the centre, something of paramount importance in bereavement counselling.

As a reflective practitioner, I have spent time exploring aspects of personality development, of what it means to be human and how we interact with others on many levels. Working within the skilled helper model allows me to draw on different concepts and theories to aid both my own and the clients' understanding of what is happening to them and their responses to it.

For many clients, their adult response to death is something learned from those around them in childhood. For instance, for the client who has come because he is struggling to deal with the death of a parent, there may be the discovery that the earlier loss of a grandparent is still with him and is unresolved. Working with this client in stage one of the skilled helper model, but using a psychodynamic viewpoint, we can begin to get an understanding of the impact of the past on his current experiencing. The enormous impact of learned patterns of behaviour can be seen in the client's suppression of grief, a response that he saw in the adults around him as a child. In using active listening, advanced empathy and normalisation of the client's response, we can allow the expression of emotions and facilitate the resolution of delayed grief and the possibility of then working with current losses.

Integration of many theoretical concepts can be useful in stage one of the model; existential thinking becomes important in consideration, both for the client and for ourselves, of our own mortality and particularly facing the death of our parents; clients can feel abandoned and unloved when someone close to them dies and the concept of life scripts from transactional analysis can bring an understanding and framework for exploration with clients whose self-esteem has been greatly affected by the loss.

The flexibility of the skilled helper model allows me to work for as long as is necessary in stage one, and sometimes this can be all that the work requires. At other times, resolution or acceptance of the loss requires further work, such as the case of a client who had been unable to be present at the death of a loved one or did not have the chance to say the things he or she wanted. In this situation, questions exploring this area and leading to stage two can be useful, such as: 'How would you have liked it to have been?' and 'What would you have liked to say?'. Allowing clients to explore what they might have gained from being able to do these things can then be rephrased into 'How would it be to gain some of that now?' and thence to 'How might you be able to achieve this?'. For some clients, this means writing a letter to the dead person, for others it may mean visiting the grave and saying the words out loud.

For some clients, moving on is important and the work then becomes more future oriented, both in terms of the model and in terms of what the client needs to achieve. Bereaved clients are, or course, left with a sense of loss. This may not just be in terms of the person who has died but may also be experienced as the loss of a sense of direction and guidance in their lives, particularly when the death is of a partner. There have been many times when a client has said to me that, whilst it is helpful to understand how and why they are in this situation, or reacting as they are, what can they do about making things different in the here and now? At times, when a client has asked this, I have been transported back to my skills practice group of my first year of training, with the step 2A question hanging in the air: 'How would you like it to be?' and we are off down a well-worn, but nonetheless worthwhile, track towards a new way of being.

Stages two and three of the skilled helper model can be used effectively to look at practical issues around day-to-day existence or sometimes more significantly at re-establishing social contact and support. Integration within the framework of the model allows for management and resolution of the strong and sometimes overwhelming emotions associated with bereavement but also encompasses the important task of maintaining and improving day-to-day functioning and the gradual development of a future-oriented view.

Endings are extremely significant in bereavement work, including the ending of the counselling relationship. Again, the skilled helper model can be used to facilitate this in a client-centred way that allows for growth and development within a 'good ending'. The stage two question of 'How would you like it (our ending) to be?' is often in the back of my mind and sometimes explicitly voiced, as a way of offering a contrast between the ending of the counselling work and that of the bereavement.

I like the thoughts of Yalom when he says that 'the therapist must strive to create a new therapy for each patient' (Yalom 2001: 34). As I move forward in my counselling work and reflect on what I do, despite my sense of moving away from the skilled helper model, I realise that I come back to it when I least expect it. In bereavement work, and in other areas, I am now using it in a flexible and individual way, sometimes just as a very light holding and framework for myself and the client and sometimes more clearly working with the stages in collaboration with the client – either way it provides a sense of direction for the work.

The skilled helper model and the art of motorcycle maintenance

Before I started training as a counsellor my background was in theatre and performance, with a specialisation in street theatre with all its rough edges and unplanned interruptions. That discipline involves a predetermined structure to the performance containing specific stages (crowd-build, applause routine, manufacture of suspense, cajoling spectators for contributions, climax and collection) that is augmented by a never-ending search for, and honing of, tricks, techniques and bits of business that manipulate the spectator towards predetermined reactions and specific mental spaces.

Unsurprisingly then, I initially found the skilled helper model very attractive, with its specific stages alongside an apparent emphasis on methodology and results. The Lazarus technique (see Egan 2002a: 238) for finding areas of leverage, brainstorming and cost/benefit balance-sheet exercises all appeared valuable bits of business to me. I regularly saw work in the preferred scenario stage initiating sudden and powerful 'AHA-type' moments of insight for clients and this convinced me that I was dealing with very powerful magic here indeed. This in turn led me to begin raiding the cupboards of other approaches and searching for similar treasures in order to build a repertoire of interventions that could be called on to meet whatever challenge the client presented.

I still believe that one of the great strengths of the skilled helper model is that it gives counsellors trained in it permission to go and explore other approaches and search for elements, including models of the personality, which may enhance their practice and understanding. It allows the individual practitioner's version of the model to remain a work in progress that can be built on or equally have components stripped away as the experience and wisdom of the helper develops. I imagine it as a lovingly home-built car or motorbike that is regularly maintained, experimented with and which improves as the owner's knowledge and expertise increase.

However, I am now personally at a point where I feel I am stripping down the vehicle, getting rid of all the unnecessary parts to try and rediscover what it is that makes the thing run unencumbered by tricks, devices and techniques. A few months ago, motivated by my frustration at what I perceived to be some students' stubborn determination to solve their clients' problems for them at any cost, I had a session with a client free of challenges, imagined futures, areas of leverage and cost/benefit analysis. All I did for the entire hour was reflect and paraphrase. I came away convinced that something special had happened (that I am still unable to fully define) and a sense that there had been a greater degree of warmth in the room than I was used to experiencing in my counselling sessions.

I have not seen Egan practise and I am convinced that I would learn a great deal from doing so. But in his writing style there is for me a hectoring quality that sounds sceptical regarding the possibility of positive change arrived at through the client's experience of the core conditions or insight – what he terms 'discretionary change' (Sugarman 1995), and a continual insistence on action leading to tangible results. I have a sense that my initial acceptance of this priority began to block out my engagement with the relationship in the room. I believe that somewhere in my desire to encourage clients to problem-manage, set SMART goals and envision preferred scenarios, the core conditions began to gradually dissipate.

Egan has written that he stands on the shoulders of Rogers. I now think that if as trainers or counsellors we stop primarily locating ourselves in the core conditions and the counsellor/client relationship then we are working with a model that has lost its foundations. It is in danger of tumbling down around us in a debris of half-formed and rarely achieved goals that can create power struggles between the counsellor and client and possibly leave the client further disempowered than she may have been at the beginning of the relationship.

I am currently entering the counselling room unencumbered by picture cards, cognitive-behavioural formulae and any other props. I am aspiring to encounter the client free of tricks, techniques and bits of business and simply to be a person in his wholeness wholly attending. I do not fully understand it but it feels as if something has shifted in my practice – that a block has been moved and there is a new momentum in the room.

In the course of one week recently, a client with quite tangible mental health issues had a sudden moment of insight as to their origin, a client with issues around addiction who had resisted all my previous attempts at goal setting announced that he had been clean for three months and I shared some time with an angry young woman where she considered her relationship to God, which I believe we both found quite profound. It is as if by finally having the resolve to steady myself and step gingerly out from behind the reassuring structure of a tried and tested model, and then daring to try and simply be one person in relationship to another, I am beginning to experience in this relationship a more profound and healing quality than I have previously found. For now I need to spend some time becoming familiar with this quality and working out how best to use it before returning to the model or maybe letting it lead me into new areas of practice.

I feel that I need to stress that this is a stripping back of Egan's model not a rejection of it. I am in agreement with Egan's perception that the skilled helper model simply makes explicit a natural human process that occurs during most successful therapy. As a practitioner I now tend to use the model as a map or a template that I can refer to whenever the client or I need to ask: 'Where are we now?' and 'Where do you think we could be headed?'. Only instead of having the model drive the process, I am now taking a deep breath and allowing the clients to spend most of the time at the steering wheel, allowing myself to travel with them on the apparent detours and short-cuts they take, and beginning to suspect that there might really be a movement by the client towards self-actualisation that is driving the process; that the detours and short-cuts might really be leading somewhere. I believe that this is in keeping with Egan's assertion that the model should be flexible and has a holographic nature. It is, however, a rejection of Egan's admonition 'that we overemphasise Stage 1' (Sugarman 1995), or his assertion that 'most benefits . . . lie down the line in helping them [the clients] determine what they want' (*ibid.*).

As a trainer, I have no issues with teaching the skilled helper model. I believe that it gives students a theoretical framework that is quite clear and tangible to work from. An advantage of its apparent lack of a model of personality is that there is no demand on the student to take a leap of faith and base her practice on concepts such as the life script of transactional analysis or the figure-and-ground of Gestalt. I also believe that this same apparent omission will encourage students to engage in continuing professional and personal development beyond their diploma training. There are a number of philosophical and conceptual questions that Egan does not answer, such as what it is in our human nature that drives us towards positive change or the search for meaning in our existence, which I believe need to be addressed as students begin to engage with the challenges of professional accreditation.

For me, the biggest issue in training emerges within the skills practice element. On the one hand, I need to insist that students locate themselves where the client actually is at a given moment without immediately feeling compelled to dutifully drag her protesting through the various steps and stages of the model. On the other hand, there is the necessity of requiring that the journey is actually undertaken in the face of reluctance or lack of confidence on the part of the student.

Using and teaching the skilled helper model: an accommodation of creativity and ambivalence

Looking back over my experience as a counsellor I would say that as a student I found the skilled helper model frustrating and prescriptive. The structure felt for me like a strait-jacket. As a result, I found it restricting and at times regretted the choice to study it as my core model.

I had initially chosen to complete my counsellor training on a course where the skilled helper was the core training model because I liked the look of the model and felt that the practical and down-to-earth aspects appealed to the pragmatist inherent in me. In my written work and in skills groups it soon became apparent that I was critical of the model at every opportunity. My interests lay more towards the humanistic end of the theoretical spectrum and that was where much of my reading was directed, and still is to this day. I would currently describe myself as an integrative counsellor who draws largely from humanistic approaches.

Once qualified and working in the first instance for a voluntary agency and subsequently for a student counselling service, I did not consciously use the model. In fact, at that time I suspect I would have argued vehemently that I was definitely not using any part of it. However, I did, on occasion, find that I was using one specific step, and that was helping clients to look at possibilities for a future that might be better or in some way different. I would offer it as a way of encouraging people to think creatively and divergently.

I can think of several clients for whom this worked very well. For one in particular it put back into her life something that had been missing for some time and that she almost forgot about. A long-held dream for this client had been to dance professionally but she had been unable to fulfil this ambition. When she looked at what she might ideally want in her life in the future she realised she wanted to dance again, which she subsequently did by joining a local dance class. I now regularly use creative material, shells, stones, paper, writing, colour and images, and have found that these work well when used as invitations to clients to draw, sculpt or shape their preferred scenarios.

Later I began to do some training work and eventually became a module tutor on a BA course in Counselling Studies. This is a degree programme for undergraduates and is not a professional counsellor training. Few of the students will go on to become counsellors and most will apply the counselling skills they have learned in other professions. After a year or so I was asked to teach the skilled helper model to first-year students, initially only the second and third stages. This meant that I went back to the book and re-read it, still with a real sense of ambivalence towards it. I would say now that I am more familiar with the model than I was whilst training and the ambivalence is still there. However, now I feel that I can see more clearly how I integrate aspects of this model into my everyday practice, which has been something of a surprise. I can also see its value as a framework, particularly as a training tool.

I am still resistant to some of the structure of the model and prefer to live with the reality of the individual client and this, for them, might not be about goal setting or action planning. I am also not comfortable with some of the notions around change that I see as inherent in the model. For instance, Egan (1998:31) states that helping is about working towards 'constructive change'. Whilst in principle I agree that counselling *can* be about constructive change, I would never presume that this is the basis for continuing with the work. I can work, and have worked with people for whom change, at least at that particular time in their life, was not possible or desirable.

I have gone on to teach all three stages of the skilled helper model and have had the experience this academic year of taking some of the current first-year cohort of students through the model in its entirety. I am now back teaching the later stages of the model with a colleague and we have been introducing these to students in a more creative way.

Recently, we took creative materials into a lecture and invited the students in training triads to explore stages two and three in as imaginative a way as possible. Our aim was to present the model in a way that was different from what we had previously done, which at times felt to us to be didactic and quite dry. We wanted to encourage the students to experience using some steps, particularly the first steps of stages two and three, and to enable them to see that asking clients to 'think outside the box' could be done successfully in this way. So we asked them, when in the helper role, to invite the client to draw how he or she would like things to be in the future, or to use stones to represent aspects of how life might look if it was better. We took in a wide range of resources: feathers, stones, shells, buttons, paper, pens, crayons, finger paints, pipe cleaners and postcards. The results were really very good, so good that many of them asked if they could continue to use creative materials in their skills groups. They had clearly enjoyed the activity and, during the debriefing afterwards, some said that they had learnt something interesting about themselves, especially when in the role of client.

When we had finished the formal teaching element of the model we asked the students to draw all the steps and stages as a way of pulling it all together. We asked them to create a visual image on paper for each of the stages and steps. Again the results were enlightening and it is interesting that some similar themes emerged. For instance, all four groups on one day drew something about a wedding, for example wedding rings, for commitment (stage 2C) and perhaps not surprisingly all had a book for story (stage 1A). There were some interesting images for change agenda (stage 2B), including a boardroom table with people seated around it. Again the level of energy and enjoyment was high – in fact when I put up the official overview of the model, the joke was that their versions were much more interesting, much less boring and certainly more creative than mine!

I suppose what I have come to understand is that there are aspects of the model that are as flexible and creative as you allow them to be. Whilst I do not use the skilled helper model as a whole, I do now recognise (and own up to the fact) that I use elements of it. Teaching it has enabled me to look at this model in a different light, and a more positive one certainly. I am now more comfortable with acknowledging that the way in which clients can be encouraged to think outside their current situation (and the limitations that go with that) is a strength of the model. However, even whilst acknowledging its strengths, it is also true for me that the model's structure, and what I consider to be its prescriptive notions around change, mean that my ambivalence lives on.

Rediscovering holy aspirations: integrating the skilled helper model as a therapist and teacher

Shortly after being invited to write this piece I was re-reading some extracts from Erving Goffman's (1969) *The Presentation of Self in Everyday Life* and was struck by a passage that seemed to describe my experience of engaging with Egan's skilled helper model. In this passage, Goffman discusses what he sees as a natural movement between cynicism and sincerity and cites the work of Becker and Greer with medical students, who describe how idealistically oriented beginners typically lay aside 'holy aspirations' for a period of time before rediscovering them. Research here suggests that medical students tend to lose sight of their formative aspirations when they are required to focus on the tasks of learning about disease and how to pass examinations, but that once their medical training has ended they then rediscover their original ideas and ideals about medical service.

I had come to training in counselling following a career in health service management, and wanting to find opportunities to work with individuals in ways in which the interpersonal relationship was the prime focus. My response to Egan's skilled helper model was therefore somewhat ambivalent. Its similarities to business management theories felt at odds with my understanding of the philosophical and psychological theories underpinning counselling. I felt as if my beliefs about the uniqueness of individuals and the myriad of ways in which people make sense of the world and in which they solve problems, needed to be held in check whilst I came to grips with working within the steps and stages of a structured model. I struggled with distinguishing between a problem-management model and my desire to become a warm, empathic presence. I came to develop a love–hate relationship with the skilled helper model, which endured throughout my Certificate and Diploma courses.

I was fortunate in being introduced to the skilled helper model by two trainers who, in addition to being well versed in the model, were also Gestalt-trained therapists. From them I obtained a sense of how the model could be used as a map in counselling and how aspects of other theories could be integrated into it, for example how Gestalt techniques could be introduced to help clients to view blind spots and new perspectives.

People often believe that change means getting rid of particular patterns of behaviour and curbing or restraining certain qualities in themselves. In contrast to this, Gestalt theory of change focuses on the notion of the paradox of change, as stated by Beisser (1970: 77): 'Change occurs when one becomes what he is, not when he tries to become what he is not.' Thus I have found integrating techniques that encourage client self-awareness useful (particularly in stage one of the skilled helper model) in relation to discovering and highlighting aspects of the client that might undermine their apparent desire to change. One way I might do this is to encourage clients to focus on and describe bodily sensations, such as a knot in the stomach. This might help them to understand that this feeling signals a chiding voice that can undermine their attempts at change by suggesting that they ought to behave or feel differently.

My growing view of the potential of the skilled helper model to provide an integrative framework was influential in my choice of advanced training at Diploma level. I had come to view the model as a foundation stone upon which I could build the subsequent development of my own style of counselling. If asked, I would now describe myself as being an integrative, humanistic counsellor. I cannot say that the skilled helper model is now foremost in my mind when sitting with an individual but it provides some of the structure to the backcloth. What *is* in the forefront of my mind is my relationship with the individual client; the backcloth is composed of all the threads of theories about development, personality and cognitive processes I have acquired. The three-stage model – the clients' current experience, how they would wish themselves and their life to be and how they might achieve this – can then provide a framework for the process.

Following training, my initial counselling work was in organisations that allowed open-ended contracts where I was counselling individuals on a relatively long-term basis. Like Becker and Greer's medical students, I found myself re-engaging with my 'holy aspirations' and drawing more on person-centred theories than using the skilled helper model in any overt way. However, in retrospect, I am aware of how much it provided a subconscious map for the counselling process.

I then began working in an organisation providing short-term counselling and drew more overtly on the model in establishing a focus for brief work. I found that in undertaking initial meetings and assessments my exploration of the client's reasons for seeking counselling, his or her desired outcomes and my ideas of how I might be of help could all be loosely framed by the stages of the skilled helper model as well as this framework being useful to guide the subsequent work.

Post-training, my counselling was supervised by a supervisor who had also trained in the skilled helper model and who was interested in and influenced by psychodynamic theories. Her support enabled me to continue a process of learning how to use the framework of the model in a way which was consistent with my own beliefs and in sympathy with different philosophical and psychological theories.

The skilled helper is a model that is characterised by logic and linear thinking, whilst I tend to value intuition, creativity and subjective experience. I am therefore drawn to elements of psychodynamic and Gestalt theory, in particular the importance of childhood experience and the significance of dreams. Supervision has enabled me to develop ways of working with my intuitive hunches and those of my clients while retaining aspects of the skilled helper model. Personally, I find metaphor a powerful means of accessing intuitive learning and will encourage clients to use metaphor as means of describing the self, either working with the images they spontaneously provide or asking them to describe or draw an image of themselves or a situation.

My initial work using counselling skills and then practising as a counsellor included bereavement work, advocacy work in the mental health field and befriending carers of people with Alzheimer's disease. I can clearly remember thinking at points during training that the skilled helper model was inappropriate for use with some of these clients – how could I ask someone who was recently bereaved what her ideal scenario looked like when the return of a loved one was impossible? Similarly, would it not be irresponsible and possibly dangerous to encourage someone whose grasp on reality was tenuous to engage in suspending judgement and brainstorming wild possibilities? However, it was through working with these client groups that I learnt about the import- ance of allowing and enabling individuals to hope and dream and the potential of stage two of the model for engendering this. This is the part of the skilled helper model that I have come to value the most and which I have found most useful in my practice. Integral to this has been developing ways of using creative media (post- cards, stones, paints, etc.) to visually represent preferred (and current) scenarios.

In view of this it is not surprising that in teaching the model to undergraduate students of counselling I have found myself empha- sising the importance of stage two and striving to find ways in which this can be taught creatively as well as fostering creative means to help clients generate possibilities. Recently, using a case study, I suggested that students draw or create a map of the counselling interaction through viewing the dialogue as a journey. I used prompts such as the following to stimulate this process:

- Were there points at which the counsellor and client climbed a hill together to get a better view of the way ahead, or to understand the terrain they had crossed and why they needed to carry with them particular equipment?

- Did they need to try several exits from a roundabout?
- If there were unexpected obstacles, did this require demolition equipment or a detour?

The pictures they created were rich and gave a visual representation of using the skilled helper model in a non-linear and flexible way.

Finally, I would add that perhaps the part of the model that has figured least in my own counselling practice has been in the detailed planning steps of stage three (i.e. 3B and 3C). This may be so because it seems to me that many students (and clients) are familiar with goal-setting and action planning but have a tendency to think only in terms of familiar strategies to achieve outcomes rather than in terms of generating lots of ideas about possible scenarios and solutions. It is the creative and expansive steps of stages two and three (2A and 3A) that I find most liberating for my clients and students in helping them think 'outside of the box'.

Never the twain?: integrating psychodynamic ways of working within the skilled helper model

I should start by explaining that my philosophical orientation is rooted in the humanistic perspective that everyone has the capacity to grow and achieve their potential given the right conditions. The importance of the therapeutic relationship using the core conditions of empathy, respect and congruence is central to my counselling practice. I believe that a balance of support and challenge has to be present to facilitate change.

I find that my training in Egan's skilled helper model, which finished over two years ago, has given me a useful, practical and flexible framework in which to operate, and I would say that my approach is becoming increasingly integrative as my knowledge base increases. The aspects that I find most useful about Egan's integrated cognitive-behavioural model in the humanistic tradition are his emphasis on the therapeutic alliance, the collaborative nature of counselling, the notion of client empowerment and the role of judicious goal setting. I have also found the future-oriented stage of his model – 'Where do you want to be?' – a particularly effective and creative way of working with some clients.

Within his model Egan promotes the idea of systematic eclecticism, whereby elements from other approaches can be located on the 'map' he provides and used in a client-responsive way. However, if the definition of eclecticism is separating out and the definition of integration is bringing together, then this latter idea of placing complementary ideas from different approaches within an existing framework is more accurately what I do.

Egan points out that his model is not the 'whole curriculum' and suggests building up a supplementary knowledge base to become a more effective helper. Early on in my counselling practice came an awareness of needing to know more when a client asked, 'Why am I in an abusive relationship when I'm not from an abusive background?'. Discussing in supervision that abused people always have low self-esteem and that low self-esteem is always rooted in the past, it seemed that here was an opportunity for exploration with a client who wanted to understand her present situation by looking at past experience.

Egan does not dwell in the past but, from my limited knowledge of psychodynamic practice and transactional analysis, I knew that these two approaches could help me with this perceived gap. I wanted to discover more about two areas of interest in particular, namely a coherent theory of personality – 'Why are we the way we are?' – and also about developmental stages, how people change over the course of their lives. Both curriculum additions are suggested by Egan with a proviso that an awareness of cultural factors goes hand in hand with these.

My subsequent work as an associate in a predominantly psychodynamic therapy centre with a psychodynamic supervisor gave me access to an enormous amount of knowledge, understanding and insightful perspectives from this different theoretical approach, which I have tried to integrate into my practice there and elsewhere. Whilst not embracing the more directive, diagnostic and interpretative ways of working from psychodynamic practice, and indeed not being qualified to do so, I have found myself able to bring in and share my understanding of aspects of transference, developmental stages, defences and the role of the subconscious in a client-responsive way. By doing this I can ask my clients, as well as myself, the question that Jacobs (1991: 160) defines as central to psychodynamic practice, namely, 'What does it . . . (this word, that action, this memory, that feeling, this aspect of our relationship, that symbol, this defence, that explanation) . . . what does it mean?'.

I have also found that my knowledge of transactional analysis, built up by teaching this approach to students on a counselling skills certificate course for the last eighteen months, has worked its way into my practice. Offering and sharing my knowledge with some clients about ego states and life scripts gives them accessible tools to understand thoughts, feelings, behaviours and their possible origins. Berne set out to demystify psychodynamic theory and place it within a humanistic context. His aim was to promote client autonomy and I find this sits well with Egan's goal of client empowerment. Both wish to give clients choice and the ability to change their situation if they so wish.

An example of the way I have integrated some of this into my practice can be illustrated by reference to my client Rachel (a pseudonym) in the abusive relationship, mentioned above. We spent several sessions looking at her past and present relationship with her dominant and critical mother and her suppression of self, which was a theme in many of her relationships. The telling of the story threw up many examples of ways in which Rachel's self-esteem had been eroded, resulting in a chronic lack of confidence and therefore a vulnerability to being dominated by a stronger personality. This, of course, is what had happened when she met the abuser at a time in her life when she was feeling particularly low. Rachel was very quick to grasp the significance of her background experiences in relation to her present difficulties – the sessions were full of insights for her and she was eager to gain some understanding.

By sharing knowledge of ego states, together with that of the victim/persecutor/rescuer drama triangle, Rachel was enabled to see that the role she played out with her mother, that of the compliant, occasionally rebellious 'adapted child' in response to her mother's 'controlling parent' was also one she was repeating in the present with the abuser, albeit with more severe physical consequences. Perversely, one of the pay-offs for staying in the relationship was an enhanced sense of self-esteem through being associated with this socially well-regarded and seemingly powerful figure.

After establishing the leverage issue from this exploration of the dynamic of her current situation, we moved on later to work with her preferred scenario. I asked Rachel ideally what she would want in a relationship. She was able to identify the goals of being in an *equal* partnership and having the confidence to be herself. By gaining insight into the power dynamics of relationships, I believe Rachel was able to engage with this stage of the model in a more meaningful way. She went on to take action, initially by establishing boundaries in the abusive relationship, with encouraging results. This led to trying out new behaviours in other relationships with similar success. After some time she was eventually able to build enough confidence and develop a strong enough sense of self to leave the relationship altogether.

I find that not all clients need to sift through the past in this way, but for some it is extremely helpful. Rachel and I met for over two years, which allowed for this more in-depth work. Much of the time I am not aware of the skilled helper model or any other theoretical approach when I am with my clients; it is only later writing up the notes that I realise how embedded this framework has become and how seamlessly other elements, including those from psychodynamic theory and practice, can be interwoven with it.

Contradictory or complementary?: using the skilled helper model in supervision to help develop 'client-centred' counsellors

When I was asked for a contribution to this book I felt very positive about having an opportunity to write about something that has become increasingly part of my conscious awareness in the supervisory relationships I experience. My own counsellor training was based on Egan's skilled helper model (Val Wosket being one of my trainers) and I remember well my own struggles with the model as a student. It often felt too complex to remember easily and yet, paradoxically, there was something very straightforward and de-mystifying about a helping process that unfolded through various steps and stages.

Many of the counsellors I offer supervision to now happen to be relatively inexperienced therapists and/or trainees and all have been schooled in the skilled helper model. I think it is fair to say that not one person has come to me as an unreservedly enthusiastic fan of the skilled helper framework. I encounter some familiar attitudes to the model. I come across comments about it being overly complicated and somewhat mechanistic, or it seeming to be rather too objective and task-focused. I hear observations about the model taking little account of the client–counsellor relationship and how this impacts upon the process of counselling in general and problem/opportunity-identification and management strategies in particular. I share some of these concerns to an extent, as well as having other questions of my own.

So how come, despite these reservations, a number of my supervisory sessions bear witness to the words 'model', 'Egan', 'helper' and 'skilled' issuing from my lips? Well, I think this is something to do with not throwing the baby out with the bath water. Sometimes, when I explore my supervisee's interventions and relating style with her client, it is as if she has had an aversion reaction to the skilled helper model and, as a consequence, the baby and the bath water have both gone. By this I mean that there has been a shift on her part completely away from anything that might feel mechanistic, or outcome-driven, or in any way questioning of the client's motivations or actual purpose. She may be working with metaphor, or artwork or something creative, but there is no real sense of the purpose or reason for its introduction into the counselling space. Instead there is just a vague sense that this is working in a 'person-centred' way because it doesn't seem to pressurise the client into accounting for why he might be there in the first place or figuring out what he might want or need.

To pursue my own metaphor further, the bath water might be the more formulaic and deterministic aspects of the model as perceived by some trainees. These elements sometimes seem to jar with their sense of the relationship needing to be at the centre of resolving longer-term inner conflict in the client. The baby, for me, is the framework, which can be useful, particularly to trainee and inexperienced counsellors, in providing them with a 'how to' guide and a sound orientation within the helping process.

Let me try to illustrate this with an example. Several sessions into a relationship with a new client, my supervisee has used some artwork. She has followed the client from metaphor to metaphor but wonders when to intervene and whether or not this might be intrusive or interpretive. She has accepted the client's movement from childhood anecdote to a description of his partner's behaviour. She introduces some pebbles to help her client explore relationships in his life. But ultimately she has become lost and unsure of herself. Her integrity and preferred orientation is apparent in our discussion in the supervision session around her wanting to offer non-directive support. But in circumstances such as this, this looks more like 'directionless' or 'indirectly directive' support, with all its attendant but unresolved confusion, anxiety and conflict – not least on the part of the client.

I hear myself, hopefully between empathic responses, attempting to facilitate some clarity for the counsellor through phrases that sound to me very much in the spirit of the skilled helper model:

- So remind me why the client has come to you in the first place.
- What is it that the client said he actually wanted from you/the helping?
- I wonder whether there is anything you might be doing that is adding to the client's sense of stuckness?
- Who has decided that this should be the focus for the counselling?
- It sounds like your client has decided that counselling is the answer – skilled helper model stage three if you like – but I don't hear anything that tells me the client is clear about what the actual issue is, which would be stage one.
- You've got a couple more sessions to go. What does he want to know, or feel, or do as a result of the counselling? What is his 'stage two' that counselling is supposed to help him achieve?

It is almost as if the desire to move away from something perceived as mechanistic into something that seems more 'human' has left the novice counsellor adrift, wanting to be 'creative' and to work empathically but feeling unsure what to do with her own part in the dynamic or how to give shape to the process. At this point I might encourage my supervisee to try and make sense of the client's position in terms of the skilled helper model:

- What did the client actually want from six counselling sessions?
- What specifically prompted the client to come to you?
- How do you think the client sees your presence within the helping process?
- What part of the skilled helper model might be accommodating the client 'going round in circles'?
- Is 'going round in circles' the problem itself or is it a difficulty in addressing another problem?
- Would it be helpful for the client to locate where 'going round in circles' is situated in the problem-management process?

and of their own position:

- What was the key difficulty for you in remaining client-centred?
- What would you ideally have liked to do in those difficult moments for you and the client?
- What would you want or need to do in order to offer more of your own experience to the client at that moment in a way that would have been more helpful?
- Is there some further self-development work that might be of help to you here?

This kind of approach does seem to allow my supervisees a reduction in feelings of confusion and anxiety sufficient for an effective level of intentionality and process-insight to occur. Here, at least, is a background framework of 'how to' and 'where we might go next' that can allow the developing counsellor to stay effective and client-focused. Working in this way in supervision does also seem to have an energising effect for my supervisees as they recognise and respond to their own feelings about the therapeutic relationship. I think they can then attend more readily to their own emotional response having more clearly and securely located themselves and their client within the skilled helper framework.

In conclusion, I would like to touch on the issue of counselling context and time limitations. Where the counsellor has relatively little experience of working in a time-limited setting, I have found the skilled helper model useful in helping my supervisee develop an ethical approach. By this I mean giving consideration to how to offer a framework of helping that allows for the client to leave counselling at a 'stage three' place, if that is what the client had indicated in some way that they wished to work towards. The framework of the model can offer a sense of containment for client, counsellor and process, so that the client who wants to walk away from (particularly short-term) counselling with a cognitive understanding of what has occurred and some plans for the future (rather than, say, merely 'an experience') does not leave feeling disenchanted, confused and wondering what it was all about.

Using the skilled helper model as a tool for analysis does also seem to help my supervisees recognise differences between the person-centred counselling they sometimes think they are engaged in and the integrative 'client-centred' styles they look, more accurately, to be in the process of developing. (I am making a necessary and important distinction here between purist person-centred counselling training – which my supervisees are *not* undertaking – and the ability to work in 'client-centred' ways that place client responsiveness at the heart of the counselling process – something that they *are* striving, through their integrative training, to acquire.)

I think what has surprised me most in considering this topic is the positive response I have had from supervisees who, as they gain experience, rediscover the framework of the skilled helper model, make friends with it and use it as a tool for orientation and creativity in their client work and indeed their own development. For less experienced and more recently qualified or training supervisees, offering the skilled helper model as a point of reference in supervision does seem to help create a sense of clarity in the work for themselves and their clients. This in turn seems to enhance client progress (whether towards a specific practical goal or towards growing self-acceptance and congruence), which might otherwise be impeded by the counsellor's lack of experience and self-awareness.

A paradoxical affair: blending relational and mechanistic elements in the teaching and learning of the skilled helper model

In this short piece I would like to explore the skilled helper model from the perspective of a trainer of helpers and counsellors. Egan's model formed the core theoretical model in which I was trained as a counsellor and I grew familiar with it over the two years I studied it. However, I think it was not until I had to teach it to others that I understood it in its entirety. This knowledge has been deepened by my reading of subsequent editions as the model has been brought up to date by its author.

It is common to hear counsellors, therapists, supervisors and trainers use the words 'model' and 'theory' as interchangeable. I feel that there is a need to distinguish between these two terms. A theory, as I see it, includes a relatively unique philosophy, one that can be largely distinguishable from another. There are a number of theoretical perspectives that can be understood in this way. Psychodynamic theory, humanistic theory and cognitive-behavioural theory are examples. Within these theoretical frameworks models have developed, many confined to one or other of them (e.g. solution-focused therapy, systemic therapy, person-centred therapy). Other models encompass or select elements from different theoretical strands and become integrative and eclectic approaches. I understand the skilled helper model to be an integrative model with a good deal of scope for including techniques and conceptual frameworks that have their roots in various theoretical soils.

I have taught elements of the model to groups of certificate-level counsellor trainees, to those studying for a professional diploma qualification, and to others – trainee teachers, careers service employees and staff colleagues. I have taught it in various degrees of complexity for about six years and I think the model's flexibility is the first quality I appreciated about it.

The skilled helper model is an integrative tool. It draws from many psychological and other perspectives and provides a strong, reliable working strategy. I find it straightforward and unpretentious. I think it reflects some of the values of its birthplace and its culture. It is forward looking and goal- and achievement-oriented. It has a no-nonsense tone to it that can be facilitating but can also feel reductionist. It can generate hope, energy and satisfying measurable outcomes. It can also not accommodate well to particular clients, contexts and therapeutic aims. I think the model is economical and functional and fits agreeably with the day-to-day experience of ordinary people in the individualised capitalist world.

I consider a strength of the skilled helper model to be that it provides a safe model for beginners. Through learning and applying this model, new helpers can increase their skills, extend their knowledge and offer some productive help to others. If novice helpers stick closely to the model guidelines, learn them thoroughly and engage in adapting them to their own style and context, I believe that they are likely to work from a sound baseline. Many will find themselves able to use elements of it in a variety of helping situations, as well as learning to use it in their day-to-day lives to identify their own goals and pursue them.

So the second quality I attribute to the model is that of a good starting point for many trainees and a sufficient finishing point for others. Employing the model well enough will produce some useful results, and if helpers keep to the map and use it flexibly, will keep them on the right road. However, as the author himself stresses, the model is not the total curriculum and consequently the map is only useful if it is used skilfully, in the context of a helping relationship imbued with the values that create and maintain an effective working alliance.

Therefore, my priority in teaching the skilled helper model is to emphasise the attitudes and values that create the potential for client–counsellor collaboration. This requires both exploration of elements of the therapeutic relationship and self-awareness on the part of the learner. The underpinning interpersonal context of helping requires a good enough relational style – one that to a minimal extent provides some psychological contact.

Helping, then, is most likely to be successful if the relationship works. How to teach relationship awareness and the communication skills required to convey that awareness is the subject of a myriad of books and Egan provides one useful source. As there is no one accepted method of setting out to do this, I will not attempt, in this brief discussion, to elaborate further on this essential element of training counsellors and helpers. I will look instead at aspects of teaching the model that assume that a helper has an adequate ability to work at relational depth together with the potential for psychological collaboration *and* that they can successfully communicate this to those they wish to help. I consider that for the model to be used ethically and productively requires that the helper must be at this point of departure. This also fits with the sequential nature of the model and how I believe it is best taught, in a logical order, where relationship comes first and foremost.

There are as many and various ways of developing the helper as there are contexts from which helpers are drawn. I think one of the major challenges of teaching the skilled helper model is to make sure that the relational and collaborative elements of helping are sufficiently in place with trainees before introducing them to the 'mechanics' of the model.

I have always taken great pains to challenge beginners to appreciate that their use of the skilled helper model should be flexible. I truly hope that not one trainee leaves a course taught by me thinking that someone has to be taken slavishly through each and every stage and step of the model. However, somewhat paradoxically, I also recognise that for trainees to be able, first, to locate themselves on the map and, second, to make best use of the model's qualities, they usually need to learn the model mechanically stage by stage.

Egan sets out the model in a logical order and I believe this is the best route for someone to learn it thoroughly. Having said this, learning to weave together the relationship qualities with the steps and stages of the model can often prove a painful stage for students to negotiate. A supportive and client-responsive trainee attempting to facilitate a client through leverage and into picturing a preferred scenario for the first time can sometimes become directive and insensitive. Trainees can quickly lose heart and find themselves returning to the security and familiarity of story-telling. In my experience, learning to move with a client from stage to stage and step to step without losing one's responsiveness and sensitivity to the client's experience is a tall order.

My colleagues and I often use modelling within teaching sessions to help illustrate for our students how the stages and steps of the model can be applied in a way that honours the therapeutic relationship. We demonstrate a listening or counselling session with one trainer as the helper and the other trainer as the client who presents a genuine and real issue with which they need help. These are not role-plays. The client brings a real issue from his or her life, one that carries some emotion and that he or she is committed to exploring. Working with a client in this way can help to clarify the different components of the model and the trainees, as observers, are invited to discuss the steps and stages they have seen demonstrated and come to some conclusions about how the model works in practice.

Another useful strategy for teaching the model is to use a case-study method and including the whole class in the process of exploring a client's issue and how they might intervene as the helper. I give each student a written copy of a (fictitious) client case study and then divide the group into four equal sections. I position three sections of the student group to form a horseshoe and I invite a further section to become the client. We then have a table which serves as stage one of the skilled helper model, another for stage two and the final arm of the horseshoe becomes the stage three table. The fourth section of the group, which represents the client, works together to build up his or her profile in private discussion. Then together, as the collective client, they attend each table as the rest of the class listens and observes. The stage one table group tries to establish the story, blind spots and leverage and the 'client' then moves on to the next table, and so on. The tutor may intervene to keep the stage table groups to their own stages to ensure that the model is worked through as clearly as possible. The 'client' can find themselves moving back and forth between the tables and this helps to illustrate the flexibility and non-linear application of the model. The session is completed when a plan is outlined by the 'client'. A debrief is usually very fruitful for questions and clarifications and to de-role the students playing the client at the end of the exercise.

I use this exercise to illustrate the need to accept that learning and applying the model includes some routine and sequential strategies that may, in the moment, feel like a lack of respect for the subtleties and complexities of helping someone in difficulties. Experiencing the momentary necessity and usefulness of such strategies can take the trainee helpers into a place where they can begin to use the model with more confidence, flexibility and sense of safety.

In conclusion, I do feel that the skilled helper model is an exceptionally useful tool and that introducing trainees to it after laying the groundwork of establishing and maintaining relationships can give helpers a push into purposefulness. The 'story' stage can so easily become an indulgence for new helpers – its seductiveness lying in the simple fact that listening to another person is so absorbing and interesting and is often greeted with enthusiasm by clients. As a consequence, new helpers, I have found, can often neglect to attend sufficiently to the client's aims and objectives in being helped. This model reminds both helper and helped that there needs to be some shared purpose in this talking and listening exchange, and that helping is more than conversation.

Endnote

In concluding this chapter and this book I hope it has become evident that the skilled helper model remains a vibrant and dynamic resource both for helpers and for their clients. I have attempted, in presenting this work, to ease the model a little from the shoulders of Gerard Egan, who has carried it pretty much single-handed for three decades. Writing this book has been an exciting journey that took my interest and attention to places I had not foreseen when I first set out. In the true spirit of the travel writer, I now rest in the anticipation and hope that what has been written on these pages, by myself and by others, may awaken or rekindle interest in a landscape (in this case a landscape of helping) that fellow travellers will now wish to explore further and in their own way.

References

Aebi, J. (1993) 'Nonspecific and specific factors in therapeutic change among different approaches to counselling', *Counselling Psychology Review*, 8, 3: 19–32.

Agnew-Davis, R. (1999) 'Learning from research into the counselling relationship', in C. Feltham (ed.) *Understanding the Counselling Relationship*, London: Sage.

Anderson, H. and Goolishian, H. (1992) 'The client is the expert: a not-knowing approach to therapy', in S. McNamee and K.J. Gergen (eds) *Therapy as Social Construction*, London: Sage.

Andrews, J. (1991) *The Active Self in Psychotherapy: An Integration of Therapeutic Styles*, Boston: Allyn and Bacon.

Aponte, H.J. (1982) 'The person of the therapist: the cornerstone of therapy', *Family Therapy Networker*, 6, 2: 19–21 and 46.

Argyle, M. (2001) *The Psychology of Happiness*, 2nd edn, London: Routledge.

Arnold, E. and Boggs, K. (1995) *Interpersonal Relationships: Professional Communication Skills for Nurses*, 2nd edn, Philadelphia: W.B. Saunders.

Aron, L. (1996) *A Meeting of Minds: Mutuality in Psychoanalysis*, Hillsdale, NJ: The Analytic Press.

Aspinwall, L. and Staudinger, U. (2003) *A Psychology of Human Strengths: Fundamental Questions and Future Directions for a Positive Psychology*, Washington, DC: American Psychological Association.

BACP (2002) *Ethical Framework for Good Practice in Counselling and Psychotherapy*, Rugby, UK: British Association for Counselling and Psychotherapy.

Baldwin, M. and Satir, V. (eds) (1987) *The Use of Self in Therapy*, Binghamton, NY: Haworth Press.

Beck, A.T., Freeman, A., Davis, D.D. and Associates (2003) *Cognitive Therapy of Personality Disorders*, 2nd edn, New York: Guilford Press.

Beisser, A.R. (1970) 'The paradoxical theory of change', in J. Fagan and I.

Shepherd (eds) *Gestalt Therapy Now*, Palo Alto, CA: Science and Behavior Books.

Beutler, L.E. and Consoli, A.J. (1993) 'Matching the therapist's interpersonal stance to clients' characteristics: contributions from systemic eclectic psychotherapy', *Psychotherapy* 30, 3: 417–422.

Bimrose, J. (1996) 'Multiculturalism', in R. Bayne, I. Horton and J. Bimrose (eds) *New Directions in Counselling*, London: Routledge.

Bordin, E.S. (1979) 'The generalizability of the psychoanalytic concept of the working alliance', *Psychotherapy: Theory, Research and Practice*, 16, 3: 252–260.

Bowlby, J. (1969) *Attachment and Loss: Vol. 1. Attachment*, London: Hogarth Press.

—— (1973) *Attachment and Loss: Vol. 2. Separation: Anger and Anxiety*, London: Hogarth Press.

—— (1980) *Attachment and Loss: Vol. 3. Loss: Sadness and Depression*, London: Hogarth Press.

—— (1988) *A Secure Base*, London: Routledge.

Bugental, J. F. (1987) *The Art of the Psychotherapist*, New York: Norton.

Burnard, P. (1996) *Acquiring Interpersonal Skills: A Handbook of Experiential Learning for Health Professionals*, 2nd edn, Cheltenham, UK: Stanley Thornes.

Callaghan, G.M., Naugle, A.E. and Follette, W.C. (1996) 'Useful constructions of the client–therapist relationship', *Psychotherapy*, 33, 3: 381–390.

Calligor, L. (1984) 'Parallel and reciprocal processes in psychoanalytic supervision', in L. Calligor *et al.* (eds) *Clinical Perspectives in the Supervision of Psychoanalysis*, New York: Plenum Press.

Carkhuff, R.R. (1969) *Helping and Human Relations*, Vols I and II, New York: Holt, Rinehart and Winston.

—— (1971) 'Training as a preferred mode of treatment', *Journal of Counseling Psychology*, 18: 123–131.

—— (1987) *The Art of Helping*, 6th edn, Amherst, MA: Human Resource Development Press.

Carr, A. (2004) *Positive Psychology: The Science of Happiness and Human Strengths*, Hove, UK: Brunner-Routledge.

Casement, P. (1985) *On Learning From the Patient*, London: Routledge.

Cassidy, J. and Shaver, P.R. (1999) *Handbook of Attachment: Theory, Research and Clinical Applications*, New York: Guilford Press.

Chaplin, J. (1988). *Feminist Counselling in Action*, London: Sage.

Clark, D.A. (2004) *Cognitive-Behavioral Therapy for OCD*, New York: Guilford Press.

Coles, A. (1996) 'From priesthood to management consultancy: Adrian Coles interviews Gerard Egan', *Counselling*, 7, 3: 194–197.

—— (2003) *Counselling in the Workplace*: Maidenhead, UK: Open University Press.

Connor, M. (1994) *Training the Counsellor: An Integrative Model*, London: Routledge.

Connor, M., Price, J. and Wash, M. (eds) (1989) *Becoming a Skilled Helper: A Collection of Training Materials Used at the 1989 York Counselling Summer School*, York, UK: The College of Ripon and York St John.

Connor-Greene, P.A. (1993) 'The therapeutic context: preconditions for change in psychotherapy', *Psychotherapy*, 30, 3: 375–382.

Culley, S. (1991) *Integrative Counselling Skills in Action*, London: Sage.

Culley, S. and Bond, T. (2004) *Integrative Counselling Skills in Action*, 2nd edn, London: Sage.

Dainow, S. and Bailey, C. (1988) *Developing Skills with People: Training for Person to Person Client Contact*, Chichester, UK: John Wiley and Sons Ltd.

Dancer, J. M, (2003) 'Mentoring in healthcare: theory in search of practice', *Clinician in Management*, 12, 1: 21–31.

Dawes, R.M. (1994) *House of Cards: Psychology and Psychotherapy Built on Myth*, New York: Free Press.

Dexter, G. and Russell, J. (1989) 'A client-centred model of supervision', in M. Connor, J. Price and M. Wash (eds) *Becoming a Skilled Helper: A Collection of Training Materials Used at the 1989 York Counselling Summer School*, York, UK: The College of Ripon and York St John.

DeYoung, P.A. (2003) *Relational Psychotherapy: A Primer*, New York: Brunner-Routledge.

Doehrman, M.G. (1976) 'Parallel processes in supervision and psychotherapy', *Bulletin of the Menninger Clinic*, 40, 1: 9–104.

Dolan, R.T., Arnkoff, D.B. and Glass, C.R. (1993) 'Client attachment style and the psychotherapist's interpersonal stance', *Psychotherapy*, 30, 3: 408–412.

Draycott, S. and Dabbs, A. (1998) 'Cognitive dissonance 1: an overview of the literature and its integration into theory and practice of clinical psychology', *British Journal of Clinical Psychology*, 37: 341–353.

Dryden, W. (1989) 'The therapeutic alliance as an integrating framework', in W. Dryden (ed.) *Key Issues for Counselling in Action*, London: Sage.

Dryden, W., Horton, I. and Mearns, D. (1995) *Issues in Professional Counsellor Training*, London: Cassell.

Dryden, W. and Neenan, M. (2004) *The Rational Emotive Behavioural Approach to Therapeutic Change*, London: Sage.

Duncan, B.L., Solovey, A.D. and Rusk, G.S. (1992) *Changing the Rules: A Client-Directed Approach to Therapy*, New York: Guilford.

D'Zurilla, T. and Nezu, A. (1999) *Problem Solving Therapy*, 2nd edn, New York: Springer Verlag.

Egan, G. (1970) *Encounter: Group Processes for Interpersonal Growth*, Monterey, CA: Brooks/Cole.

—— (1973) *Face to Face: The Small Group Experience and Interpersonal Growth*, Monterey, CA: Brooks/Cole.

—— (1976) *Interpersonal Living: A Skills-Contract Approach to Human Relations Training in Groups*, Monterey, CA: Brooks/Cole.

—— (1977) *You and Me: The Skills of Communicating and Relating to Others*, Monterey, CA: Brooks/Cole.

—— (1984a) 'People in systems: a comprehensive model for psychosocial education and training', in D. Larson (ed.) *Teaching Psychological Skills: Models for Giving Psychology Away*, Monterey, CA: Brooks/Cole.

—— (1984b) 'Skilled helping: a problem-management framework for helping and helper training', in D. Larson (ed.) *Teaching Psychological Skills: Models for Giving Psychology Away*, Monterey, CA: Brooks/Cole.

—— (1985) *Change Agent Skills in Helping and Human Service Settings*, Monterey, CA: Brooks/Cole.

—— (1988a) *Change Agent Skills A: Assessing and Designing Excellence*, San Diego, CA: University Associates Inc.

—— (1988b) *Change Agent Skills B: Managing Innovation and Change*, San Diego, CA: University Associates Inc.

—— (1993) *Adding Value: A Systematic Guide to Business-Driven Management and Leadership*, San Francisco: Jossey-Bass.

—— (1994) *Working the Shadow Side: A Guide to Positive Behind-the-Scenes Management*, San Francisco: Jossey-Bass.

—— (1998) *The Skilled Helper: A Problem-Management Approach to Helping*, 6th edn, Monterey, CA: Brooks/Cole.

—— (2002a) *The Skilled Helper: A Problem-Management and Opportunity-Development Approach to Helping*, 7th edn, Pacific Grove, CA: Brooks/Cole.

—— (2002b) *Exercises in Helping Skills: A Manual to Accompany The Skilled Helper, 7th edn*, Pacific Grove, CA: Brooks/Cole.

—— (2006) *Essentials of Skilled Helping: Managing Problems, Developing Opportunities*, Pacific Grove, CA: Brooks/Cole.

Egan, G. and Cowan, M.A. (1979) *People in Systems: A Model for Development in the Human-Service Professions and Education*, Pacific Grove, CA: Brooks/Cole.

—— (1980) *Moving into Adulthood: Themes and Variations in Self-Directed Development for Effective Living*, Monterey, CA: Brooks/Cole.

Epston, D., White, M. and Murray, K. (1992) 'A proposal for re-authoring therapy: Rose's revisioning of her life and a commentary', in

S. McNamee and K.J. Gergen (eds) *Therapy as Social Construction*, London: Sage.

Fear, R. and Woolfe, R. (1996) 'Searching for integration in counselling practice', *British Journal of Guidance and Counselling*, 24, 3: 399–411.

—— (2000) 'The personal, the professional and the basis of integrative practice', in S. Palmer and R. Woolfe (eds) *Integrative and Eclectic Counselling and Psychotherapy*, London: Sage.

Feltham, C. (1995) *What is Counselling?*, London: Sage.

—— (1996) 'The place of counselling in the universal scheme of suffering and folly', in S. Palmer, S. Dainow and P. Milner (eds) *Counselling: The BAC Counselling Reader*, London: Sage.

—— (1997a) 'Challenging the core theoretical model', *Counselling*, 8, 2: 121–125.

—— (ed.) (1997b) *Which Psychotherapy?*, London: Sage.

—— (ed.) (1999a) *Controversies in Psychotherapy and Counselling*, London: Sage.

—— (ed.) (1999b) *Understanding the Counselling Relationship*, London: Sage.

Feltham, C. and Horton, I. (eds) (2000) *Handbook of Counselling and Psychotherapy*, London: Sage.

Festinger, S. (1957) *A Theory of Cognitive Dissonance*, New York: Harper and Row.

Fetherston, B. (2002) 'Double bind: an essay on counselling training', *Counselling and Psychotherapy Research*, 2, 2: 108–125.

Fine, C.G. (1999) 'The Tactical-Integration Model for the treatment of dissociative identity disorder and allied dissociative disorders', *American Journal of Psychotherapy*, 53, 3: 361–376.

Fowler, D., Garety, P. and Kuipers, E. (1995) *Cognitive Behaviour Therapy for Psychosis*, Chichester, UK: John Wiley and Sons.

Frank, J.D. (1961) *Persuasion and Healing*, Baltimore: Johns Hopkins University Press.

—— (1989) 'Non-specific aspects of treatment: the view of a psychotherapist', in M. Shepherd and N. Sartorius (eds) *Non-Specific Aspects of Treatment*, Toronto: Hans Huber.

Frankland, A. and Sanders, P. (1995) *Next Steps in Counselling: A Student's Companion for Certificate and Counselling Skills Courses*, Ross-on-Wye, UK: PCCS Books.

Franklin, L. (2003) *An Introduction to Workplace Counselling: A Practitioner's Guide*, Basingstoke, UK: Palgrave.

Freedman, J. and Combs, G. (1996) *Narrative Therapy: The Social Construction of Preferred Realities*, New York: Norton.

Freshwater, D. (2003) *Counselling Skills for Nurses, Midwives and Health Visitors*, Maidenhead, UK: Open University Press.

Friedman, M. (1992) *Religion and Psychology: A Dialogical Approach*, New York: Paragon House.

Gabriel, L. (2005) *Speaking the Unspeakable: The Ethics of Dual Relationships in Counselling and Psychotherapy*, London: Brunner-Routledge.

Geller, J.D., Cooley, R.S. and Hartley, D. (1981–82) 'Images of the psychotherapist: a theoretical and methodological perspective', *Imagination, Cognition and Personality*, 1, 2: 123–146.

Gergen, K.J. (1977) 'The social construction of self-knowledge', in T. Mischel (ed.) *The Self, Psychological and Philosophical Issues*, Oxford: Blackwell.

—— (1985) 'The social constructionist movement in modern psychology', *American Psychologist*, 40: 266–275.

—— (1994a) 'Exploring the postmodern', *American Psychologist*, 49: 412–416.

—— (1994b) *Realities and Relationships*, Cambridge, MA: Harvard University Press.

—— (1994c) *Towards Transformation of Social Knowledge*, 2nd edn, London: Sage.

—— (1996) 'The healthy, happy human being wears many masks', in W.T. Anderson (ed.) *The Fontana Postmodernism Reader*, London: Fontana Press.

—— (1997) 'The place of the psyche in a constructed world', *Theory and Psychology*, 7, 6: 724–745.

—— (1999) *An Invitation to Social Construction*, London: Sage.

Gergen, K.J. and Kaye, J. (1992) 'Beyond narrative in the negotiation of therapeutic meaning', in S. McNamee and K.J. Gergen (eds) *Therapy as Social Construction*, London: Sage.

Gergen, M.M. and Gergen, K.J. (2000) 'Qualitative inquiry: tensions and transformations', in N.K. Denzin and Y.S. Lincoln (eds) *Handbook of Qualitative Research*, 2nd edn, Thousand Oaks, CA: Sage.

—— (eds) (2003) *Social Construction: A Reader*, London: Sage.

Gilligan, C. (1982) *In a Different Voice: Psychological Theory and Women's Development*, Cambridge, MA: Harvard University Press.

Goffman, E. (1969) *The Presentation of Self in Everyday Life*, London: Allen Lane/Penguin.

Gold, S.N., Elhai, J.D., Rea, B.D., Weiss, D., Masino, T., Morris, S.L. and McIninch, J. (2001) 'Contextual treatment of dissociative identity disorder: three case studies', *Journal of Trauma and Dissociation*, 2, 4: 5–36.

Goldfried, M.R. (ed.) (1982a) *Converging Themes in Psychotherapy: Trends in Psychodynamic, Humanistic and Behavioral Practice*, New York: Springer.

—— (1982b) 'Towards the delineation of therapeutic change principles', in M.R. Goldfried (ed.) *Converging Themes in Psychotherapy: Trends in Psychodynamic, Humanistic and Behavioral Practice*, New York: Springer.

Grencavage, L.M. and Norcross, J.C. (1990) 'Where are the commonalities among the therapeutic common factors?', *Professional Psychology: Research and Practice*, 21, 5: 372–378.

Hall, L. and Lloyd, S. (1993) *Surviving Childhood Sexual Abuse: A Handbook for Helping Women Challenge their Past*, 2nd edn, London: Falmer Press.

Hardy, G.E., Stiles, W.B., Barkham, M. and Startup, M. (1998) 'Therapist responsiveness to client interpersonal styles during time-limited treatments for depression', *Journal of Consulting and Clinical Psychology*, 66, 2: 304–12.

Hayes, J. (2002) *Interpersonal Skills at Work*, 2nd edn, Hove, UK: Routledge.

Henderson, P. (2001) 'Supervision and the mental health of the counsellor', in M. Carroll and M. Tholstrup (eds) *Integrative Approaches to Supervision*, London: Jessica Kingsley.

Heppner, P.P. (1988) *The Problem Solving Inventory*, Palo Alto, CA: Consulting Psychologists Press.

Heppner, P.P. and Baker, C.E. (1997) 'Applications of the problem solving inventory', *Measurement and Evaluation in Counseling and Development*, 29: 229–241.

Hill, C.E. (1996) *Working with Dreams in Psychotherapy*, New York: Guilford Press.

—— (ed.) (2004) *Dream Work in Therapy: Facilitating Exploration, Insight, and Action*, Washington, DC: American Psychological Association.

Hobson, R.F. (1985) *Forms of Feeling: The Heart of Psychotherapy*, London: Routledge.

Hollanders, H. (1999) 'Eclecticism and integration in counselling: implications for training', *British Journal of Guidance and Counselling*, 27, 4: 483–500.

—— (2000) 'Eclecticism/integration: historical developments', in S. Palmer and R. Woolfe (eds) *Integrative and Eclectic Counselling and Psychotherapy*, London: Sage.

—— (2003) 'The eclectic and integrative approach', in R. Woolfe, W. Dryden and S. Stawbridge (eds) *Handbook of Counselling Psychology*, London: Sage.

Hollanders, H. and McLeod, J. (1999) 'Theoretical orientation and reported practice: a survey of eclecticism among counsellors in Britain', *British Journal of Guidance and Counselling*, 27, 3: 405–414.

Horton, I. (1996) 'Towards the construction of a model of counselling', in

R. Bayne, I. Horton, and J. Bimrose (eds) *New Directions in Counselling*, London: Routledge.

—— (2000a) 'Integration', in C. Feltham, and I. Horton (eds) *Handbook of Counselling and Psychotherapy*, London: Sage.

—— (2000b) 'Principles and practice of a personal integration', in S. Palmer and R. Woolfe (eds) *Integrative and Eclectic Counselling and Psychotherapy*, London: Sage.

House, R. (1999) 'Limits to therapy and counselling: deconstructing a professional ideology', *British Journal of Guidance and Counselling*, 27, 3: 377–392.

Howard, G.S. (1986) 'The scientist-practitioner in counseling psychology: toward a deeper integration of theory, research and practice', *The Counseling Psychologist*, 14, 1: 61–105.

Hudson-Allez, G. (1997) *Time-Limited Therapy in a General Practice Setting*, London: Sage.

Hutchins, D.E. (1989) 'Improving the counselling relationship', in W. Dryden (ed.) *Key Issues for Counselling in Action*, London: Sage.

Hycner, R.H. (1991) *Between Person and Person: Towards a Dialogical Psychotherapy*, Highland, NY: The Gestalt Journal.

Inskipp, F. (1993) 'Beyond Egan', in W. Dryden (ed.) *Questions and Answers on Counselling in Action*, London: Sage.

—— (1996) *Skills Training for Counselling*, London: Cassell.

Inskipp, F. and Johns, H. (1984) 'Developmental eclecticism: Egan's skills model of helping', in W. Dryden (ed.) *Individual Therapy in Britain*, Milton Keynes, UK: Open University Press.

Ishiyama, F. (1988) 'A model of visual case processing using metaphors and drawings', *Counselor Education and Supervision*, 28: 2, 153–161.

Ivey, A.E. and Authier, J. (1971) *Microcounseling*, 2nd edn, Springfield, IL: Charles Thomas.

Jacobs, M. (1999) *Psychodynamic Counselling in Action*, 2nd edn, London: Sage.

Jenkins, J., Hildebrand, J. and Lask, B. (1982) 'Failure: an exploration and survival kit', *Journal of Family Therapy*, 4: 307–320.

Jenkins, P. (1993) 'The search for a system', *Counselling News*, December 1993: 26–27.

—— (2000) 'Gerard Egan's Skilled Helper Model', in S. Palmer and R. Woolfe (eds) *Integrative and Eclectic Counselling and Psychotherapy*, London: Sage.

Jinks, G.H. (1999) 'Intentionality and awareness: a qualitative study of clients' perceptions of change during longer term counselling', *Counselling Psychology Quarterly*, 12, 1: 57–71.

Johns, H. (1996) *Personal Development in Counsellor Training*, London: Cassell.

Jones, A. (1998) '"Out of the sighs" – an existential-phenomenological method of clinical supervision: the contribution to palliative care', *Journal of Advanced Nursing*, 5: 905–913.

Joseph, S. and Worsley, R. (eds) (2005a) *Person-Centred Psychopathology: A Positive Psychology of Mental Health*, Ross-on-Wye, UK: PCCS Books.

—— (2005b) 'Shared roots', *Counselling and Psychotherapy Journal*, 16, 5: 24–26.

Jourard, S.M. (1971) *The Transparent Self*, revised edn, New York: Van Nostrand Reinhold.

Karasu, T.B. (1996) *Deconstruction of Psychotherapy*, Northvale, NJ: Jason Aronson.

Kaye, J. (1999) 'Toward a non-regulative praxis', in I. Parker (ed.) *Deconstructing Psychotherapy*, London: Sage.

Keyes, C.L.M. (2002) 'The mental health continuum: from languishing to flourishing in life', *Journal of Health and Social Behavior*, 43: 207–222.

Kidd, J. (2003) 'Career development work with individuals', in R. Woolfe, W. Dryden and S. Stawbridge (eds) *Handbook of Counselling Psychology*, London: Sage.

Kingdon, D.G. and Turkington, D. (1995) *Cognitive-Behavioral Therapy of Schizophrenia*, London: Brunner-Routledge.

Kivlighan, D.M. (1990) 'Relation between counselors' use of intentions and clients' perception of working alliance', *Journal of Counseling Psychology*, 37, 1: 27–32.

Kivlighan, D.M. and Arthur, E.G. (2000) 'Convergence in client and counsellor recall of important session events', *Journal of Counseling Psychology*, 47, 1: 79–84.

Kivlighan, D.M. and Schmitz, P.J. (1992) 'Counselor technical activity in cases with improving working alliances and continuing-poor working alliances', *Journal of Counseling Psychology*, 39, 1: 32–38.

Lambert, M. (1992) 'Psychotherapy outcome research: implications for integrative and eclectic therapists', in J. Norcross and M. Goldfried (eds) *Handbook of Psychotherapy Integration*, New York: Basic Books.

Lambert, M. and Barley, D. (2002) 'Research summary on the therapeutic relationship and psychotherapy outcome', in J. Norcross (ed.) *Psychotherapy Relationships that Work*, New York: Oxford University Press.

Lapworth, P., Sills, C. and Fish, S. (2001) *Integration in Counselling and Psychotherapy: Developing a Personal Approach*, London: Sage.

Larson, D. (ed.) (1984) *Teaching Psychological Skills: Models for Giving Psychology Away*, Monterey, CA: Brooks/Cole.

Lawton, B. and Feltham, C. (eds) (2000) *Taking Supervision Forward: Enquiries and Trends in Counselling and Psychotherapy*, London: Sage.

Lazarus, A.A. (1993) 'Tailoring the therapeutic relationship or being an authentic chameleon', *Psychotherapy*, 30, 3: 404–407.

Leahy, R.L. (2001) *Overcoming Resistance in Cognitive Therapy*, New York: Guilford Press.

—— (ed.) (2003) *Roadblocks to Cognitive-Behavioral Therapy: Transforming Challenges into Opportunities for Change*, New York: Guilford Press.

Leiper, R. and Kent, R. (2001) *Working Through Setbacks in Psychotherapy: Crisis, Impasse and Relapse*, London: Sage.

Leiper, R. and Maltby, M. (2004) *The Psychodynamic Approach to Therapeutic Change*, London: Sage.

LeShan, L. (1996) *Beyond Technique: Psychotherapy for the 21st Century*, Northvale, NJ: Jason Aronson.

Lindon, J. and Lindon, L. (2000) *Mastering Counselling Skills: Information, Help and Advice in the Caring Services*, Basingstoke, UK: Macmillan.

Lomas, P. (1981) *The Case for a Personal Psychotherapy*, Oxford: Oxford University Press.

Mabey, J. and Sorensen, B. (1995) *Counselling for Young People*, Buckingham, UK: Open University Press.

McLennan, J. (1996) 'Improving our understanding of therapeutic failure: a review', *Counselling Psychology Quarterly*, 9, 4: 391–397.

McMillan, M. (2004) *The Person-Centred Approach to Therapeutic Change*, London: Sage.

McNamee, S. and Gergen, K.J. (1992) *Therapy as Social Construction*, London: Sage.

Mahrer, A.R. (1993) 'The experiential relationship: is it all-purpose or is it tailored to the individual client?', *Psychotherapy*, 30 (3): 413–416.

Martin, P. (1997) 'Counselling skills training for managers in the public sector', in M. Carroll and M. Walton (eds) *Handbook of Counselling in Organisations*, London: Sage.

Maslow, A.H. (1968) *Toward a Psychology of Being*, 2nd edn, New York: Van Nostrand Reinhold.

Mattinson, J. (1977) *The Reflection Process in Casework Supervision*, London: Institute of Marital Studies, Tavistock Institute of Human Relations.

Miller, S.D., Duncan, B.L. and Hubble, M.A. (1997) *Escape from Babel: Toward a Unifying Language for Psychotherapy Practice*, New York: Norton.

Morrison, A.P. (ed.) (2002) *A Casebook of Cognitive Therapy for Psychosis*, London: Brunner-Routledge.

Morrison, A.P., Renton, J.C., Dunn, H., Williams, S. and Bentall, R.P. (2003) *Cognitive Therapy for Psychosis: A Formulation-Based Approach*, London: Brunner-Routledge.

Morss, J. and Nichterlein, M. (1999) 'The therapist as client as expert:

externalizing narrative therapy', in I. Parker (ed.) *Deconstructing Psychotherapy*, London: Sage.

Nelson-Jones, R. (1982) *The Theory and Practice of Counselling Psychology*, London: Holt, Rinehart and Winston.

—— (1990) *Human Relationship Skills*, 2nd edn, London: Cassell.

—— (2000) *Introduction to Counselling Skills: Text and Activities*, London: Sage.

—— (2002) *Essential Counselling and Therapy Skills: The Skilled Client Model*, London: Sage.

Norcross, J.C. (1991) 'Prescriptive matching in psychotherapy: an introduction', *Psychotherapy*, 28, 3: 439–443.

Novak, M. (1979) 'Rethinking social policy', *Worldview*, 22 (7–8): 40–44.

O'Brien, M. and Houston, G. (2000) *Integrative Therapy: A Practitioner's Guide*, London: Sage.

O'Connell, B. (1998) *Solution-Focused Therapy*, London: Sage.

Owen, I. (1993) 'The personalility of psychotherapists', *Counselling Psychology Review*, 8, 3: 10–14.

Page, S. and Wosket, V. (2001) *Supervising the Counsellor*, 2nd edn, London: Brunner-Routledge.

Palmer, S. and Szymanska, K. (1995) 'An introduction to cognitive therapy and counselling', *Counselling*, November: 302–306, Rugby, UK: BAC Publications.

Palmer, S. and Woolfe, R. (eds) (2000) *Integrative and Eclectic Counselling and Psychotherapy*, London: Sage.

Palombo, J. (1987) 'Spontaneous self disclosures in psychotherapy', *Clinical Social Work Journal*, 15, 2: 107–120.

Parker, I. (ed.) (1999) *Deconstructing Psychotherapy*, London: Sage.

Parkes, C.M. (1996) *Bereavement: Studies of Grief in Adult Life*, 3rd edn, London: Routledge.

Patterson, C.H. and Hidore, S.C. (1997) *Successful Psychotherapy: A Caring, Loving Relationship*, Northvale, NJ: Jason Aronson.

Payne, N. (2000) *Narrative Therapy*, London: Sage.

Pinsof, W.M. (1995) *Integrative Problem-Centred Therapy: A Synthesis of Family, Individual, and Biological Therapies*, New York: Basic Books.

Plummer, D. (1999) *Using Interactive Imagework with Children: Walking on the Magic Mountain*, London: Jessica Kingsley.

Rappaport, R.L. (1991) 'When eclecticism is the integration of therapist postures, not theories', *Journal of Integrative and Eclectic Psychotherapy*, 10, 2: 164–172.

Rappoport, L., Baumgardner, S. and Boone, G. (1999) 'Postmodern culture and the plural self', in J. Rowan and M. Cooper (eds) *The Plural Self: Multiplicity in Everyday Life*, London: Sage.

Reddy, M. (1987) *The Manager's Guide to Counselling at Work*, London: British Psychological Society/Methuen.

Reinharz, S. (1997) 'Who am I? The need for a variety of selves in the field', in R. Hertz (ed.) *Reflexivity and Voice*, Thousand Oaks, CA: Sage.

Rennie, D.L. (1994) 'Clients' accounts of resistance in counselling: a qualitative analysis', *Canadian Journal of Counselling*, 28, 1: 43–57.

Rogers, C.R. (1951) *Client-Centred Therapy*, Boston: Houghton Mifflin.

—— (1957) 'The necessary and sufficient conditions of therapeutic personality change', *Journal of Consulting Psychology*, 21: 95–103.

—— (1965) *Client-Centred Therapy: Its Current Practice, Implications and Theory*, Boston: Houghton Mifflin.

Rollnick, S., Mason, P. and Butler, C. (1999) *Health Behavior Change: A Guide for Practitioners*, Edinburgh: Churchill Livingstone.

Russell, J. (1993) *Out of Bounds: Sexual Exploitation in Counselling and Therapy*, London: Sage.

—— (1996) 'Feminism and counselling', in R. Bayne, I. Horton and J. Bimrose (eds) *New Directions in Counselling*, London: Routledge.

—— (1999a) 'Counselling and the social construction of self', *British Journal of Guidance and Counselling*, 27, 3: 339–352.

—— (1999b) 'Professional and socio-cultural aspects of the counselling relationship', in C. Feltham (ed.) *Understanding the Counselling Relationship*, London: Sage.

Ryff, C.D. (1989) 'Happiness is everything, or is it? Expectations of the meaning of psychological well-being', *Journal of Personality and Social Psychology*, 57, 1069–1081.

Ryff, C.D. and Keyes, C.L.M. (1995) 'The structure of psychological well-being revisited', *Journal of Personality and Social Psychology*, 69, 719–727.

Safran, J.D. (1990) 'Towards a refinement of cognitive therapy in light of interpersonal theory: 1. Theory', *Clinical Psychology Review*, 10: 87–105.

Safran, J.D., McMain, S, Crocker, P. and Murray, P. (1990) 'Therapeutic alliance rupture as a therapy event for empirical investigation', *Psychotherapy*, 27, 2: 154–165.

Safran, J.D. and Muran, J.C. (2000) *Negotiating the Therapeutic Alliance: A Relational Treatment Guide*, New York: Guilford Press.

Safran, J.D. and Segal, Z.V. (1990) *Interpersonal Process in Cognitive Therapy*, New York: Basic Books.

Salovey, P., Rothman, A.J., Detweiler, J.B. and Steward, W.T. (2000) 'Emotional states and physical health', *American Psychologist*, 55: 110–21.

Schön, D.A. (1983) *The Reflective Practitioner: How Professionals Think in Practice*, New York: Basic Books.

Scott, J. (1992) 'Chronic depression: can cognitive therapy succeed when other treatments fail?', *Behavioural Psychotherapy*, 18: 63–72.

Searles, H.F. (1955) 'The informational value of the supervisor's emotional experience', *Collected Papers on Schizophrenia and Related Subjects*, London: Hogarth Press.

Segal, Z.V., Williams, J.M.G. and Teasdale, J.D. (2001) *Mindfulness-Based Cognitive Therapy for Depression: A New Approach to Preventing Relapse*, New York: Guilford Press.

Seligman, M. and Csikszentmihalyi, M. (2000) 'Positive psychology: an introduction', *American Psychologist*, 55: 5–14.

Shapiro, D.A., Firth-Cozens, J. and Stiles, W.B. (1989) 'Therapists' differential effectiveness: a Sheffield Psychotherapy Project addendum', *British Journal of Psychotherapy* 154: 383–385.

Shaw, B.F. and Dobson, K.S. (1988) 'Competency judgements in the training and evaluation of psychotherapists', *Journal of Consulting and Clinical Psychology*, 56, 5: 666–672.

Shepherd, M. and Sartorius, N. (eds) (1989) *Non-Specific Aspects of Treatment*, Toronto: Hans Huber.

Sherwin, S. (2001) 'Feminist reflections on the role of theories in a global bioethics', in R. Tong, G. Anderson and A. Santos (eds) *Globalizing Feminist Ethics*, Boulder, CO: Westview Press.

Skovholt, T.M. and Rønnestad, M.H. (1992) *The Evolving Professional Self: Stages and Themes in Therapist and Counselor Development*, Chichester, UK: Wiley.

Slade, P. and Haddock, G. (1995) *Cognitive-Behavioural Interventions with Psychotic Disorders*, London: Brunner-Routledge.

Snyder, C. and Lopez, S. (2002) *Handbook of Positive Psychology*, New York: Oxford University Press.

Speedy, J. (2001) 'Narrative approaches to supervision', in M. Carroll and M. Tholstrup (eds) *Integrative Approaches to Supervision*, London: Jessica Kingsley.

Spinelli, E. (1994) *Demystifying Therapy*, London: Constable.

Sprull, D.A. and Benshoff, J.M. (2000) 'Helping beginning counsellors develop a personal theory of counseling', *Counselor Education and Supervision*, 40, 1: 70–80.

Stein, S. (1999) 'Student empowerment, staff support and organizational stress', in J. Lees and A. Vaspe (eds) *Clinical Counselling in Further and Higher Education*, London: Routledge.

Stiles, W.B., Elliott, R., Llewelyn, S.P., Firth-Cozens, J.A., Margison, F.R., Shapiro, D.A. and Hardy, G. (1990) 'Assimilation of problematic experiences by clients in psychotherapy', *Psychotherapy*, 27, 3: 411–420.

Strong, S.R. (1968) 'Counseling: an interpersonal influence process', *Journal of Counseling Psychology*, 15: 215–224.

—— (1991) 'Social influence and change in therapeutic relationship', in C.R. Snyder and D.R. Forsyth (eds) *Handbook of Social and Clinical Psychology*, New York: Pergamon Press.

Strupp, H.H. (1986) 'Psychotherapy: research, practice and public policy (how to avoid dead ends)', *American Psychologist*, 41, 2: 120–130.

Strupp, H.H. and Hadley, S.W. (1979) 'Specific vs nonspecific factors in psychotherapy: a controlled study of outcome', *Archives of General Psychiatry*, 36: 1125–1136.

Sugarman, L. (1995) 'Action man: an interview with Gerard Egan', *British Journal of Guidance and Counselling*, 23, 2: 275–286.

Sutton, C. (1989) 'The evaluation of counselling: a goal attainment approach', in W. Dryden (ed.) *Key Issues for Counselling in Action*, London: Sage.

Talley, P.F., Strupp, H.H. and Morey, L.C. (1990) 'Matchmaking in psychotherapy: patient–therapist dimensions and their impact on outcome', *Journal of Consulting and Clinical Psychology*, 58: 182–188.

Taylor, S.E., Kemeny, M.E., Reed, G.M., Bower, J.E. and Gruenewald, T.L. (2000) 'Psychological resources, positive illusions, and health', *American Psychologist*, 55: 99–109.

Totton, N. (2003) *Body Psychotherapy*, Maidenhead, UK: Open University Press.

Tryon, G.S. and Kane, A.S. (1993) 'Relationship of working alliance to mutual and unilateral termination', *Journal of Counseling Psychology*, 40, 1: 33–36.

Tyndall, N. (1993) *Counselling in the Voluntary Sector*, Buckingham, UK: Open University Press.

Viorst, J. (1987) *Necessary Losses*, New York: Fawcett/Ballantine.

Wheeler, S. (1998) 'Challenging the core theoretical model: a reply to Colin Feltham', *Counselling*, 9, 2: 134–138.

White, M. and Epston, D. (1990) *Narrative Means to Therapeutic Ends*, New York: Norton.

Wills, F. and Sanders, D. (1997) *Cognitive Therapy: Transforming the Image*, London: Sage.

Wills, T.A. (1982) 'Nonspecific factors in helping relationships', in T. Wills (ed.) *Basic Processes in Helping Relationships*, New York: Academic Press.

Winslade, J. and Monk, G. (1999) *Narrative Counselling in Schools: Powerful and Brief*, Thousand Oaks: Sage.

—— (2000) *Narrative Mediation: A New Approach to Conflict Resolution*, San Francisco, CA: Jossey-Bass.

Winter, M. and Holloway, E.L. (1991) 'Relation of trainee experience, conceptual level, and supervisor approach to selection of audiotaped counseling passages', *Clinical Supervisor* 9, 2: 87–103.

Worden, J.W. (1991) *Grief Counselling and Grief Therapy*, 2nd edn, London: Routledge.

Wosket, V. (1999) *The Therapeutic Use of Self: Counselling Practice, Research and Supervision*, London: Routledge.

—— (2006) 'The skilled helper model (Gerard Egan)', in C. Feltham and I. Horton (eds) *Handbook of Counselling and Psychotherapy*, 2nd edn, London: Sage.

Wosket, V. and Page, S. (2001) 'The cyclical model of counsellor supervision: a container for creativity and chaos', in M. Carroll and M. Tholstrup (eds) *Integrative Approaches to Supervision*, London: Jessica Kingsley.

Yalom, I. (2001) *The Gift of Therapy*, London: Piatkus.

Index

DATE DUE

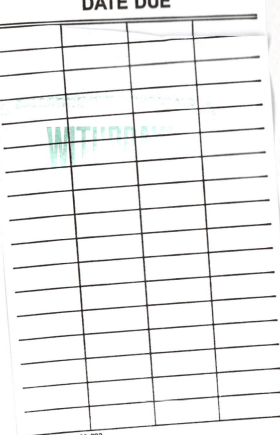

WITHDRAWN

Demco, Inc. 38-293